BODIES, PLEASURES, AND PASSIONS

BODIES, PLEASURES, AND PASSIONS

Sexual Culture in Contemporary Brazil

Richard G. Parker

Beacon Press
Boston

Beacon Press
25 Beacon Street
Boston, Massachusetts 02108-2800

Beacon Press books
are published under the auspices of
the Unitarian Universalist Association of Congregations.

97 96 95 94 93 92 91   8 7 6 5 4 3 2 1

Excerpts from *Casa-Grande e Senzala: Formação da Família Brasileira sob o regime da Economia Patriarcal*, 22d edition, by Gilberto Freyre, Rio de Janeiro, Livraria José Olympio Editora, 1983 (*The Masters and the Slaves: A Study in the Development of Brazilian Civilization*, New York, Alfred A. Knopf, 1956, reprinted by permission of Fundacao Gilberto Freyre.

Text design by Hunter Graphics

Library of Congress Cataloging-in-Publication Data

Parker, Richard G. (Richard Guy), 1956–
    Bodies, pleasures, and passions : sexual culture in contemporary
Brazil / Richard G. Parker.
        p. cm.
    Includes bibliographical references and index.
    ISBN 0-8070-4102-5
    1. Sex customs—Brazil. 2. Sexual ethics—Brazil. 3. Sexual
behavior surveys—Brazil. I. Title.
HQ18.B7P37 1990
306.7'0981—dc20   90-52586
                                                        CIP

Ah esse brasil lindo e trigueiro,
É o meu brasil brasileiro,
Terra de samba e pandeiro,
Brasil, para mim . . .
Brasil, para mim . . .
  —Ary Barrosa,
   "Aquarela do Brasil"

Ah that Brazil, dark and beautiful,
Is my Brazilian Brazil,
Land of samba and tambourine,
Brazil, for me . . .
Brazil, for me . . .
  —Ary Barrosa,
   "Watercolor of Brazil"

Contents

Acknowledgments

Over the course of a number of years, one acquires many debts. While it hardly erases such debts, it is at least possible to thank some of the individuals and institutions that have most directly helped to make this work possible.

My field research in Brazil has been supported at various points by grants from the Tinker Foundation and the Center for Latin American Studies; by a Robert H. Lowie Scholarship from the Department of Anthropology, a Traveling Fellowship in International Relations, and two Graduate Humanities Research grants, all from the University of California, Berkeley; as well as by a Fulbright grant and two grants from the Wenner-Gren Foundation for Anthropological Research. Rewriting and revision of the text, as well as ongoing field research, has been made possible by the Fundação de Amparo à Pesquisa do Estado do Rio de Janeiro.

During my initial periods of field research in Brazil, I was fortunate to be associated with the Programa de Pós-Graduação em Antropologia Social at the Museu Nacional, and I would like to thank especially Roberto Da Matta, Anthony Seeger, and Gilberto Velho for helping to facilitate this affiliation.

The first version of this text was written over a number of years at the University of California, Berkeley, and I owe a special debt to my doctoral dissertation committee, Alan Dundes, Nancy Scheper-Hughes, and Robert N. Bellah, for their insights, their kindness, and their patience. Nancy Scheper-Hughes, in particular, has continued to offer support and advice, which has been invaluable in the completion of the final manuscript.

A revised version of the manuscript was written in Rio de Janeiro, and I would like to thank Gilberto Velho of the Museu Nacional for helping me to begin this process. More recently, I owe special thanks to Benilton Bezerra, Jr., Claudio J. Struchiner, Joel Birman, Jurandir Freire Costa, Maria Andrea Loyola, and Sérgio Carrara, my colleagues in the Instituto de Medicina Social at the Universidade do Estado do Rio de Janeiro, for the intellectual environment that they have offered me, and to Regina Marchese for her help on all manner of issues.

While the list of friends and colleagues who have offered help and encouragement is too long to include in its entirety, I would particularly like to thank Antônio J. C. Mazzi, Samina Bashirudden, Carmen Dora Guimarães, Herbert Daniel, Paul Kutsche, Stanley Brandes, Ondina Fachel Leal,

Teresa Caldeira, Luiz Mott, Edward MacRae, Nancy Lutz, and Jackie Urla. I must also thank Peter Fry, whose work has done much to shape my own, and whose kindness and generosity during my early days in the field helped to keep me going, and Gilbert Herdt, for his cogent advice and suggestions.

Special thanks go, as well, to Rosemary Messick for her constant support and encouragement. She has shared Brazil with me in a way that I think no one else possibly could, and she has helped to shape not only my work, but my life.

Finally, thanks are hardly enough for Vagner de Almeida. More than anyone else, he opened Brazil up for me, taught me about myself, and made it possible to go on. He has lived with this project from beginning to end, and, in a very real sense, it is his as much as it is mine.

A Note on Translations

Published English translations of original Portuguese texts have been used whenever available and accurate. All other translations of both published texts and informant quotations have been made by the author. Throughout the text, Portuguese terms and expressions have been maintained in referring to key cultural categories, even in some instances where there seems to be a relatively straightforward English translation. This was a conscious decision, aimed not at making the reader's task more difficult, but at underlining the extent to which these categories are in fact highly complex cultural constructs whose full range of meanings can never be completely translated.

1

Introduction

This is a book about Brazilian sexual culture. It focuses, above all else, on the question of diversity, and on the social and historical construction of sexual diversity in Brazilian culture. It is clearly situated, then, within a wider understanding of sexual life that has begun to emerge over a number of years and within a variety of different disciplines: a sense that sexual experience, like all human experience, is less the result of some immutable human nature than the product of a complex set of social, cultural, and historical processes.[1] More specifically, it emerges from a particular tradition within social and cultural anthropology—a tradition that focuses on the symbolic dimensions of human experience, and that thus draws special attention to the intersubjective cultural forms that shape and structure the subjective experience of sexual life in different social settings.[2]

Because so much of the best anthropological work on sexual life has been carried out within the context of relatively small-scale societies, however, questions of sexual diversity and difference have often emerged more clearly at the level of cross-cultural comparison than in the analysis of sexual life within any particular society or culture (see Davis and Whitten 1987). Only very recently, as anthropologists have begun to turn their attention to more complex societies, have these questions been raised within specific settings (see, for example, Rubin 1984). Yet in turning to contemporary Brazil—a society that is nothing if not complex—such questions of diversity or difference, within a wider whole, are central to any attempt to understand the character of sexual life (see, for example, Parker 1985b, 1987, 1989a, 1989b). Sexual experience takes shape in Brazil, as in other profoundly complex societies, less in the singular than in the plural, and it is thus less accurate to speak of a single, unified system of sexual meanings in contemporary Brazilian culture than to think in terms of multiple subsystems, recurring yet often disparate patterns, conflicting, and sometimes

1

even contradictory, logics that have somehow managed to intertwine and interpenetrate within the fabric of social life (Parker 1989a).

These subsystems lie at the heart of the Brazilian sexual universe and open up its most fundamental possibilities. They offer what might be described as frames of reference, culturally constituted perspectives or vantage points, that Brazilians can draw on in building up and interpreting their own experiences. They are thus essential to understanding the constitution of meaningful sexual realities in contemporary Brazilian life. Because they coexist, and even intersect in the flow of daily life, however, drawing lines between these different subsystems is by no means an easy task. On the contrary, any analytic distinction between them is necessarily tenuous— and at least somewhat artificial. Still, in examining the symbolic configurations, the cross-cutting logics, that emerge most clearly and seem to play the greatest roles in the constitution of daily life, it is possible to make a number of useful distinctions that may open the way for further analysis (see Parker 1989a).

Traditionally, for example, the question of gender has defined the Brazilians' interpretation of their own sexual practices (Parker 1985b). Situated within the context of a profoundly patriarchal social order, conceptions of male and female, of masculinity and femininity, have provided the foundations upon which the world of sexual meanings has been built up in Brazil. Both in an understanding of a patriarchal past as well as in the informal language of contemporary daily life, perceived anatomical differences have been gradually transformed into culturally defined notions of gender in Brazil, as in every society. Through a range of symbolic forms that shape the human body and its practices, the distinctions between two sharply opposed anatomical types have been transformed into notions of masculinity and femininity that encode a particular system of cultural values. As culturally elaborated, these notions have become the basis for a complex system of symbolic domination, establishing hierarchical relationships not only between men and women in general, but between an even broader set of classificatory types which structure the traditional sexual landscape in Brazilian culture and, in so doing, offer Brazilians perhaps the single most important perspective for the interpretation and evaluation of their sexual universe.

As influential—and as widely held—as this gender system has been in Brazilian culture, however, it is but one perspective among a number of other possibilities for the organization of sexual life. Constituted in relatively informal terms within the discourse of folk or popular culture, it has been tied, traditionally, to a more formal system of religious interdictions focused not only on the body and its acts, but on the implications of these acts for the soul. From the early colonial period to the present day, a relatively formal—if not always unbending—system of religious prohibitions has reinforced the divisions of gender while at the same time extending the implied significance of sexual practices themselves, implicating them in a different symbolic economy, interrogating them in terms, not merely of their significance in normal daily life, but of their meaning for eternal life.

This emphasis on the internal implications of sexual acts, while clearly confirming the central assumptions of the ideology of gender, has thus provided a slightly different take, a slightly different angle, for the perception of the sexual universe. Its more formal discourse, in turn, has gradually given way, through the processes of modernization that have rocked Brazilian life since at least the late nineteenth century, to what might at first seem to be a very different conceptual framework: a highly rationalized set of scientific and pseudo-scientific ideas about sexual life drawn largely from developments in European psychology, sexology, and sociology. Like the strictures that it has at once opposed and reaffirmed, this scientific sexuality has signaled a fundamental shift of emphasis from the external manifestations of sexual life to the internal significance of sexual existence, from a concern with the body and the ways in which bodies combine to a preoccupation with what might be described as the sexual self (see, for example, Costa 1979; see also Parker 1985b, 1987, 1989b).

Central to this new way of thinking, and distinguishing it from the religious perspective with which it otherwise seems to have shared a good deal, was an extremely utilitarian approach to the whole question of sexual behavior—a new cultural emphasis on reproduction as the proper aim of sexual encounters, not simply as a duty to one's family, or even to God, but to one's fellows, to one's society, to the Brazilian people as a whole. Sexual energy channeled in this legitimate direction was thus contrasted with sexual energy expended solely in the pursuit of pleasure. This outlook, in turn, set off a flurry of scientific and medical investigation aimed at uncovering the roots of sexual promiscuity. As in Europe and the United States, sex became sexuality—an object of knowledge. In practical terms, probably the most important result of such highly rationalized investigation was the emergence of a new system of sexual classifications built up in the terminology of science. First in the works of pioneering medical doctors, and later in the more popular treatments of newspapers, magazines, films, and television, sexual normality and abnormality were carefully mapped and analyzed, and new sets of classificatory categories, based on the hidden secrets and desires of the sexual self, have been developed for the organization of the sexual universe. Increasingly, sexuality has become a focus for discussion and debate within Brazilian society, and its importance has become even more pronounced as controversies such as abortion, the rights of sexual minorities, and most recently, the alarmingly rapid spread of AIDS have all come to the center of public attention in contemporary life.

Within the terms of this new frame of reference, the traditional distinctions of gender in Brazilian life have hardly lost their significance. On the contrary, it would be more accurate to suggest that analytically distinct, and obviously diverse, sets of interpretive practices have been built up and superimposed on the definitions of gender in approaching and articulating the significance of sexual life in Brazil. Rather than eclipsing other possibilities, these more rationalized interpretive frameworks have served to diversify the wider structure of sexual meanings in Brazilian culture. And they have thus been linked to different systems of power, in which the failure to adhere to relatively formal, institutionalized strictures can invoke not simply the censure of the local community, but the disciplinary proceedings of various authorities. Because the fit between these various perspectives is imperfect, their simultaneous existence offers contemporary Brazilians a number of diverse problems and possibilities as they approach the whole question of sexuality. And while these problems and possibilities are socially and culturally ascribed or determined, their resolution is less so—there is room for choice, for both the conscious and unconscious manipulation of cultural meanings.

Nowhere, I think, is the variability, the fundamental multiplicity, of this configuration more evident than in what I would describe as the domain of erotic experience (Parker 1989a). Linking the question of meaning to the question of power, and existing, as they do, simultaneously for the vast majority of contemporary Brazilians, the conceptions of gender in popular culture, the renunciation of the flesh in religious ideology, and the interrogation of dangerous desires in modern medical and scientific thinking map out an elaborate set of possible sexual practices—some defined as permissible, others as prohibited. The very notion of prohibition, however, also implies the possibility of transgression—a possibility which is itself no less culturally defined. For Brazilians, it is in the erotic domain (quite "publicly" viewed as an eminently "private" realm) that sexual transgression becomes not only possible, but in fact highly valued. Indeed, the private undermining of public norms would seem to play a particularly important role in the constitution of meaningful erotic practice in Brazilian life. It is here, then, that the body, the soul, and the self are most clearly brought together in a way that relativizes the categories and classifications of other perspectives through the articulation of a distinct symbolic construct: a world of erotic meanings.

Here, within this erotic world, sexual transactions acquire their significance neither as an expression of social hierarchy nor as an external indication of inner truth, but as an end in themselves: as a realization of desire in the achievement of pleasure and passion. And this realization places central emphasis on those sexual practices which, in the public world, dominated by notions of sinfulness and abnormality, are the most questionable and problematic. Erotic ideology thus structures an alternative universe of sexual experience—a universe that takes concrete shape not only in erotic practices themselves, but in the language and the popular-festive forms that Brazilians use to play with sexual definitions, in the stories which they tell themselves about themselves as sensual beings (Parker 1987, 1989a).

Once again, this does not mean that the various categories and classifications of other perspectives somehow cease to function within the erotic world. On the contrary, as I hope to make clear, erotic experience and erotic meanings are built up with constant reference to these structures (just as other perspectives are constructed with constant reference to erotic practice). In shifting frames of reference, however, the significance of these structures is radically transformed. The classifications which, in the public domain, map out the sexual universe can be, in the world of erotic experience, inverted, distorted, and even transcended. They can be played with in such a way as to relativize and even undercut the limitations which they outwardly impose. Indeed, it is characteristic of Brazilian life that the cultural system itself, in the ideology of eroticism and in the interpretation of sexual practices which this ideology makes possible, not only recognizes but incites such a process (Parker 1989a).

Taken together, then, these frames of reference cut across the Brazilian sexual landscape. Far from absolute, either in their number or their boundaries, they constantly generate and make possible still other perspectives, other vantage points for the interpretation of the sexual world in Brazil. In this sense, then, as I hope will become increasingly apparent, they should be thought of less as delimiting the sexual field (which permeates all aspects of Brazilian culture) than as opening it up. It is through the terms such frames of reference provide and the orientations they make possible that meaningful sexual realities can be built up in contemporary Brazilian life. In using the tools they offer, social actors are able to shape and mold the contours of their own sexual universes. To understand these processes, however, and the profound implications that they can have for the lives of particular human beings, we must look not merely to the similarities, the patterns of cultural coherence, that exist between these highly diverse configurations, but also to the crucial differences which separate them—the logical and emotional contradictions which flow from them. We must turn, in short, to the ambiguities which permeate so much of modern Brazilian life (see, for example, Da Matta 1978, Fry 1982, Velho 1981).

The pages that follow constitute my own attempt to work through these many layers of meaning—to open the Brazilian sexual universe up to readers who have little or no familiarity with it, to enable those who are already intimate with its contours to reflect upon it in new ways, and ultimately, to suggest some of the ways in which an understanding of its particularity might offer new insights about human sexual experience more generally. With these goals in mind, as a way of introducing the reader to this unique universe, in the following chapter I turn to the peculiar myths of origin that have been built up in relation to Brazil: stories which have been told about Brazilians, and which Brazilians have told (and continue to tell) themselves about their history as a people, about their historical roots and their sensual orientation to the world, about their identity as sexual beings, and about their sexual identity as Brazilians.

In the third chapter, I move into the heart of the text—the ideology of gender in Brazilian life, the social and cultural mechanisms capable of transforming the world of perceived anatomical differences into hierarchically related values associated with masculinity and femininity. In the fourth chapter, I move from the relatively informal constructs which have traditionally structured the ideology of gender to the far more formal and rationalized constructs that have structured the religious, medical, and scientific interrogation of the sexual—to a consideration of these more rationalized discourses, of their historical interrelationships, and of the ways in which they influence the Brazilian sexual vocabulary and constitute an understanding of sexuality in modern life. In the fifth chapter, I turn to what I have discussed as the ideology of eroticism itself—to the culturally encoded erotic meanings and practices which are both produced by and yet, ironically, manage to undercut the hierarchical classifications which structure so much of modern sexual life in urban Brazil.

Having worked through these key domains, in the sixth and penultimate chapter, as a way of bringing the discussion back to the more general question of Brazilian identity, I want to turn to the Brazilian *carnaval* (perhaps itself best understood as yet another frame of reference), the popular-festive cultural form through which Brazilians may most clearly comment upon and critique the nature of their sexual universe. Finally, in the concluding chapter, I try to bring back together the many strands of argument and interpretation, and to offer some thoughts not only on the Brazilian case, but on the social and cultural construction of sexual meanings more generally. Without presuming to have fully answered all, or perhaps even any, of the questions that I have raised, I nonetheless seek to repay at least some small part of the debt that I owe to my Brazilian friends in attempting to underline how very much it is that they have to teach us.

2

Myths of Origin

I still remember being struck, during one of my first trips to Brazil, by the comments of a Brazilian friend. It was an unusually hot day, even for Rio, and the late afternoon sun was shining through the western window of the room where we sat. We had eaten a late lunch and were now discussing my plans for field research during the coming year. My friend had asked me about the difficulties of adapting to life in the tropics, Brazilian life, and I had responded, truthfully, that I could hardly remember having been happier and that it was difficult for me to imagine ever wanting to leave. He smiled, as Brazilians do when they sense a certain affinity with an outsider—an even nascent appreciation of their reality. "Be careful," he warned, "Brazil can be seductive."

His choice of words was insightful on a number of levels. On the one hand, it expressed an ethos or world view that strikes me as particularly Brazilian. Indeed, it is impossible, I think, for anyone who spends any real amount of time in Brazil, or with Brazilians, to ignore the extent to which a notion of sexuality, or perhaps better, sensuality, plays a role in their own understanding of themselves (see Wagley 1971, 255–56). The most striking quality of this fact is the degree to which this notion is tied not simply, as North Americans or Europeans are accustomed, to the perception of individual existence, but to the self-interpretation of an entire society. Indeed, Brazilians view themselves as sensual beings not simply in terms of their individuality (though this too is important), but at a social or cultural level—as sensual individuals, at least in part, by virtue of their shared *brasilidade,* or "Brazilianness." [1] And this view, in turn, seems to play a key role in defining the nature of Brazilian life both in and of itself and in relation to the world around it, the outside world, the world of the foreigner.

At the same time, however, as the exhortation to take care in the face of Brazil's seductive charms might indicate, the emphasis on the particularly sexual nature of Brazilian life has long been viewed with a certain wariness by Brazilians. It has been both celebrated and scorned. It has been seen, traditionally at least, more as a source of shame than as a reason for pride. Even today, in the most modern sectors of Brazilian society, it tends to be viewed with an underlying uneasiness. To even begin to understand the character of sexual life in contemporary Brazil, then, we must confront both the remarkable importance that Brazilians have traditionally given to sex in their own interpretations of themselves as a people and the fundamental ambiguities which these interpretations have encoded.

The first step toward such an understanding lies in an apprehension of the historical depth of this often contradictory emphasis on the importance of sexual life in Brazilian culture. Far from being the recent creation of an export economy, it is a view that is nearly as old as Brazil itself. It seems to be rooted in the very earliest reflections of the European explorers and travelers who first began to map the Brazilian landscape—in their vivid representations of a new world in the tropics. First articulated in the words of the outsider, the explorer and, later, the traveler, this characterization of Brazilian life has been reproduced, in a variety of ways and under a variety of circumstances, by Brazilians themselves throughout at least the past two centuries of their history. It is a view that has become increasingly salient during recent years in the stories that Brazilians have chosen to tell about themselves as a people.[2] Indeed, it has been central to what we might describe as Brazil's own myths of origin—myths which tell, for better or worse, of the formation of a uniquely sexual people in an exotic land, and which give meaning simultaneously to the past and the present by providing one of the most powerful and troubling self-interpretations in contemporary Brazilian life.[3]

To grasp all that is involved in the Brazilian understanding of sexual life, and its role in their understanding of their society, then, it is necessary to take a step back in time. We must examine the development of such interpretations in historical perspective and investigate the conditions of their production and reproduction. It is thus necessary to confront at least some of the texts in which the Brazilian spirit and the sensual ethos of Brazilian life have been articulated and explored, to examine the relationships that exist between these texts, and the transformations that take place within them. By focusing in detail on several key texts (texts in which the structures of Brazilian thought emerge with particular clarity and which, for this reason, seem to have exerted unusual influence in Brazilian cultural history), it may be possible to grasp some of the multiple, and often highly ambiguous, meanings that have been tied to sexual life in Brazilian culture, and to use them as a point of departure for a more extended examination of sexual meanings in Brazilian life.

Out of Eden

Many of the central themes that will mark the discourse about Brazil and Brazilians throughout history are present in the very earliest European descriptions of the strange new world in the tropics. Indeed, as early as the first known text written about the discovery of Brazil—the famous *carta,* or "letter," of Pero Vaz de Caminha, the scribe who sailed with Pedro Álvares Cabral in 1500, and who reported for Cabral to the Portuguese monarch, Dom Manoel, on the discovery of an unknown land south of the equator—at least one key component of this discourse seems to have been clearly formed (see Cortesão 1943, Greenlee 1937). For Caminha, as for many who would follow him, this new world was apprehended and described (not surprisingly, given the major currents of thought of his day) as an earthly paradise, a kind of tropical Eden.[4]

Nowhere, of course, was this Edenic character more obvious than in the immense richness of the land itself. As Caminha reported to the king, it was this natural wealth which made the new discovery so potentially valuable to the interests of the Crown. While Caminha and his fellow explorers had no way of knowing what this new land might ultimately offer in terms of much sought after precious metals such as gold or silver, they could attest its remarkable natural abundance: "Here, up to now, we cannot know if there is gold or silver, nor anything of metal or iron, nor have we seen it. However, the land itself has very good air, cool and temperate. . . . The waters are many, infinite" (Caminha 1943, 239–40). However, what most seemed to fascinate Caminha were the inhabitants themselves. In their presence, and in their potential for salvation, he suggested, lay the true value of this new discovery: "But the best fruit, that from this land might be taken, it seems to me, will be to save this people. It is this that should be the principal seed that Your Highness should sow in her" (ibid., 240). Indeed, in the European's perception of the natives, savage yet savable, the Edenic metaphor seems both to complete and to contradict itself. It is with them that Caminha's own seduction seems to have played itself out.

Reading through Caminha's text, it is difficult not to be impressed by the mixture of desire, fascination, and genuine intellectual curiosity that underlie his vision of the local population. In describing their appearance, he returns repeatedly to their most striking characteristic—their nakedness—and to the combination of beauty and innocence which seems to distinguish them from their European counterparts. It is this quality that stands out most clearly in his description of the group's initial encounter with a pair of native men:

> In appearance, they are dark, a bit reddish, with good, well formed faces and noses. They go naked, without any covering. They pay no attention to conceal-

ing or exposing their shameful parts, and in this they have as much innocence as in showing their face. (Ibid., 204)

And it is this same innocent nakedness that provides the focus for virtually every description of the native women:

> There walked among them three or four maidens, young and gracious, with very black, shoulder length hair, and their shameful parts so high, so tight and so free of hair that, though we looked at them well, we felt no shame. And one of those maidens was completely dyed, both below and above her waist, and surely was so well made up and so round, and her shameful part (that had no shame) so gracious, that many women from our land, seeing her countenance, will feel shame in not having theirs like hers. (Ibid., 210–11)

In terms that barely conceal his own excitement, Caminha's report seems intended to entice as well as to scandalize. The beauty and the innocence of the natives are extolled through vivid references to precisely those parts that, within the moral universe of Caminha's own society, ought to be most hidden and unmentioned.

Indeed, it is through such potentially dangerous references that Caminha's text achieves its most remarkable goal—it manages to link these otherwise distant savages to both the Europeans of the modern day and their Edenic ancestors. In their shameless genital displays, according to Caminha, this new population can be distinguished from the more familiar infidels of African or the Middle East and identified with the contemporary Christian: "Not one of them was circumcised, but, all as we are" (ibid., 212). This identification, implicit in the simple innocence of their nakedness, brings Caminha's set of associations to their logical conclusion and links these new-found children of God to Europe's own mythic past as well as to its spiritual mission: "Thus, Sir, the innocence of this people is such that that of Adam would not be greater in respect to shame. Now Your Highness may see if those who live in such innocence will convert or not, teaching them what pertains to their salvation" (ibid., 238–39). Because of their innocence, these otherwise savage individuals might be intellectually assimilated and spiritually saved. And it was in the name of salvation, of course, that both exploration and exploitation would ultimately be justified and legitimized throughout the New World.

The obvious fascination with the natives, expressed on a variety of levels in Caminha's text, was not entirely shared, however, by all of the explorers who followed him to this new land—and many of whom would dedicate their lives to the spiritual mission that Caminha had first suggested. During the same period that an idealized image of the Brazilian Indian was taking shape in the thought of Europeans such as Montaigne and Rousseau, Caminha's vision of paradise had already begun to be transformed in the eyes of observers such as Amerigo Vespucci, Hans Staden, André Thevet, Jean de Léry, and Gabriel Soares de Sousa.[5] No writer, of course, could deny the natural grandeur first pointed to by Caminha; for these later explorers and travelers, however, the view of an overpowering and abundant nature would tend to merge with a far more negative (or, at the very least, ambivalent) vision of Caminha's innocent human inhabitants. Indeed, the sins and transgressions of the savages would be carefully cataloged and, as a result, the New World would soon emerge in European accounts as much a green hell as a tropical paradise.

Many of the themes first stressed by Caminha can thus be found, as well, in Amerigo Vespucci's early letter to Lorenzo de Medici reporting on his own voyage commissioned by the Portuguese crown to follow up on the discoveries of Cabral. Like Caminha, Vespucci found this new land as close to an earthly paradise as he could imagine: "In truth, if the terrestrial paradise is located in any part of this earth, I judge that it is not far from those regions" (Vespucci 1954, 165). And like Caminha, he was especially struck by the native inhabitants:

> All the people, of both sexes, go naked, without covering any part of their bodies: and as they leave their mothers' wombs so they go until death. They have robust bodies, of medium stature, well formed and well proportioned, and reddish in color, which comes to them, I think, from the fact that they walk naked and are colored by the sun. Their hair is abundant and black. In their gait and when playing games they are agile and noble. (Ibid., 162)

In much the same terms as Caminha, Vespucci painted a picture which fit neatly with contemporary European beliefs concerning an earthly paradise, and which situated this paradise in the newly discovered land of the Brazilians.

In Vespucci's narrative, however, there emerges a darker side to this vision—a set of images which, while clearly no less linked than Caminha's to the fantasies of the European, leave the reader with a far less simple and innocent understanding of the Indians. Indeed, as described by Vespucci, their customs are grotesque and savage:

> They are handsome, though they nevertheless deform themselves, perforating their cheeks, lips, noses and ears. And don't think that those holes are small nor that they have only one: some that I have seen had, in the face alone, seven orifices, any one of which could hold a plum. They stop up these holes with blue stones, fragments of marble, beautiful crystals of alabaster, white bones, or with other ingeniously worked objects. If you could contemplate a thing so strange and monstrous as, for example, a man having in his cheeks no fewer than seven stones, some of which are a span and a half in length, you would certainly not fail to become stupefied. (Ibid., 162)

Nowhere is their savagery more apparent than in their transgression of the most fundamental taboos in European culture, their perverse sexual practices and their consumption of human flesh:

> There is among them another custom, excessively monstrous and aberrant, of the highest degree of human cruelty. It happens that their women, being libidinous, make swell the genital members of their husbands to such a size that it seems hideous and repellent: and they achieve this with a ruse of theirs and with the bite of venomous animals. Because of this, many husbands become eunuchs, losing the member, that, for lack of care, decays. . . . They take as many wives as they like, and the son has intercourse with the mother, and the brother with the sister, and the male cousin with the female cousin, and the one who is out walking with the first woman whom he meets. And as often as they like they also dissolve their marriages, with regard to which they observe no formality. (Ibid., 162–63)

> They live according to nature and should be considered Epicureans rather than Stoics. There are neither markets nor commerce among them. The tribes wage war against one another without any art or discipline. Haranguing the young, the elders are able to bend them to their will and excite them for the wars, where they barbarously kill one another. And as to those who become captives of war, they preserve them not to generously save their lives, but with the end of killing them for food: for victors and vanquished devour one another and human flesh is a common item of their diet. Have no doubt as to the veracity of this fact, because they take it as a natural right of the father to devour his wife and his children, and I myself met a man with whom I also spoke and who was reputed to have eaten three hundred human bodies. (Ibid., 163)

In Vespucci's text, the vision of paradise is contrasted with its horrifying opposite: an image of hell on earth as profound as the wildest creations of the European mind. And it is in the natives themselves, in their grotesque and distorted bodies, and in their savage and perverse customs, that this image is located and built up.

The emphasis on the perceived aberrations of native life first articulated by Vespucci would remain a common theme in written accounts of Brazilian life throughout the sixteenth and the seventeenth centuries. Vivid accounts of the sexual customs of the native Brazilians—in particular, their apparent polygyny and, to the eyes of the early European travelers, their lack of a clear incest taboo—appear repeatedly in the late sixteenth-century texts of writers such as the French priest André Thevet (1944, 252–53), the Calvinist missionary Jean de Léry (1941, 202–4), and the Bahian planter Gabriel Soares da Sousa:

> The Tupinambás are so lecherous that there is not a lascivious sin that they do not commit. Even at a very young age they have contact with women, because

the old women, not highly valued by the men, attract these boys, offering them gifts and favors, and teach them to do what they do not know, and do not leave them by day nor by night. These heathens are so lustful that seldom do they have respect for sisters or aunts, and, as this sin goes against their customs, they sleep with them in the forest, and some with their own daughters; and they do not content themselves with a single woman, but have many, as is indicated by the fact that many die worn out. And in conversation, they know of nothing to speak about except these filthy acts, which they commit constantly. Indeed, they are such friends of the flesh that they are not content, in order to follow their appetites, with the genital member as nature formed it. On the contrary, there are many who are accustomed to pass their spare time in putting on the fur of an animal so venomous that it makes them become swollen and causes great pain for more than six months. This makes the penis so thick and deformed that the women cannot wait for nor suffer them. And not being content, these savages, to naturally commit in such bloodthirsty fashion this sin, many of them are addicted to the nefarious sin, and among them it is no affront. And the one who serves as the male is considered valiant, and they tell of this bestiality as of a feat. And in their villages in the interior, there are some who have public tents for those who want prostitutes. (Soares de Sousa 1971, 308)

Drawing on the key images of good and evil, of taboo and transgression, within their own tradition, and superimposing these images upon the radically different reality of the New World, writers such as Thevet, Léry, and Soares de Sousa, following in the footsteps of Vespucci, began to build up a representation of Brazilian life as a primitive Sodom and Gomorrah, a repository of the gravest sins known to contemporary European society. In less than a hundred years, Caminha's Edenic metaphor had incorporated a profound sense of human frailty and failure, and the notions of innocence and simplicity that had marked that first encounter had begun to give way to the images of evil that most disturbed Christian consciousness.

The perceived failings of these nefarious savages were especially evident, of course, in what would become the dominant image of the *índio* during the sixteenth and seventeenth centuries: the bloodthirsty cannibal. Thanks to the writings of Staden and Léry, and to the illustrations of de Bry's *Great Voyages* based upon these writings, the Brazilian cannibal was soon a central figure in European thought. As described by these early writers, cannibalism takes shape as a highly ritualized—and, in various ways, eroticized—set of ceremonies linked to warfare and the taking of prisoners.[6] The rites recall, on a number of levels, the pagan feasts, the intoxicated orgies, of the Greek and Roman worlds—at least as interpreted by the Christian eye:

Then the assassin strikes a blow to the nape of the neck, the insides of his head are knocked out and the women take his body, pulling it to the fire; they skin it until it is very white and insert a small stick from behind so that nothing

will escape. . . . Once skinned, a man takes him and cuts the legs, above the
knees, and also the arms. Then the women come; they grab the four pieces
and run to their huts, making a great uproar. After this they open up the back,
separating it from the front side, and dividing it among themselves. But the
women keep the intestines, boil them, and from the broth make a soup that
they call Mingau, which they and the children drink. They eat the intestines
and also the meat of the head; the brains, the tongue, and whatever else remains are for the children. (Staden 1955, 253–54)

It is hardly surprising that these cannibalistic rites should have captured the
European imagination of the day—indeed, they must be understood as reflections of that imagination rather than as accurate depictions of native
Brazilian practices. Their immense power as representations cannot be
underestimated, however, for they capture more clearly than any other image the darkest side of the European vision of life in this mysterious tropical
land. Merging with and reproducing the most extreme perversions of sexual
transgression, their evocative power would ultimately stretch much further
than the texts from which they first emerged or even the reading public for
which they were first intended.

The representation of Brazilian life that began to take shape in the texts
of these early writers, then, was already a highly ambiguous one. It combined both the most positive and the most negative images available to the
European mind. It was at one and the same time a vision of paradise and a
vision of the inferno. It was a vision centered on the question of sexual life,
sensuality, and eroticism no less than on the obvious potential for economic
exploitation and colonization. Whether seen as childlike innocents or perverse savages, the native Brazilians were repeatedly analyzed and interpreted
in sexual terms. Against the lushness of the Brazilians' natural surround-
ings, such conflicting interpretations gave rise, in the eyes of the European
observers, to both the deeply felt seduction of the tropics and the no less
strong sense of horror in the face of savagery. This contradictory sense of
excitement, fascination, and horror defined the foreign view of Brazil during
these early years.

The Brazilian Sadness

While originating, of course, from without, in the eyes of the European
seeking to distinguish himself from a strange and frightening other, this
highly ambivalent view of Brazil has exercised a profound influence over
Brazilians in their own attempts to distinguish themselves from the European and the North American (on the broad question of national identity,
see Burns 1968, Cândido 1968). If the vision of the outsider has been reproduced and appropriated by Brazilians, however, it has been articulated

alongside a set of additional tales—tales which have both deepened and broadened its constellation of meanings. Nowhere has this been more true than in the story of three races—in the emphasis placed, at least since the early nineteenth century when the declaration of Brazilian independence gave rise to a new concern with national identity, on the question of *miscigenação* or *mestiçagem* (miscegenation or cross-breeding), of *mistura racial* (racial mixture), as somehow central to the formation of the Brazilian people (see Haberly 1983, Ortiz 1985, Skidmore 1974). Because of the emphasis that Brazilians have placed on the mixture of three races, the Indian, the Portuguese, and the African, as the key to their own historical constitution, the question of sexuality, of sexual interaction as the concrete mechanism of racial mixture, has taken on an almost unparalleled importance in modern Brazilian thought. Superimposed on the ambivalent visions of the early explorers, it has become central to the Brazilians' own interpretation of themselves and of their history—to their own myths of origin.[7]

Attention to the highly charged erotic atmosphere of early Brazilian life, and of its impact on racial mixture, is nearly as old as Brazil itself. While not always a primary theme in their work, it is clearly present during the colonial period in the writings of Jesuit missionaries such as Joseph de Anchieta and Manoel da Nobrega—perhaps the earliest writers to address their texts to Brazilians themselves rather than to write *about* Brazil for a European audience (see Anchieta 1933, Nobrega 1931; see also Haberly 1983). And, whether in the romantic novels of José de Alencar, the naturalistic work of Aluízio Azevedo, Adolfo Caminha, and Julio Ribeiro, or even the more difficult to classify masterpieces of Graça Aranha or Euclides da Cunha, the questions of sexual interaction and racial mixture are constant themes in Brazilian letters (see, for example, Alencar 1984; Azevedo 1941, 1943; Caminha 1983; Cunha 1940; Graça Aranha 1913). They have been the key issues around which the relatively small intellectual elite has sought to explore its own identity, both in relation to the outside world of the foreigner and in relation to the wider Brazilian population. Given the continued presence of the Judeo-Christian moral order, along with the recent emergence of the kind of scientific racism that so marked the thought of the nineteenth century, however, it is hardly surprising that the perceived centrality of both uninhibited sexual activity and unrestricted racial mixture should have been viewed by this elite with more than a little ambivalence. Indeed, throughout much of the late nineteenth and early twentieth centuries, the tragic consequences of such unbridled sensuality dominated Brazilian letters (see Haberly 1983). And in perhaps no other single text is this tradition played out more clearly or more influentially than in Paulo Prado's remarkable *Retrato do Brasil: Ensaio sobre a Tristeza Brasileira* (Portrait of Brazil: An essay on the Brazilian sadness), first published in 1928 at the height of the turbulent modernist movement in Brazil (Prado 1931).

The modernist movement itself seems to have marked an especially important (and in many ways contradictory) moment in Brazilian cultural history (see Haberly 1983, Martins 1970, Brito 1971). Drawing primarily on contemporary European forms, whether in art or in literature, the modernists launched a paradoxical attack on the imitation of European models that had, in their view, long characterized Brazilian cultural life. They set out to discover the Brazilian past, to reinvent it through the process of artistic creation, in order to invent its future. In attempting to achieve such a goal, of course, the various intellectuals loosely associated with the movement followed various paths—yet they returned, repeatedly, to the descriptions of the early European explorers in their recreation and mythologization of Brazilian history. Oswald de Andrade, for example, produced a *Manifesto Antropófago* (Anthropophagist manifesto), suggesting that the cannibalism of the native Brazilians should serve as a model for the cultural relations between Brazil and the outside world—that foreign models should not be copied, but incorporated and digested in the creation of a uniquely Brazilian culture. He suggested sardonically a new national chronology beginning in 1556, when the Indians of Rio Grande do Norte killed and consumed Antônio Sardinha, Brazil's unfortunate first bishop (Oswald de Andrade 1967; see also Burns 1968, Haberly 1983). Mário de Andrade, in his highly celebrated *Macunaíma: O Herói sem Nenhum Caráter* (Macunaíma: The hero without character) seems, in many ways, to have taken Oswald's call to heart. Drawing on a series of Amerindian folktales first recorded by Koch-Grünberg, he creates an almost Rabelaisian hero as a kind of metaphor for Brazil's racial and cultural diversity, tracing his circuitous path from the depths of a primordial jungle through the modern hell of urban São Paulo and beyond (Mário de Andrade 1983). Yet it is in Prado's *Retrato do Brasil,* published in the same year as both the *Manifesto Antropófago* and *Macunaíma,* that the mythologization of the Brazilian past as well as the many contradictions of the modernist project are most clearly evident—and it is surely in *Retrato do Brasil* that the intellectual elite's pessimism over the apparent role of sexuality in their nation's formation takes its most extreme form.

At one level, simply a modernist attack upon the artifices of the romantics, *Retrato do Brasil* is a much more complex and important text than one might at first assume. Just as the earliest explorers had marveled at the contrast between Brazil's natural splendor and its human impoverishment, so also does *Retrato do Brasil* situate its problematic in the disparity between the land and the people—between what Prado describes, following the early European writers, as the radiance of the tropical landscape and, what he focuses on, drawing on a long-standing Brazilian tradition, as the sadness of the Brazilian people. This Brazilian sadness, Prado argues, can be tied to the very impulses which characterized both its discovery and its colonization: to *luxúria* (lust) and *cobiça* (greed). Any attempt to understand fully the contradictions of contemporary life must therefore turn to an analysis of these historical forces:

> In a radiant land there lives a sad people. This melancholy is the inheritance of its discoverers, who revealed it to the world and peopled it. The splendid dynamism of these crude people obeyed two great impulses that dominated the psychology of the discovery and that never generated happiness: the ambition for gold and the free and unbridled sensuality that, like a cult, the Renaissance had revived. (Prado 1931, 11)

Through its fundamental humanism and its revival of the pagan pleasures, Prado suggests, the European Renaissance created a morality ideally suited to the age of discovery—an emphasis on worldly ambition that encouraged exploration, and an imagination that endowed the unknown with an almost erotic sense of excitement.

Drawing on the texts of those early explorers—simultaneously situating and reproducing them—Prado reaffirms the vision of paradise that greeted the first explorers and that, as Prado's own text makes so clear, has played a lasting role in the Brazilian perception of their own physical environment:

> In this atmosphere of ideal heroism and impatient ambition, and with uncommon pomp, the squadron of Pedro Álvares left Restello in March of 1500. Upon dropping anchor in Cahy bay, in front of the blue sawhorse of the coastline, the expedition had a vision of a paradisiacal life, with the verdure of the tropical country and the swarming potency of the virgin land. The letter of Caminha, in its idyllic naïveté, is the first hymn dedicated to the splendor, the force and the mystery of the nature in Brazil. . . . Pero Vaz was, for us, the chronicler of the marvelous find. (Ibid., 16)

As Vespucci had suggested, if this was not the terrestrial paradise itself, it was surely not far from it. Yet as Prado takes pains to point out, nature alone was hardly responsible for such a vision:

> The edenic impression that assaulted the imagination of the recently arrived exalted itself in the total nakedness of the indigenous women. The letter of Caminha itself speaks clearly of the surprise that was caused to the navigators by the unexpected aspect of the gracious figures that enlivened the landscape. (Ibid., 33–34)

Combined with the climate and the geography of the new land, then, the grace and beauty of its native inhabitants set the scene for what is in fact Prado's real interest: for what he describes, in precisely the same terms as my anthropological colleague, as the *sedução,* or "seduction," of the European in tropical Brazil.

As Prado explains it, not all of the early travelers were completely taken with this new land as they first entered Guanabara Bay, later the site of Rio de Janeiro, but there were few who could resist completely the seduction of its tropical atmosphere. Paradise or not, here in Brazil the sensuality of the weary explorers, many of whom were little more than boys, could be given free reign in a way that would have been unthinkable in the established order of temperate Europe:

> The seduction of the land was joined in the adventurer to the boldness of the adolescent. For men who came from a restrained Europe, the ardor of the temperments, the amorality of the customs, the absence of civilized shameful-ness—and all the continual voluptuous tumescence of the virgin nature— were an invitation to the free and unrestrained life in which all was permitted. The native, in his turn, was a lascivious animal, living without any constraint in the satisfaction of his carnal desires. . . . They returned themselves to the simple law of nature, and the heathen was well suited to the sexual fantasy of the young and ardent adventurer at the height of his vigor. (Ibid., 35–36)

Freed from the constraints of traditional European morality, set loose in this strangely sensual land, the heretofore repressed and restricted sensuality of the European adventurer could thus run its natural course. It could play itself out in harmony with the apparently no less strong sensualism of the natives themselves:

> They encountered no obstacle to the satisfaction of the vices and immodera-tions that in Europe were repressed by a more severe law, a more strict moral-ity, and a stronger sense of shame. They gave themselves with the violence of the times to the satiation of the passions of their crude souls. One of these was the lasciviousness of the white man unleashed in the paradise of the strange land. Everything favored the exaltation of his pleasure: the impulses of the race, the listlessness of the physical environment, the complicity of the desert and, above all, the easy and admiring submission of the indigenous woman, more sensual than the male as in all primitive peoples, who, in love, gave pref-erence to the European, perhaps for priapic considerations insinuated the se-vere Varnhagen. She sought out and entreated the white men in the ham-mocks in which they slept, wrote Ancieta. She was nothing more than a machine for enjoyment and work in the rural gynoeceum of the colonies. (Ibid., 39)

For Prado, then, as for so many of his contemporaries, the seduction of the land itself is linked to the naturally seductive charms of the natives in such a way as to free the inherent sensuality of the young explorers. Perceived as the source of both pleasure and productivity, the bodies of the native women (as elaborated, of course, in this fundamentally male discourse) would thus take shape as particularly complex symbols—at once the initial site of the European's essential loss, both of himself and of the moral baggage that he brought with him, and the womb which would give rise to Brazil's own distinct population.

The emphasis on the native women, on the pleasures and products of their bodies, on their unrestrained sensuality and their easy seduction of the European male is crucial in the configuration of Brazil's own myths of origin. As Prado's text makes abundantly clear, however, the symbolic configuration surrounding the Brazilian woman is in fact even more complex, for it makes possible, as well, the integration of the third and final component of the Brazilian racial trinity—the African—and thus provides the transition to a new phase of Brazilian history in which the early and unruly days of the colonial encounter give way to a secure patriarchal order built up on the foundation of slavery. Implicit throughout *Retrato do Brasil*, this configuration becomes explicit as Prado moves from the *mulher indigena* (indigenous women) to the *negra africana* (African negress) and the *mulata* (mulatto woman):

> In the colony the African factor was not isolated from contributing to the fusion of elements peopling the land. On the contrary. Just as the arm of the Negro substituted for the labor of the natives, considerably inferior to that of the Africans, in the same way the *negra,* more affectionate and submissive, took the place of the Indian woman in the gynoeceum of the colony. (Ibid., 192)

Unlike the North American case, at least as perceived from a Brazilian perspective, such sexual interaction made possible an extension of the same racial amalgamation that had marked the contact of the European and the Indian:

> Being a feature so peculiar to the ethnic development of our land, the sexual hyperesthesia that we have seen in the course of this essay avoided the segregation of the African element that occurred in the United States dominated by racial prejudice and antipathy. Here lust and social laxity brought together and united the races. Nothing and nobody repelled the new afflux of blood. Except for one or another aristocratic objection, that no longer exists, the amalgam was freely made, by chance sexual meetings, without any physical or moral repugnance. It repeated what had happened with the Indian crossing with the European spurred on by the polygyny of the first peopling. On the contrary, the seduction of the Portuguese settler by the *negra* and the *mulata* would become legendary. (Ibid., 192–93)

Within the confines of the patriarchal order, then, the contact between races was played out along sexual lines. The lust and sensuality that, according to Prado, typified both the European and the Indian are certainly no less present in the African. Especially evident in the body of the *negra* or the *mulata,* it is this sensuality that will continue to mark the unique course of Brazilian history—and to distinguish Brazil from both Europe and North America.

If the mythic dimensions of such a powerful self-interpretation seem clear in Prado's text, however, so too is the profound ambivalence with which the Brazilian elite has often approached its own past. Indeed, placed within a historical context, the *Retrato do Brasil* summarizes a long line of late nineteenth- and early twentieth-century Brazilian thought—a line of thought in which recognition of Brazil's multiracial formation is colored by the fear that the mixture of Brazil's races has somehow indelibly marked the character of the Brazilian people and doomed them to a degeneration at once moral and physical:

> From the weakening of physical energy, from the absence or diminution of mental activity, one of the characteristic results both in men and in collectivities is, without doubt, the development of a melancholy propensity. *Post coitum animal triste, nisi gallus qui cantat;* it is the "collapse" of the doctors, a physical and moral depression, which continues in cases of repeated excess. In Brazil, sadness flows out of the intense sexual life of the colony, set loose by the erotic perversions, and ultimately emphatically atavistic. (Ibid., 127–28)

It is ultimately in this lascivious mixture of three races that Prado locates the source of that peculiar sadness which his *Retrato do Brasil* pictures as so characteristic of the Brazilian soul. If lust for gold had originally drawn European explorers to Brazilian shores, and continued to motivate the colonial enterprise and to structure the course of Brazilian history, sexual lust had uniquely marked the formation of the Brazilian people. Taken together, these two central vices had given rise to a third, to what Prado describes as "the romantic evil": the sense of "melancholy" that seemed, at least to the intellectual elite, to typify the Brazilian spirit, and to contrast so sharply with the more positivistic goals that they would prefer to hold up for their nation.

Bringing together so many strands of Brazilian thought, *Retrato do Brasil,* much like *Macunaíma,* can be taken as a quintessential realization of the goals outlined by Oswald de Andrade in his *Manifesto Antropófago.* It is a text which consumes and ingests not merely the forms of European thought, but the very words and images of the earliest European explorers of Brazil. It succeeds in transposing one set of signs onto another. The ambivalent vision of the savage handed down from the earliest explorers is thus transformed in the no less ambivalent self-image of the modern Brazilian, who identifies himself at the point of intersection between European and Savage. In both visions, the question of sexuality is obviously central; and however ambivalent, or, indeed, even negative, the emphasis placed upon sexuality seems to have been, its role in framing a myth of origins, or more accurately, a cultural framework for the self-interpretation of Brazilian society in which history and myth merge, can hardly be ignored. Because of this, the possibility for a fundamental reinterpretation of this problematic seems to have been opened up.

New World in the Tropics

Retrato do Brasil must be understood as both a culmination and a begin-ning—certainly not the last, but probably the greatest, the most influential, in a long line of works exploring the Brazilian sadness, and at the same time, among the first in series of widely read interpretive works which would open up a new intellectual space for "Brazilian studies" in the twentieth century (see Martins 1970, 185). While this tradition has by no means exhausted itself, it clearly reached its high point but a short time after the appearance of Prado's *Retrato,* with the publication in 1933 of Gilberto Freyre's *Casa-Grande e Senzala,* translated into English as *The Masters and the Slaves* (Freyre 1956, 1983). However ambiguous the argument might at times seem, *Casa-Grande* provides a fundamental rethinking of the problem of miscegenation that has so troubled the elite, emphasizing more positively the mixture of cultures and the creation of a new civilization in the tropics as a result of this mixture.

The great innovation of *Casa-Grande,* as has often been pointed out, was Freyre's shift from the question of race, as an essentially biological phe-nomenon, to the question of culture, and to the social context in which the mixture of distinct cultural traditions had become possible in Brazilian his-tory (see Ortiz 1985). This shift itself, of course, can be understood at least in part as an attempt to escape or displace the anxiety that he shared with other members of the (predominantly white) Brazilian intellectual elite when faced with the undeniable empirical reality of miscegenation in the population as a whole (see Haberly 1983, 162). Yet it was also tied, as Freyre himself explains in his preface to the first edition of *Casa-Grande,* to his encounter with twentieth-century anthropology during his years as a stu-dent of Franz Boas at Columbia University:

> It was my studies in anthropology under the direction of Professor Boas that first revealed to me the true value of the Negro and the mulatto—racial char-acteristics separated from the effects of environment or cultural experience. I learned to consider as fundamental the difference between *race* and *culture,* to discriminate between the effects of purely genetic relations and those result-ing from social influences, cultural heritage and milieu. (Freyre 1983, lvii–lviii)

Taking this distinction as central to his own approach to Brazilian reality, Freyre by no means denies the mixture of races that was so obviously essen-tial to the formation of the Brazilian population. On the contrary, he loudly affirms it. He clearly perpetuates the notion of the Brazilian people as the product of racial mixture and asserts that such mixture has left its mark not merely on the Brazilian body, but perhaps even more fundamentally, on the Brazilian soul: "Every Brazilian, even the light-skinned fair-haired one, car-ries about with him on his soul, when not on soul and body alike—for there are many in Brazil with the mongrel mark of the *genipap*—the shadow, or at least the birthmark, of the aborigine or the Negro" (Freyre 1956, 278). If he insists that racial mixture be understood as the unifying element in Brazilian life, he also asserts that it offers Brazilians their greatest potential— the potential to create, through the cultural fusion (built up, one might say, on top of the foundation that racial mixture provided) of Amerindian, European, and African traditions, a distinctly new civilization, or what he later describes as a "new world in the tropics."

Yet even within Freyre's new configuration, the importance placed upon sexuality in the texts of earlier writers is preserved. In Freyre's interpretation, cultural interpenetration was both concretely achieved and metaphorically represented by the miscegenation of races. Once again, then, the question of sexual practice, like that of racial difference, is held up and displayed as definitive of Brazilian civilization as a whole. Freyre's particular version of "genital history" (Haberly 1983, 168) takes its place, if not above, then certainly alongside the texts of earlier writers as among the most powerful interpretations of the Brazilian self and its unique formation. It has become, no less than the texts of the early explorers, or for that matter, of more contemporary Brazilian writers such as Prado, yet another version of this peculiarly Brazilian theme.

Indeed, Freyre's construction is itself clearly another transposition of these earlier versions, and it is in relation to them that he situates his own *história* (the Portuguese term for both "story" and "history") in *Casa-Grande e Senzala*. Like Prado, then, Freyre gives special emphasis to the perceived character of early Brazilian life and describes it in terms of its extremely erotic atmosphere: "The milieu in which Brazilian life began was one of sexual intoxication" (Freyre 1956, 85). In Freyre's discussion, as in Prado's, the startling sexual freedom of the initial colonial encounter is primary.

> No sooner had the European leaped ashore than he found his feet slipping among the naked Indian women, and the very fathers of the Society of Jesus had to take care not to sink into the carnal mire; for many of the clergy did permit themselves to become contaminated with licentiousness. The women were the first to offer themselves to the whites, the more ardent ones going to rub themselves against the legs of these beings whom they supposed to be gods. They would give themselves to the European for a comb or a broken mirror. (Ibid., 85)

Freyre also suggests that the Portuguese of the sixteenth century were particularly well suited to the process of colonizing and peopling their new discovery. Given the relatively limited size of their own population, it was largely through *miscibilidade,* or "miscibility," rather than *mobilidade,* or "mobility," that the Portuguese were able to achieve their goals as coloniz-

ers. The unusual openness to racial mixing that their colonization entailed
had itself been conditioned, Freyre argues, by the course and character of
Portugal's own historical experience:

> Long contact with the Saracens had left with the Portuguese the idealized fig-
> ure of the "enchanted Moorish woman," a charming type, brown-skinned,
> black-eyed, enveloped in sexual mysticism, roseate in hue, and always engaged
> in combing out her hair or bathing in rivers or in the waters of haunted foun-
> tains; and the Brazilian colonizers were to encounter practically a counterpart
> of this type in the naked Indian women with their loose-flowing hair. These
> latter also had dark tresses and dark eyes and bodies painted red, and, like the
> Moorish Nereids, were extravagantly fond of a river bath to refresh their ar-
> dent nudity, and were fond, too, of combing their hair. What was more, they
> were fat like the Moorish women. Only they were a little less coy, and for some
> trinket or other or a bit of broken mirror would give themselves, with legs
> spread far apart, to the "*caraibas*" (Europeans), who were so gluttonous for a
> woman. (Ibid., 12–13)

Added to this general predisposition, this general moral climate, was the
sharp sense of sexual liberation experienced, as Prado also notes, by the
explorers and adventurers upon their arrival in a new world free from
the restrictions of traditional European life (ibid., 29). Set loose within this
climate, the Europeans (and their sexual activities) would prove central to
the earliest processes of colonization in Brazil:

> The lustful inclinations of individuals without family ties and surrounded by
> Indian women in the nude were to serve powerful reasons of State, by rapidly
> populating the new land with mestizo offspring. One thing is certain, and that
> is that the bulk of colonial society throughout the sixteenth and seventeenth
> centuries was founded and developed upon the basis of a widespread and deep-
> going mixture of races that only the interference of the Jesuit fathers kept
> from becoming an open libertinism, by regularizing it to a large extent
> through the sacrament of Christian marriage. (Ibid., 85)

The "sexual intoxication" of the New World, first realized in the contact between the Portuguese and the Amerindian, later opened the way for a complete integration of the African as well, giving rise, ultimately, to the almost
total mixture of three previously distinct races that would, for all Brazilians,
but perhaps most self-consciously for members of the intellectual elite such
as Freyre, define the unique nature of their national reality.

The fundamental ambivalence that characterizes, in a text such as *Retrato do Brasil,* this understanding of sexual life as central to Brazilian reality, is no less present in *Casa-Grande e Senzala.* It is especially evident, for
example, in Freyre's constant emphasis on the question of *sífilis* (syphilis),
which functions symbolically, much as the notion of "sadness" does in Prado's text, as the dark underside to the definitive process of miscegenation:

The advantage of miscegenation in Brazil ran parallel to the tremendous dis-
advantage of syphilis. These two factors began operating at the same time: one
to form the Brazilian, the ideal type of modern man for the tropics, a European with Negro or Indian blood to revive his energy; the other to deform
him. Out of this there arises a certain confusion of thought on the subject of
responsibilities, many attributing to miscegenation effects that are chiefly due
to syphilis. (Ibid., 70–71)

Brought to Brazil by the European explorers, the impact of syphilis in the
New World can thus hardly be separated from the moment of contact that
would first give rise to racial mixture in Brazil (ibid., 71). On the contrary,
it influenced the wider patterns of Brazilian history, having its greatest effect during a time that for Freyre is most definitive: within the context of
the great sugar plantations of northeastern Brazil during the seventeenth
and eighteenth centuries. It was here, in the *casa-grande,* or "big house,"
and the *senzala,* or "slave quarters," that the reign of syphilis, like the reign
of sex itself, was most intense:

> Syphilis invariably had its own way in patriarchal Brazil. It killed, blinded,
> deformed at will. It caused women to abort. It took "little angels" off to
> heaven. It was a serpent brought up in the house, with no one taking any
> notice of its venom. . . . The syphilization of Brazil—granted its extra-
> American origin—dates from the beginning of the sixteenth century; but in
> the voluptuous atmosphere of the Big Houses, filled with young Negro girls,
> with *mulecas* and *mucamas,* it and kindred affections were propagated more
> freely through domestic prostitution, which is always less hygienic than that
> of the brothels. (Ibid., 326)

Tied to the unbridled sensuality of the Brazilian past, then, syphilis marks
the Brazilian body no less than miscegenation marks the Brazilian soul.
Indeed, in Freyre's text the disease emerges as a symbolic construct of central importance. On the one hand, it gives expression to the profound uneasiness of the Brazilian elite in the face of their mixed racial origins—origins
that were unavoidably acknowledged to be a product of the sexual interaction responsible for the spread of venereal disease. At the same time, however, it provides an apparently scientific position from which to counter ar-
guments about the negative biological effects of miscegenation itself. It
identifies physical degeneration as the product, not of racial mixture, but of
syphilitic infection.

Subtly shifting the terms of the debate, then, this emphasis on syphilis
in *Casa-Grande e Senzala* ironically undermines the view of miscegenation
that had characterized Brazilian thought during the nineteenth and early
twentieth centuries, holding out the hope that the negative effects of this
process are essentially superficial and ultimately corrigible through the
techniques of modern medical science. This fundamental transformation is

completed, in turn, by Freyre's historicization of the whole issue of sexuality—his viewing the question of sex in Brazilian life as itself the product of a specific social setting. Just as Paulo Prado had reworked the texts of the early explorers into a troubled and guilt-ridden interpretation of the Brazilian self, through his historical/sociological lens, Freyre revises the texts of writers such as Prado. For Freyre, the Portuguese colonists themselves, far from being the victims of the seductive tropics and of the apparently inferior natives that they encountered there, were implicated in the sins associated with *luxúria,* or lust: "It was natural that Europeans, surprised at encountering a sexual code so different from their own, should have come to the conclusion that the aborigines were extremely lustful, whereas, of the two peoples, the conquerer himself was perhaps the more lascivious" (ibid., 96). And just as this disparity was evident in the relationship between the European and the native Brazilian, it was also present in the encounter between the white planters and their African slaves: "Eroticism, lust, and sexual depravity have come to be looked upon as a defect in the African race; but what has been found to be the case among the Negro peoples of Africa, as among primitive peoples in general . . . is a greater moderation of the sexual appetite than exists among the Europeans" (ibid., 323).

Indeed, the heightened sensuality of Brazilian life after the arrival of the European must be tied, as Prado had implicitly sensed, to the social and economic milieu which shaped its participants. It must be understood as a direct result of the relations of power and domination and the system of economic production that had marked colonial life—that had distinguished the conquerers from the conquered, the colonists from the colonized, the masters from the slaves. Slavery itself, by its very nature as a social institution, was in large part responsible for the moral laxity, the sexual excess, that so disturbed writers such as Prado:

> There is no slavery without sexual depravity. Depravity is the essence of such a regime. In the first place, economic interests favor it, by creating in the owners of men an immoderate desire to possess the greatest possible number of *crias* (slaves reared in the *casa-grande*). From a manifesto issued by slaveholding planters Nabuco quotes the following words, so rich in significance: "The most productive feature of slave property is the generative belly." (Ibid., 324)

Far from being the product of the inherent degeneration of a mongrel people, the sexual character of Brazilian life was tied, not to miscegenation itself, but to the social context which produced miscegenation. The notion of slavery, in turn, could thus be employed metaphorically in describing the relations of power, of domination and oppression, that marked the whole process of conquest and colonization. The regime of slavery was clearly linked to a particular sexual ethic dominated by differences in power, by sadism and masochism, by activity and passivity. It was in the institution of slavery itself that the sexual depravity of Brazilian life took shape, manifested most clearly, as Freyre repeatedly emphasizes, in the perverse pleasures of the planters' sons:

> The planters' sons fell into other vices; and at times, owing partly to the effect of the climate, but chiefly as the result of conditions of life created by the slave-holding system, they would precociously engage in sadistic and bestial forms of sexuality. The first victims were the slave lads and domestic animals; but later came the great mire of flesh: the Negro or mulatto woman. This was a quicksand in which many an insatiable adolescent was hopelessly lost. (Ibid., 394–95)

This emphasis on the most questionable excesses of sexual life under the regime of slavery enables Freyre to avoid much of the pessimism that characterizes the work of writers such as Prado. Without ever doubting the importance (or, for that matter, the perverse undercurrent) of sexuality in the formation of Brazilian life, in *Casa-Grande e Senzala,* Freyre transforms its implications. He preserves the notion of sexual interaction—indeed, of sexual intercourse—as a metaphor for the formation of the Brazilian people. But he undercuts the self-doubt that had previously been associated with that metaphor by tying all that had once seemed most troubling in it to an era now gone, an outmoded social and economic system which, while leaving an indelible mark upon the Brazilian spirit, had nonetheless been passed by in the creation of a new world.

At the same time, by yet another metaphoric transposition, *Casa-Grande e Senzala* opens the way for an even more fundamental reorientation. It seeks to reappropriate even the tragically flawed plantation past by focusing on it as the arena of cultural fusion. Nowhere is this more clear than in the language of nurturance and sexual initiation that runs throughout the text. Indeed, in Freyre's construction, it was the gentle, almost loving contact between master and slave within the *casa-grande* that counteracted the abuses of the slave-holding system elsewhere:

> But admitting that the influence of slavery upon the morality and character of the Brazilian of the Big House was in general a deleterious one, we still must note the highly special circumstances that, in our country, modified or attenuated the evils of the system. First of all, I would emphasize the prevailing mildness of the relations between masters and household slaves—milder in Brazil, it may be, than in any other part of the Americas. (Ibid., 369)

Within the intimacy of the *casa-grande*, the relations between masters and slaves were, in Freyre's interpretation, transformed and redeemed:

> The Big House caused to be brought up from the *senzala,* for the more intimate and delicate service of the planter and his family, a whole set of individu-

als: nurses, house-girls, foster-brothers for the white lads. These were persons whose place in the family was not that of slaves, but rather of household inmates. They were a kind of poor relations after the European model. Many young mulattoes would sit down at the patriarchal board as if they were indeed part of the family: *crias* (those who have been reared in the house), *malungos* (foster-brothers), *muleques de estimação* (favorite houseboys). (Ibid., 369)

Freyre argues in *Casa-Grande e Senzala* that it was through the dark-skinned *ama-leite,* or "wetnurse," that the most positive values of the non-European cultures were first transmitted to the European masters. It is in the intimacy of this exchange that Freyre locates the historical center, the truest expression, of the Brazilian spirit:

In our affections, our excessive mimicry, our Catholicism, which so delights the senses, our music, our gait, our speech, our cradle songs—in everything that is a sincere expression of our lives, we almost all of us bear the mark of that influence. Of the female slave or "mammy" who rocked us to sleep. Who suckled us. Who fed us, mashing our food with her own hands. The influence of the old woman who told us our first tales of ghost or *bicho* (animal). Of the mulatto girl who relieved us of our first *bicho de pé* (a type of flea), of a pruriency that was so enjoyable. Who initiated us into physical love and, to the creaking of a canvas cot, gave us our first complete sensation of being a man. (Ibid., 278)

As much as the physical reality of miscegenation and the sadistic sexuality of a slave-holding society, then, the tender intimacy of the *casa-grande* defines the Brazilian past in Freyre's interpretation. Symbolized most vividly in the act of suckling, in the milk of the *ama-leite,* and even more intriguingly in the nostalgic description of the sexual initiation of the plantation lad, it is this characterization that transforms the fundamentally negative view of Brazil's past with its legacy of racial mixture and degeneration, replacing it with an image of cultural fusion and creativity.[8] The importance of sexual interaction clearly remains, but it is situated within an interpretive framework focused as much on nourishment and sensitivity as on sadism, syphilis, and sadness.[9]

While *Casa-Grande e Senzala* is hardly less ambiguous than *Retrato do Brasil* in its internal structure, it nonetheless develops an interpretation of the Brazilian past that opens itself up to a radically different reading on the part of both the intellectual elite and the general public. It emphasizes the processes of sexual interaction and racial mixture as essentially positive in nature. Even more explicitly than the modernist texts of writers such as Oswald de Andrade, Mário de Andrade, or Paulo Prado, in its nostalgia, its attempt to reappropriate what Freyre saw as the best of the traditions of the Brazilian past, *Casa-Grande e Senzala* lends itself with unusual ease to the process of myth-making, to the legitimation of Brazilian society as a new world in the tropics. As even its detractors would agree, it has proved to be the most influential interpretation of Brazilian civilization ever produced, striking a chord in popular culture that has played easily into the increasingly nationalistic political discourse of the twentieth century (see Burns 1968). It again reaffirms—as if, for the vast majority of Brazilians, it really needed to be reaffirmed—that the nature of Brazilian reality has been specially marked.

Sensuality

Casa-Grande e Senzala, like the writings of the early travelers or of later intellectuals such as Paulo Prado, was of course directed to a very specific audience: the well-to-do white males who made up the Brazilian intellectual elite of Freyre's day, and who identified themselves in terms of their European roots. Nowhere is this more evident than in the language of "us" and "them," of "ours" and "theirs," that marks Freyre's discussion of nursing, nourishment, and racial contact in the closing sections of *Casa-Grande*—in his description of the white sons of the plantation owners nursing at the black breast of the African slave woman, and coming to their first and fullest understandings of themselves as men within her arms. Perhaps unconsciously, however, Freyre's text seems to have tapped into, to have uncovered, and, no doubt, even extended, a broader ideological context or base. Indeed, after years of popularization—whether in the textbooks of Brazilian school children, the theatrical works and musical compositions based upon it, or the *samba enredos* ("*samba* plots") built up around it during Brazilian *carnaval*—it is difficult to know to what extent Freyre's text really shaped this wider context and to what extent it was itself shaped by it (see Freyre 1983, xxvii). Whichever the case may be, perhaps all that really matters is the fact that *Casa-Grande e Senzala* has given the fullest and most vivid expression to what has been a far wider reaching, and, I suspect, more deeply rooted, ideological configuration: the sense, at once pronounced yet troublesome, of the uniquely sensual character of Brazilian life and of the Brazilian people. This understanding, although most elaborately articulated in the constructs of certain intellectuals, has nonetheless been present as well in the forms and structures of popular culture. While sexual life in North America or Europe has been treated as an essentially individual phenomenon, in Brazil it has also emerged as a central issue at a social or cultural level, and has been taken, for better or worse, as a kind of key to the peculiar nature of Brazilian reality.

Texts such as Prado's *Retrato do Brasil* or Freyre's *Casa-Grande e Senzala* clearly play on such understandings of self. In so doing, they have in

large part succeeded in grounding these interpretations in a particular reading of Brazilian history (a reading which was itself culturally patterned and
structured), and have thus provided them with a new and unusually powerful authority. If they play upon and legitimate such interpretations, however, they did not produce them. On the contrary, it would be much more
accurate to suggest that they shaped and molded the raw material provided
by the broader ideological context in giving these interpretations their most
concentrated and elaborate expression. These texts thus point us in the direction of the wider context and can be understood completely only when
situated within its terms.

As one steps back to view the larger picture, however, the understandings that at first seemed so clear and simple begin to give way. The relatively
neat and tidy connections that take one from the texts of writers such as
Pero Vaz de Caminha through those of Paulo Prado or Gilberto Freyre gradually begin to dissolve into a far more complicated set of transpositions and
transformations as one moves to the more encompassing ideological configurations that have made such texts possible. These clearly defined texts begin to disintegrate, much like one's own image in a house of mirrors, leaving not an underlying essence—a natural sensuality, produced by racial
mixture and peculiar to life in the tropics—but a multiplicity of reflections,
of representations or cultural meanings, which cut across the fabric of social
life but converge in the texts that we have discussed here and in the interpretations of the Brazilian self that such texts encode. It is this wider, more
complex, cultural context—as well as the often contradictory cultural logics
which seem to organize it—that we must now seek to understand.

3

Men and Women

As important as their myths of origin have been to modern Brazilians seeking to interpret their own cultural history and to give meaning to their contemporary sexual existence, they are obviously incomplete: they rely on a wider range of concepts drawn from at least partially distinct domains of cultural reality. This is especially true in their use of a whole set of assumptions related to the question of gender: definitions of _macho_ (male) and _fêmea_ (female), conceptions of _masculinidade_ (masculinity) and _feminilidade_ (femininity), notions of what it is to be an _homem_ (man) as opposed to a _mulher_ (woman) in Brazilian society, and perhaps most important, understandings of the ways in which such notions shape one's sexual experience in contemporary Brazilian life. These understandings are present everywhere in daily life; indeed, they are so central as to be taken largely for granted, internalized almost unthinkingly, by particular individuals. Given this fact, it is best to begin, once again, by contextualizing such concrete notions within a wider discourse and turning, first, to the legacy of patriarchal authority in Brazilian history and to the significance that this legacy continues to hold for the understanding of gender and sexual life in contemporary Brazil.[1]

The Patriarchal Tradition

Certainly no less than the interpenetration of three distinct races, over the course of at least the past fifty years, the legacy of a patriarchal past has become essential to the movement of self-interpretation in Brazilian society (see Freyre 1956, 1963, 1970; see also Faoro 1979; Vianna 1955). The question of patriarchal authority, in turn, has been linked to the perceived salience of the patriarchal family in Brazilian history—not simply as a form of

30

social organization but as an ideological construct, a system of representations, that continues to influence the ways in which contemporary Brazilians understand the proper order of things in their universe, structure their social interactions, and interpret the meaning of their social relations.

As writers such as Gilberto Freyre, Oliveira Vianna, and Antônio Cândido have suggested, the classic model of the patriarchal family handed down from the colonial period was dualistic (Cândido 1951, Freyre 1956, Vianna 1955). It consisted of a nucleus composed of the patriarch and his wife as well as their legitimate children, all living together under the single roof of the plantation's *casa-grande*. On the periphery of this core, however, there existed a much more extensive and less well delineated set of individuals, constituted as a group principally through their various links to the patriarch himself: his concubines or mistresses, his illegitimate children, his slaves and tenant farmers, his friends and clients (see Cândido 1951).

The figure of the patriarch, and the authority which emanated from him, clearly lay at the heart of this system, effectively linking the core to the periphery and uniting them as a single, functional unit. The almost unlimited nature of patriarchal power within this unit has traditionally been interpreted as a response to the contingencies of the colonial situation: the difficulties of establishing a social order in an immense geographical region which lacked any effective coercive apparatus but which was characterized by an economy dependent upon an extensive force of slave laborers. Within this context, then, the patriarchal family rapidly became the dominant social unit—essential to the processes of social integration as well as individual socialization. Yet because of the nature of its organization, its dual structure and its heavy dependence on the seemingly unlimited power of the patriarch himself, the distances between its various members were rigidly marked and ordered in terms of an almost absolute hierarchy (see ibid.).

This hierarchical structure seems to have been based, above all else, on the exercise of force by the patriarch: his right to invoke violence. At its most extreme—as Freyre, for example, has described it in recounting the relations between fathers and their children in patriarchal Brazil—this right to violence could indeed be taken to its logical end, as a right to death:

> In patriarchal Brazil the authority of the father over a minor son—and even one who was of age—was carried to its logical conclusion: the right to kill. The patriarch had absolute power in the administration of justice in the family, some fathers reproducing, in the shade of the cashew grove, the severest acts of classic patriarchalism: killing and ordering killed, not only Negroes, but white boys and girls, their own children. (Freyre 1963, 59)

The hierarchical structure of patriarchal domination was thus crystallized in both the image and the reality of violence. The authority of the patriarch himself rested in large part upon the social distance which this potential for violence established between him and his followers—between the master and his slaves, the father and his children, the male and his females.

Indeed, the symbolism of violence (all too often played out in reality), is crucial to any full understanding of the relations between men and women in patriarchal Brazil. Perhaps nowhere was the distance between the sexes that typified the patriarchal structure more clearly articulated than in its images of male and female. As described by Freyre, for example, the relations between the sexes under the patriarchal system were based upon a principle of extreme opposition or differentiation: "It was also characteristic of the patriarchal regime for man to make of woman a being as different from himself as possible. He, the strong, she, the weak; he the noble, she, the beautiful" (ibid., 73). The *homem* and the *mulher,* and by extension, the very concepts of masculinity and femininity, were thus defined in terms of their fundamental opposition, as a kind of thesis and antithesis. With power invested entirely in his hands, the *homem* was characterized in terms of his superiority, his strength, his virility, his activity, his potential for violence, and his legitimate use of force. The *mulher,* in contrast, was defined in terms of her obvious inferiority, as in all ways the weaker of the two sexes— beautiful and desirable, but nonetheless subject to the absolute domination of the patriarch.

This extreme differentiation carried with it an explicit moral dualism which fed back to legitimate and reinforce the apparently natural order of the gender hierarchy:

> The exploitation of woman by man, characteristic of other types of society or social organization too, but notably of the patriarchal-agrarian type which prevailed for a long time in Brazil, is favored by marked specialization or differentiation of the sexes. This justifies a double standard of morality, permitting man complete freedom in the pleasures of carnal love and only permitting the woman to go to bed with her husband when he feels like procreating. And for the woman this pleasure goes hand in hand with the obligation to conceive, give birth to, and raise the child. (Ibid., 73)

Assured, through his unquestioned domination, of his fundamental physical and moral superiority, the *homem* enjoyed an almost absolute sexual freedom. The patriarch could enter into and maintain ongoing sexual relations not simply with his wife, but with any number of mistresses or concubines as well (a fact which, in Freyre's characterization, tended to give the patriarchal structure of plantation life a haremlike quality and made it so uniquely well suited to the processes of racial mixture). The sexual activities of his women, on the other hand, were strictly regulated and controlled by the patriarch himself. His wife, invariably a white woman, was expected to be available to him, principally for procreation, as he desired. And his concubines—more often than not, the most favored of the dark-skinned female slaves on his plantation—were equally circumscribed, expected to await his call and subject to his wishes.

This dualistic sexual morality permeated and effectively divided all aspects of daily life. On the one hand, it successfully mapped out sharply opposed male and female domains, carving out contrasting sets of male and female space, opposing notions of proper male and female activities. While the activities of the male were directed toward the wider social world of economic, political, and social interactions beyond the family domain, the activities of his wife and daughters were sharply restricted, limited to the domestic world of the family itself. Thus the *casa* (house) was reserved as both fortress and prison for his wife and daughters, and the *engenho* (sugar factory) and, increasingly, the *cidade* (city), the *praça* (city square), and the *rua* (street) were the territory of men, the domain of the patriarch. His world was one of action and was sharply opposed to the relatively inactive, or, probably more accurate, the guarded and bounded society of his women.

Just as this double moral standard resulted in the sharp differentiation of male and female spheres within the patriarchal family, it also appears in what Antônio Cândido has described as the clear-cut separation of legal procreative functions from the sexual and affectual realm in patriarchal society (Cândido 1951). On the one hand, tied to the Christian ideal of monogamous family life, the legal core or nucleus seems to have provided what Cândido terms "a stabilizing force" in the otherwise chaotic sexual life of colonial Brazil, ensuring political and economic continuity by confirming set lines of inheritance running from the patriarch to his legitimate male offspring (ibid., 302–3). At the same time, however, thanks to the dual structure of the patriarchal system and the colonists' apparent taste for non-European women, the sexual and affectual interests of the patriarch seem more often than not to have been directed away from this legal core and toward the periphery—toward a de facto set of polygynous relationships with any number of his female slaves (see Cândido 1951, Freyre 1956).

While the illegitimate children produced by these relationships seem to have been afforded unusually high status in colonial society, it was through the patriarch's legal sons and daughters that the continuity of the patriarchal structure was assured—through marriage alliances arranged between patriarchal families and through the inheritance of the patriarch's wealth by his legitimate sons. Within the context of this structure, the double standard which so completely characterized the relations between the patriarch and his women was reproduced in the socialization of his sons and daughters. Indeed, the daughter was subject to an even more rigid set of controls than was her mother. In the interests of protecting her *virgindade* (virginity), her *honra* (honor)—and by extension, the honor of her father—her freedom of movement was almost completely curtailed. Entrusted during the day to the vigilance of a favorite *mucama* (female house servant), she was at night relegated to the secure interior of the *casa-grande,* to chambers which resembled more a prison cell than anything else:

> We have but to recall the fact that during the day the white girl of whatever age was always under the eye of an older person or a trusted *mucama,* and this vigilance was redoubled during the night. A small room or bedroom was re-served for her in the center of the house, and she was surrounded on all four sides by her elders. It was more of a prison than the apartment of a free being. A kind of sick-room, where everyone had to keep watch. (Freyre 1956, 353)

This almost Arabian seclusion was maintained throughout her childhood, until, at the age of twelve, thirteen, or fourteen, a marriage was arranged for her with another suitable member of the patriarchal class—often many years her senior. At this point, of course, control over her conduct passed to the hands of her husband, and she began her career as both the mistress of his estate and yet another subject of his dominion.

The early experiences of the son, however, contrast sharply with this picture. Like the daughter, from his very earliest days, his contact with the black slave population on the plantation was extensive and intimate. Yet in the case of the son, as Freyre has suggested, such contact provided less an extension of paternal vigilance than a basic sexual education—the boy's ini-tiation, at a very early age, into sexual maturity. Far from the strict sexual prohibitions applied to the daughter, whose virginity was a commodity for exchange under the patriarchal system, this early sexual initiation of the son was expected and encouraged as a mark of masculinity and, for that matter, as a potential contribution to the plantation labor force:

> No Big House in the days of slavery would want any effeminate sons or male virgins. In the folklore of our old sugar and coffee zones, whenever there is reference to sexually pure youths, it is always in a tone of mockery, by way of holding the ladylike fellow up to ridicule. The one always approved was the lad who went with the girls at as early an age as possible. A *"rapariqueiro,"* as we would say today. A woman-chaser. A ladies' man. A deflowerer of maidens. One who lost no time in taking negro women that he might increase the herd and the paternal capital. (Ibid., 395)

A younger version of the patriarch, then, with his masculinity staked at least in part upon his early sexual activities and his reputation for promiscuity, the image of the young male provides a sharp contrast to that of the female. Taken together, the two figures seem not only to reproduce, but in a funda-mental way to deepen the structure of the gender hierarchy—to add new nuances to it.

The vision of masculinity that emerges here seems reasonably clear-cut and unified. It is a vision of power, of action and virility encompassed in the patriarch's absolute domination over all those around him. The comple-mentary vision of femininity, however, is rather more complicated. It is,

without question, a vision of inferiority and submission in the face of patriarchal authority. But the separations between monogamy and polygyny,
between legal endogamy and sexual/affectual exogamy, and between the legal and the sexual/affectual functions within the family have been tied to a
far more ambivalent characterization of the *mulher* than of the *homem*.

While the *homem* was largely synonymous with the figure of the patriarch himself, a more diversified characterization of the *mulher* seems to
have been built up, linking and yet simultaneously differentiating visions of
the legal wife and mother, on the one hand, from images of the concubine,
on the other. That these figures could so easily be combined in a single
representation of the *mulher* is clearly of crucial importance, for it allowed
the notion of the *mulher,* as an ideological structure, to be far more easily
manipulated in a variety of ways to reinforce and legitimate the structure of
patriarchal domination. And, equally important, at least from our own perspective, it provided an ideological model which has continued to exercise
profound influence over the ways in which Brazilian women have been con-
ceptualized and categorized—the ways in which an understanding of femininity has been built up in the course of normal daily life.

Ultimately, it is here that the importance of the patriarchal legacy described by writers such as Cândido and Freyre takes on its fullest significance. The historical circumstances that made possible the classic patriarchal configuration have clearly long since vanished. Indeed, the extent to
which such a structure was ever in fact fully realized, even when historical
circumstances might have permitted, is a question open to debate (see, in
particular, Almeida et al. 1982). In the present context, however, this question is perhaps less important than the fact that a socially constituted vision
of the patriarchal family (as opposed to its empirical reality) has continued
to affect Brazilian thought, the ways in which Brazilians view not only their
own history but their current social milieu as well. And perhaps in no other
area has the impact of patriarchal ideology been more powerfully felt than
in the construction of gender—in interpretations of masculinity and femininity and understandings of the relationships which should exist between
men and women in contemporary social life. While these understandings
have been transformed in a variety of ways over the course of many years, a
lingering vision of patriarchal life nonetheless remains and must still be
confronted as at least one important foundation for contemporary Brazilian
thought.

The Language of the Body

While a certain image of the patriarchal tradition provides a context within
which Brazilians continue to interpret the relations between men and
women, it is in the language of daily life that their most salient understand-

ings of masculinity and femininity are first built up. It is in the expressions, terms, and metaphors that are used to speak about the body and its practices that the child's relation to reality begins to take shape and that the meanings associated with gender in Brazilian life are most powerfully expressed.

When viewed from this perspective, the differentiation between two fundamentally distinct physical types—one male and the other female—is taken as a simple fact of nature. While the manifestations of this apparently natural differentiation are varied, it is in the existence of two opposed anatomical structures—the *pênis* and the *vagina*—that the distinction between male and female is literally embodied. This initial classification of anatomical difference is but the first step, however, in a much more extended process of cultural elaboration that ultimately transforms the apparently given nature of the human body into a set of socially significant distinctions: the hierarchical relations of gender in Brazilian life. From this perspective, the penis and the vagina begin to take on meaning not simply as markers of a natural order, but as representations of a particular set of cultural values (see Rubin 1975).

The character of this process, and the underlying structure of values that it encodes, becomes quickly evident as one turns from these relatively neutral, infrequently used terms to the more common slang expressions that have been developed in Brazilian Portuguese in order to speak about the genital organs in daily life. While the list of synonymous terms is remarkably etensive, those most frequently cited by informants and most commonly used in colloquial speech consistently articulate a distinction between the male and female bodies that is anything but neutral. On the contrary, their implicit associations, and, no less important, their explicit use in particular speech acts, repeatedly elaborate the strength and superiority of the male genitals at the expense of the deficient and patently inferior female anatomy.

Among the most consistently cited terms for the penis, for example, are expressions such as *pau* (stick), *caralho* (small stick), *madeira* (wood), *cacete* (club, cudgel), *pica* (prick, from *picar,* to prick or pierce), *mastro* (mast or staff), *vara* (pole, shaft, stick), *arma* (weapon), *faca* (knife), *ferro* (iron, iron tool, iron weapon), *bicho* (animal), and *cobra* (snake). While this brief list by no means exhausts the available vocabulary (see Almeida 1981, Maior 1980, Rasmussen 1971), the pattern that it establishes is clear: drawing on the observed, physical qualities of the penis, virtually all of these expressions describe an elongated object, phallic in the most obvious sense. But they do much more than this, as well, for they place emphasis on the potentially active quality of the phallus—on its aggressive quality, on its potency not merely as a sexual organ, but, in the language of metaphor, as a tool to be wielded, as a kind of weapon intimately linked to both violence and violation (see Rasmussen 1971, 176–81).

The complexity of the associations involved here comes through clearly in my discussion below with João, a twenty-six-year-old bisexual male from a lower-middle to lower-class background (see Appendix 2):

RP: And the words for the penis, the stick (*caralho*), what are the most common that you use?

João: Prick (*pica*) . . .

RP: Prick . . . and prick has another sense?

João: It has, to bite (*morder*) . . .

RP: To bite?

João: That's it, a prick (*uma picada*), understand? You were stung, you were pricked . . . A snake, when it bites you . . . you don't say that it bit you—the snake pricks you (*te picou*).

The associations here seem to be largely unconscious. They are implicit. They begin to emerge more explicitly, however, as the discussion continues:

RP: And what else?

João: Club (*cacete*).

RP: Club . . . what does club mean? Is it something else as well as the penis?

João: It is. The penis has this term of club. Club also means beating (*porrada*). "I'm going to give you a clubbing (*cacetada*)" means that you're going to receive a beating (*porrada*). But the club is the piece of wood that (*pedaço de pau*) I get and hit you with. Then, I'm with a club (*cacete*), and I'm going to give you a clubbing (*cacetada*). And joking, I can give a clubbing with my club (penis) too. Do you understand?

In the play of words, the phallus becomes, figuratively if not literally, an *arma*—a weapon, an instrument of metaphoric aggression, or in an extension of Pierre Bourdieu's expression, of symbolic violence (Bourdieu 1977, 237; Bourdieu and Passeron 1977, x–xii).

This set of associations becomes even clearer when we turn to the use of the term *porrada*—literally, a "blow" or a "beating." But *porrada* is also used to mean the sexual act itself. It is closely linked to the term *porra*, which is at once an angry interjective expression, yet another synonym for the penis (once again, from its association as a *clava*, a "club" or "cudgel"), and the most frequently used popular term for *sêmen* (semen) or *esperma* (sperm). *Porra*, in turn, is tied to the terms *esporrar* and *esporro*, which are used to describe the ejaculation of sperm as well as a verbal rebuke or aggression.

Understood as both phallus and semen, as well as in its relation to anger and violence, then, *porra* becomes a kind of essence of masculinity—a symbol of creative power, of *potência* (potency) and *vida* (life):

> In Brazil, when you hear someone speak really about a symbol of fertility, the people are going to refer to "my *porra.*" "My *porra*" is positive. "My *porra*" is ... it gives life. "My *porra* made a child." "My *porra,* you know, created a new being." (João)

This emphasis on potency or creativity that is so clear in the symbolic associations of *porra* can be tied, ultimately, to the role played, not simply by the penis, but by the entire genital region, the *virilha* (groin), as the locus of masculine strength and will. It is in the *ovos* (literally, "eggs," essentially equivalent to "balls" in English) or the *testículos* (testicles), and the *saco* (sack) or *escroto* (scrotum), that *porra* is most obviously thought to be located and in which the strength and courage associated with masculinity are most definitively embodied.[2]

In the language of daily life, for example, *saco* becomes a kind of barometer of patience and will: expressions such as *estar com saco cheio* (literally, "to be with a full sack") and *encher o saco* (literally, "to fill the sack") mean to be "fed up" or "bothered" by something, and the expression *puxar saco* (literally, "to pull someone's sack") is roughly equivalent to the notion of "kissing ass" in English. Such essentially nonreferential usage is made possible by the metaphoric connection between the male genitals and masculine strength, stamina, force, and virility. Indeed, when used with the augmentative suffix *-udo,* any number of these terms (for example, *pirocudo, ovudo,* or *sacudo*) can acquire connotations of both virility and courage. Much like the notion of "having balls" in English, the idea of "big balls" or a "big sack" implies "guts" or "manliness" in Brazilian Portuguese.

Ultimately, then, it is in such symbolic structures that an understanding of masculinity is first built up in Brazilian life. It is through such structures that the perceived reality of the male body is culturally elaborated and articulated—that the penis is transformed into the *falo* or *fálus* (phallus).[3] In the symbol of the phallus the diverse meanings associated with masculinity in Brazilian culture merge and intertwine. It links notions of virility and potency to notions of force, power, and violence in varying degrees of conscious and unconscious understanding. And it is in the semantic configuration of these associations in the discourse of daily life that the meaning of masculinity in Brazil must initially be apprehended.

A different, and far more complicated, picture emerges as one turns to the female body and the representations of femininity that it encodes. Just as the phallus takes shape as a kind of weapon, an instrument of force and potential violence, the female body seems to emerge, through much the same process of linguistic association, as both the object of such violence and, paradoxically, a locus of danger in its own right. The list of synonymous terms employed to speak about the vagina in everyday conversation is certainly no more limited than the list that has been developed to speak about the penis. As in the case of the penis, the terminology is varied; nonetheless, here too the most commonly used terms seem to cluster around and elaborate upon the most basic of observed physical characteristics: they include expressions such as *boceta* or *buceta* (a box or receptacle), *buraco* (hole), *gruta* (cave), *racha* (a split or fissure), *chochota* or *xoxota* (from *chochar*, to become dry, weak, or insipid), *greta* (crack), *carne mijada* (meat covered with urine), *boca* (mouth), *boca mijada* (mouth covered with or filled with urine) and *boca de baixo* (mouth underneath, below), *perereca* (small tree frog), *aranha* (spider), and *baratinha* (small cockroach) (see Almeida 1981, Maior 1980, Rasmussen 1971).

If the terms most commonly used to speak about the penis emphasize its strength and its potential for violence, the terms used to discuss the vagina conjure up a sense of inferiority and incompleteness. While the male is characterized by his possession of a potential weapon, the female is characterized in terms of the fissure between her legs—the mysterious entrance that somehow defines her entire being. For both male and female informants, however, it would seem that in the darkness and obscurity of this emotionally charged image, mystery itself gives way to a sense of danger: the vagina is transformed, in almost classically Freudian terms, into the *boca de baixo,* the mouth below, the threatening *vagina dentata.* No less menacing, and more pejorative, the *boca de baixo* is simultaneously a *boca mijada*—a mouth contaminated with urine. In the most vulgar metaphor, it is *carne mijada*—meat contaminated with urine—and is laughingly said to possess the unpleasant *cheiro de bacalhau,* the "smell of dried codfish." As one riddle puts it:

> Question: What is the similarity between the cunt (*boceta*) and the fish?
>
> Answer: They both stink equally and they both swallow worms!

These symbolic connections are described as an obvious gloss on the natural processes of the female body associated with the vagina:

> They speak this way because it has all the impurities of the body . . . urine, menstruation . . . Understand? (Rose, a twenty-five-year-old heterosexual woman from a lower-middle-class family)

Linked to the waste products of the body, to urine and to the flow of menstrual blood, the vagina thus becomes a focal point for notions of impurity in Brazilian life. As is so often the case cross-culturally, it comes to stand for uncleanliness, pollution, and contamination. And, by extension, these negative images are associated with the most deeply rooted understandings of women and femininity in Brazilian culture.[4]

Nowhere is this linkage more clearly played out than in the symbolic complex developed around the notion of *menstruação* (menstruation). At its most neutral, the *mênstruo* (menses) of the female is described as her *ciclo mensal* (monthly cycle). More metaphorically, however, it is referred to as a kind of *hóspede incomodo*—as an "annoying, troublesome, or unwanted guest" named Chico or Jacinto. The flow of menstrual blood itself is spoken of as *corrimento* (discharge or secretion caused by infection), as *pa-quete* (literally, "a steamship") or *sangria* (red wine mixed with pieces of fruit), as a *bandeira vermelha* (a red flag, associated by informants with the flags placed on beaches to prohibit entry on particularly rough days as well as with the various materials which women use to catch the menstrual discharge), as an unpleasant *regra* (rule) of nature, or most forcefully, as a *mal-de-mulher* (an evil or a sickness of women). The woman suffering from such a condition can thus be described as *menstruada* (menstruant), as *incomodada* (incommodated), or simply *regrada* (ruled).

Once again, an extremely complicated set of associations is at work. At the heart of this complex is the association that is built up between notions of menstruation, sickness, and a contamination that is at once physical and spiritual. The term *corrimento*, for example, describes not merely the discharge of menstrual blood but also the genital secretions caused by venereal infection. The notion of a *mal-de-mulher* develops this connection even further, conjuring up a whole set of similar expressions used to describe venereal infection—for example, *mal-de-amores* (sickness-of-lovers), *mal-de-cristãos* (sickness-of-Christians), and *mal-de-Vênus* (sickness-of-venus). It plays on the double meaning of *mal* as both "sickness" and "evil," linking together images of disease, evil, contagion, and femininity:

> Look, there's a saying in Brazil that I don't remember well, but that says: "The woman is satanic because she spits fire . . . no, she spits *blood!*" Because you know that the cunt (*boceta*) has the same ideology as the mouth (*boca*), right? Therefore she spits blood during the days of menstruation. Then this connotation of something evil already comes from the woman in relation to the Devil. Blood . . . not blood as a life factor, because blood is the energy of life, but because she is . . . is throwing out [wasting] the blood, there is already that connotation of something evil.
>
> . . . .
>
> It's like the term *mal-de-mulher* . . . *Mal-de-mulher* can be the name of a sickness . . . Understand? "Ah, careful, don't touch because this is the *mal-de-mulher* . . ." In the same way that in certain regions of Brazil it happens that when the woman is menstruating it's as if it were a sickness. Understand? Then, the man doesn't even dare to kiss her because he could get the *mal-de-mulher* . . . They think that it's a disease . . . like this . . . you make it with a woman with gonorrhea, you put your dick in, and right away you know that you're going to come out with gonorrhea. You kiss a person with syphilis and you know that you're going to get syphilis. So, the one man says to the other: "Look, don't go with that whore, no, because she's got the *mal-de-mulher,* and be careful, because you could get sick." (João)

Just as the conceptualization of semen elaborates a set of qualities implicit in the representation of the phallus, the cultural articulation of menstruation extends the apparent perplexities of the vagina. Taken together, these symbolic complexes simultaneously bind and separate. They define male and female as opposed, hierarchically related categories within a system of cultural values. Yet at the same time, they link the two through the threat that each potentially poses to the other—through the violent attacks which seem always ready to be unleashed by the male against the female as well as through the physical and even spiritual pollution passed from the female to the male.

The physical reality of the body itself thus divides the sexual universe in two. Perceived anatomical differences begin to be transformed, through language, into the hierarchically related categories of socially and culturally defined gender: into the classes of *masculino* (masculine) and *feminino* (feminine). The nature of this distinction becomes even more explicit and more complicated as one moves from the terms that Brazilians use in speaking about the organs of the body to the ways in which they describe and comment upon the combination of these organs. As in other parts of the Latin world, these forms of speech in Brazil tend to develop a basic distinction between *atividade* (activity) and *passividade* (passivity)—between culturally defined "active" and "passive" roles during sexual interactions. Building upon the perception of anatomical difference, it is this distinction between activity and passivity that most clearly structures Brazilian notions of masculinity and femininity and that has traditionally served as the organizing principle for a much wider world of sexual classifications in day-to-day Brazilian life (see Fry 1982, 1985; Misse 1981; Parker 1985b, 1987, 1988, 1989b).

The importance of this distinction between activity and passivity is especially apparent in the language that is used to describe sex itself—in expressions such as *comer* (to eat), *dar* (to give), *entregar* (to deliver), *foder* (to fuck), *ficar por cima* (to be on top), and *abrir as pernas* (to open one's legs). *Comer*, for example, used in the active voice, functions metaphorically to describe the act of penetration in sexual intercourse. It implies an act of control, an act of domination:

> The one who eats is on top . . . he's the one who dominates . . . (Telma, a
> twenty-year-old heterosexual female, originally from a very poor rural family)

In a variety of different contexts, *comer* can thus be used synonymously with terms such as *vencer* (to conquer, vanquish) and *possuir* (to possess, own). When one soccer team defeats another, for example, its fans claim that their team has "eaten" its opponents. And through the act of *comendo*, the active partner metaphorically consumes the passive: *possuindo*, taking possession, asserting ownership.

Dar, in contrast, describes the passive role of being penetrated in either genital or anal intercourse:

> The one who gives (*dá*) opens his (or her) legs . . . delivers himself to the
> other one . . . (Antônio, a twenty-nine-year-old gay man from a middle-class
> background)

Just as *comer* suggests an act of control or domination, *dar*—or, synony-mously, *entregar*—connotes a process of submission or subjugation. Again, the metaphors can be carried out of the sexual realm: *abrir as pernas* can describe any variety of personal defeats, while the saying *entregar ouro para o bandido* (to deliver gold to the bandit) functions as well to describe a loss of valuables as it does a sexual performance. Through the act of *dando* (giv-ing), the passive partner is offered up to be penetrated and possessed (Fry 1982, 1985; Parker 1985b, 1987, 1989b).

This set of relationships is also captured in the use of *foder,* perhaps the strongest of any of the terms used to describe sexual exchanges:

> To fuck (*foder*) . . . when you're fucking (*fodendo*) someone, when you're eat-ing (*comendo*) someone, when you're possessing (*possuindo*) someone with authority . . . then you are above someone . . . You have a superiority . . . You're on top of someone . . . You're in a position of dominator, of trainer . . . You're being the king during that moment. (José, a thirty-two-year-old bisex-ual male from a working-class background)

And as in the case of *comer,* in the passive voice, *foder* implies far more than a simple sexual position: it can be used both literally and figuratively, much as one speaks of having been "fucked over" in English:

> You can be fucked (*fodido*) because someone is eating (*comendo*) you, in sex . . . But a person who is *fodido* . . . ah, there are so many things . . . Look, my country can be totally fucked because of who is in power . . . Do you under-stand? You can be fucked because you have cancer . . . You can be fucked be-cause this month you don't have any money in the bank, and a mountain of debts to be paid. You use this term a lot with money. (José)

In short, like terms such as *comer* and *dar, foder* does not simply describe a sexual act. On the contrary, it simultaneously encodes in a sexual idiom a system of cultural values, a set of social relationships. Like synonymous terms and expressions, it develops a field of power and organizes this field around the culturally defined poles of activity and passivity which them-selves translate into sharply contrasted notions of masculinity and feminin-ity (Fry 1982, 1985; Parker 1985b, 1987, 1989b).

The language of the body in contemporary Brazilian life thus plays a crucial role in the construction of gender as a social, rather than a strictly biological, fact. It is through language that the body is not only categorized, but described and interpreted—invested with multiple meanings and ana-lyzed in terms of differential values. The Brazilians' most profound under-standings of themselves as men and women are intimately bound to the language through which their culture has enabled them to think about themselves as embodied beings—and about their bodies as sexual objects. Still, this experience and understanding of the body remains but the first step in what is a far more extended process of cultural elaboration—a process in which the relatively limited possibilities of anatomic form, as culturally classified and articulated, give way to increasingly nuanced notions of gender as a system of socially determined categories.

Sexual Categories

Through its description and interpretation of the natural world, the language of the body transforms biological reality into social significance. A system of sexual classification is built up and a hierarchy of values between the various classes is established. Playing upon deeply ingrained notions of activity and passivity, domination and submission, violence and inferiority, these structures split the sexual universe in two—opposing, without compromise, the world of men, penetrating and metaphorically consuming their partners during sexual exchanges, against the world of women, passively offering themselves up to be penetrated and possessed.

As clear as these oppositions seem to be in traditional Brazilian life, however, the full range of their meaningful potential is a good deal less straightforward than it might at first appear. While an opposition between activity and passivity seems to translate into a stark contrast between masculinity and femininity, it can simultaneously be employed to articulate a more subtle set of distinctions. Culturally defined notions of biological gender and social role can be manipulated, arranged and rearranged, combined in a variety of ways, in order to build up more diverse (and hence more ambiguous) images of masculinity and femininity—composite visions of male and female potential that encode a more elaborate system of sexual definitions.

The most obvious extensions of the traditional *homem* and *mulher* can be found in categories such as the *esposo* (husband) and *esposa* (wife) or *pai* (father) and *mãe* (mother). Linked through their marital relationship, through the act of *coito* (coitus) which symbolizes this relationship, and through the underlying notions of dominance and submission which structure it, these figures reproduce and reinforce the fundamentally hierarchical distinctions implicit in the more general categories of *homem* and *mulher*. Among the most concrete symbols or embodiments of cultural values such as virility and fertility, they serve as examples of masculinity and femininity played out to their fullest potential, and they function as models for the construction of male and female roles.

But if we take a step back and examine these oppositions within a slightly broader context, it becomes apparent that they function in concert with a range of other sexual classifications. *Homem* and *mulher,* for example, are defined not only with reference to one another, but also with reference to a variety of additional figures which embody a complex array of both positive and negative male and female possibilities. An understanding of the *homem* is constructed not merely through opposition to the *mulher,* but, at the same time, through his relation to figures such as the *machão* (macho or he-man), the *corno* (cuckold), and the *bicha* or *viado* (queer or faggot). And the *mulher,* like the *homem,* must be apprehended not merely in her opposition to him, but through figures such as the *virgem* (virgin), the *piranha* or *puta* (whore), and even the *sapatão* (literally, "big shoes," but best translated into English as "dyke"). These additional figures may be lesser players in the cast of characters that make up the Brazilian sexual drama, but they all nonetheless perform crucial roles in the construction of gender in daily life.

It is hardly surprising, given our understanding of both the patriarchal tradition and the language of the body in contemporary Brazil, that the figure of the *machão* should be as important as either the father or the husband in constructing a popular definition of masculinity. As much as any other single figure, the *machão* embodies the values traditionally associated with the male role in Brazilian culture—forcé and power, violence and aggression, virility and sexual potency:

> To be a man, a real man, you have to be a *machão.* A *machão* in bed and in the street: you have, or you think that you have, huge sexual potential, a big cock, and you fuck with anything that's a woman. The *machão* is a roughneck too, you know . . . He goes out into the street and he's always ready to fight in order to defend his honor. (João)

Indeed, sexual prowess and readiness to fight in order to defend one's honor are themselves indicative of a certain kind of power or dominance—a dominance which is perhaps the key characteristic of the *machão,* and in which he clearly begins to merge with the figure of the *pai:*

> But it isn't just that, no, you know . . . It isn't just sex. It's the thing about domination. Because I remember my father. He was the father. Everything there at home was his. He had to have charge of everything because he was the man, he was the father, he was the he-man . . . He had to dominate in everything. (Maria, a twenty-seven-year-old woman from a very poor family in Rio)

Together the *machão* and the *pai* provide a portrait, or at the very least, an ideal, of the modern *homem* as hardly distinguishable from the traditional patriarch. They embody a deeply rooted set of values that continues to function even today in structuring the world of gender in Brazilian life—a set of values in which the symbolism of sexuality, violence, and power are clearly linked in the cultural configuration of masculinity.

If an image of the true *homem* is built up, at least in part with reference to positively valued figures such as the *pai* and the *machão,* however, it is not solely with reference to these figures that the *homem* is defined. Just as the *homem,* as *homem,* must be understood at least in part through his opposition to the *mulher,* so too the *homem,* as *machão* or *pai,* must be understood in contrast to additional figures such as the *viado* and the *corno.* Understood, in the eyes of their fellows, as biological males who have in one way or another failed to live up to the masculine ideal articulated so forcefully in Brazilian culture, these characters seem to have taken on special significance as negative images in relation to the *homem.* The "queer" and the cuckold are visions of masculinity somehow lost or gone astray; they are visions of all that the true *homem* can never be:

A *viado* or a *corno* isn't a true man, you know! (Rose)

The crucial point is not simply that neither the *viado* nor the *corno* is a "true" man, but that both figures function—no less than the *mulher*—as negative alternatives in building up a positive image of what the true man in fact should be: the *homem,* the *machão,* the *pai.* For this reason, the neither truly masculine nor truly feminine figure of the *viado* or the *corno* opens up a particularly ambiguous cultural space vis-à-vis both the *homem* and the *mulher.*

Nowhere is this more obvious than in the case of the *viado* (taken, originally, from the term *veado* or "deer," but more commonly spelled and pronounced with an accentuated "i" replacing the "e"), the *maricas* (sissy) or *bicha* (literally, a "worm" or an "intestinal parasite," again, probably best translated into English as "faggot" or "queer")—terms applied principally to individuals who are thought to take the passive (and thus, symbolically, feminine) role of being penetrated. In a system that places such great emphasis on the distinction between activity and passivity, and which links this distinction to the categorical opposition of male and female, the *viado* or *bicha* is assigned a particularly problematic status. Like the *mulher,* such individuals are said to *dar,* or give—in this case, in passive anal intercourse. Regardless of their objectively male physiognomy, then, they are no less clearly opposed in popular conception to the active, eating *homem* than is the *mulher.* Yet they are not *mulheres,* and the ambiguities which such inversions of normally accepted cultural categories produce invest the symbolic space of the *viado* with an especially powerful emotional charge (see Fry 1982, 1985; Misse 1981; Parker 1985b, 1987, 1989b).[5]

What seems to be central here is the essentially anomalous effeminacy of what should rightfully be male virility and activity. This is evident in the use of terms such as *viado* or *bicha.* The use of *viado,* for example, is linked to a popular perception of the *veado* (deer) as the most frail and delicate, the most effeminate, of animals:

It's because the animal is so delicate—almost feminine. (Dora, a twenty-two-year-old woman from a middle-class family in Rio)

Indeed, a number of informants went so far as to situate the term historically and link it directly to Walt Disney's popular film *Bambi:*

> This came, historically, after Walt Disney when he invented Bambi. You
> understand? Because he was a very fragile animal, very delicate, without
> strength. In spite of being "male" he was very effeminate. Before this, the cre-
> ation by Walt Disney, the terms were *maricona, pederasta, a florzinha, ma-
> rica* . . . (João)

Much the same set of associations is tied, in popular conception, to the term
bicha. A word designating a variety of intestinal parasites, *bicha* is also the
feminine form of *bicho* (a class of "unspecified animals" which can range
from insects to mammals), and it is this second meaning, with its emphasis
on an animallike femininity, that most clearly catches popular imagination:

> It's principally this business of femininity . . . When we think of a *bicha,* we
> think of a feminine animal. (Katia, a twenty-three-year-old heterosexual fe-
> male from an upper-middle-class family in south Brazil)

Indeed, as at least one highly educated informant explained, the term *bicha*
itself might well have been recently imported from France—a variation on
the French term *biche,* or "doe." With the underlying connection "female
deer," it would thus tie together the whole set of associations suggested by
other informants.

The structure of male/female relations in Brazil has therefore also
served as a model for same-sex interactions as well. A sharp distinction between culturally defined "active" and "passive" partners in anal intercourse
has been central to the traditional understanding of sexual relations between men. While the "active" partner in same-sex relations would be unlikely, in light of the Catholic condemnation of both pederasty and sodomy,
to give public notice of his activities, he is nonetheless able, thanks to his
sexual activity, to maintain an essentially masculine identity. The *viado* or
bicha, the "passive" partner in such exchanges, on the other hand, is unavoidably transformed, not merely in his own eyes, but in the eyes of his
partner or partners and in the eyes of any other individuals around him who
might happen to have knowledge of his sexual practices. He is emasculated.
He becomes, through his sexual role, a symbolic female:

> Look, the *viado* gives ass . . . He serves as the woman. (Rose)

He is referred to, often mockingly, in terms otherwise reserved for the biological female: as the feminine *ela* (she) rather than the masculine *ele* (he),
as *a donzela* (the little virgin), *a moça* (the girl, young woman), or *a menina*
(the little girl). He tends to be at least partially ostracized, finding employ-
ment only in highly marginal lines of work or in jobs traditionally reserved
for women. And he often seems to adopt a highly exaggerated feminine manner in both movement and speech—acting out, through his caricature, the

role of *bicha louca,* or "flaming queen." Yet regardless of the mockery and pretense, even the *bicha louca* is not, in fact, *uma mulher verdadeira,* "a true woman." On the contrary, he remains a dangerous and disturbing anomaly. Genitally male, yet having abandoned the true *homem*'s identity as both *machão* and *pai* by adopting the passive sexual role, the *bicha* becomes a kind of female animal, betwixt and between the accepted categories of normal human life (see Fry 1985, Parker 1985b).

Because of the emphasis it places upon culturally defined notions of activity and passivity as criteria for sexual classification, along with the clear differentiation it seems to articulate between culturally defined anatomical structure and social role, the distinction here is crucial to an understanding of the Brazilian sexual universe. Within the terms of this cultural frame, relations between men are structured along the same lines as those between men and women, that is, in terms of sex and power. It is possible, though certainly not unproblematical, for a man to enter into sexual relations not only with women but also with other biological males without really sacrificing his fundamentally masculine identity. In taking the active role of penetration during anal intercourse, his hierarchical dominance is preserved. In performing the passive role in such exchanges, however, the *viado* or *bicha* gives up his masculine identity—he comes to be defined as essentially feminine in terms of social role and as at best a poor imitation of the biological female in terms of social status, socially inadequate as a man and a biological failure as a woman. The threat of anal penetration, whether symbolic or real, thus defines the underlying structure of masculine relationships, and defense against the phallic attacks of other males becomes an almost constant concern during the ordinary interactions of daily life.[6]

Although there are certainly important differences between the two figures, an analogous symbolic configuration also emerges as one turns from the *viado* to the *corno*—literally, the "horn on an animal's head," but in popular speech, a "cuckold," an *homem* who has been betrayed by his *mulher.* As in the case of the *viado* or *bicha,* the list of synonymous terms and expressions developed in order to speak about the *corno* is extensive. While offering up a range of meanings and implications, however, these expressions virtually all tie back, in one way or another, to the verb *cornear*— literally, "to gore with horns," but figuratively or colloquially, "to cuckold":

> Everything comes from the verb *cornear,* you know. The *corno* is the man who was betrayed or is being betrayed by his wife—he is the cuckold. *Cornudo* means the same thing. And along with being called *corno* and *cornudo,* he can also be called *puto* or *chifrudo.* You know what a horn (*chifre*) is, don't you? A horn is that thing that the ox has on his head, that the deer has on his head . . . Instead of saying *corno, cornudo,* or *puto,* you can say *chifrudo*—"he's a *chifrudo*" instead of "he's a *cornudo*." And you can also say: "He's getting branches on his head . . . he's got a fucking set of branches on his head." It's a

metaphor . . . the branches of a tree and their similarity to the horns of the
man. (José Carlos, a thirty-two-year-old heterosexual male from the working
class)

The betrayal by the *mulher* thus wounds and transforms the *homem;* it
gores him and simultaneously places horns upon his head. It constitutes a
symbolic onslaught—a frontal attack upon the masculine identity of the
homem which, when successfully carried out, reduces him to the moral
equivalent of the *viado.*

In the animal imagery applied to both, the link between the *viado* and
the *corno* is explicit. As one informant described it to me, it is an association
which rests on the *corno*'s inability to protect and control the *mulher*, on
the impotence that such inability implies, and on the symbolic emasculation
that it produces:

> The *corno* is being fucked over . . . he is being fucked over without knowing
> it. He's a *viado*; in the Brazilian conception, he's a *viado*. Look, the man who
> lets his woman screw with another man, he's a *viado* because he isn't paying
> attention to the woman. He doesn't pay attention to his woman, so she ar-
> ranges another man. It is always said: "Ah, she arranged another man in the
> street because he wasn't any good in bed . . . she had to go out in the street
> and find another man." Do you understand? So you have this business of the
> *viado*, the horns, the person with horns, the branches, the antlers. And what's
> more, you still have that business: the *corno* is being screwed by the woman
> because she's betraying him. (José Carlos)

The notion of impotence is rapidly translated into an even stronger image of
passivity, and the figure of the *corno* merges with that of the *viado:*

> You talk about horns, about antlers or branches, because of the *viado*. The
> antlers are the antlers of the deer. It's this passive business. You understand?
> He's being screwed, metaphorically, by the woman who's betraying him. It's
> because of this that the *corno* is also called a "banana"—because he's com-
> pletely limp . . . he's like a queer. (João)

The figures of the *viado* and the *corno* are thus quite consciously associated
in popular thought. Each reinforces the other, while at the same time articulating, through the conceptual power of the negative, a certain vision of
masculinity as properly realized in Brazilian life.

For all the similarities that exist in the popular conception of the *viado*
and the *corno*, however, there is nonetheless at least one crucial difference
between the two: while another male is the key agent acting to produce the
symbolic space of the *viado*, it is the action of the *mulher* that places horns
upon the head of the *corno*.[7] Just as the *homem* penetrates the *viado*, the
mulher symbolically gores the *corno:*

> It's the *mulher* who makes a cuckold . . . Even if it was my best friend who
> fucked with her, you know, it wasn't him who made a *corno* out of me, no. I

would call him a "son of a bitch"—but she was the one who betrayed me.
(João)

Indeed, the *mulher* herself can be described as a *cornoateira* or, loosely
translated, a specialist in the art of cuckoldry; and the threat posed by the
cornoateira seems to be understood in Brazilian life as an almost ever-
present danger. Just as so much male anxiety seems to be focused on the
figure of the *viado* and the whole notion of passivity in sex, the possibility
that one's *mulher* might at any instant be betraying one seems to haunt the
Brazilian male.

Ultimately, then, if the *homem,* the proper *machão,* must be understood in terms of his activity and virility, this understanding must be played
off against the passivity and impotence that continually threaten the self-
assurance of male identity. The emotional contradictions of this structure
are projected outward in the symbolic complexes that mark off the *viado*
and the *corno* as traditional categories in the Brazilian sexual universe. In
the ridicule and disgust which so often accompany these figures, the Brazilian male is not simply the unquestioned dominator of patriarchal ideology,
but a potential victim—constantly open to symbolic attack, not only by
other men, but by women as well.

Recognizing that women can be seen at once as fundamentally inferior,
as desirable, and as threatening and dangerous is crucial to any full understanding of the Brazilian system. Indeed, the ambiguities inherent in such
an understanding are central to the popular conception of the *mulher.* As in
the case of the *homem,* a vision of the *mulher* has traditionally been built
up in relation to a variety of other figures: the *virgem* (virgin), the *piranha*
or *puta* (whore), and to a slightly lesser extent, the *sapatão* (big shoes or
dyke). Like their male counterparts, these female figures function symbolically in marking off as well as opening up the feminine domain as a semantic
field. They articulate both positive and negative aspects of a socially constructed feminine role.

Technically, at least, the *virgem* is defined according to her lack of sexual experience. Known also as a *donzela* (damsel), a *moça* (maiden) or *mo-
çinha* (little maiden), or even a *santinha* (a little saint), she is characterized
by her *castidade* (chastity) and, consequently, by her fundamental innocence and purity:

> In Brazil, virginity means purity. A virgin girl is a pure girl. And she has to
> marry as a virgin. This is what is correct. (Angela, a forty-eight-year-old
> housewife from a lower-middle-class family in Rio)

The innocence and purity of the *virgem* is concretely symbolized in her *cabaço* (hymen):

> The *cabaço* is what the woman loses when she fucks for the first time . . .
> Understand? In Brazil, you call this the *cabaço* . . . "She lost the *cabaço* of the

dove (vagina)!" It's when the prick enters, bursts the *cabaço,* that the woman loses her virginity. (João)

The social recognition of a girl's innocence is thus tied to the condition of her body—to its freedom from sexual contact, attested in the unbroken hymen. According to the dictates of popular morality, it is the hymen that the *virgem* must preserve until she marries (see Alves et al. 1981, Willems 1953).

Within the traditional context of sexual life in Brazil, the *cabaço* thus becomes a key representation not only of female sexuality, but of the control over that sexuality which is rightfully exercised by men. In the case of the *virgem,* such control lies, first, in the hands of her father and, by extension, of his sons, her brothers. Her *cabaço* is a symbol of her own innocence and purity, but it is simultaneously a mark of male dominion, a sign of the father's authority, and a symbol of family honor. It is clearly expected that such dominion will pass, at the time of marriage, from her father and brothers to the bride's new husband—a transfer of powers symbolized in the initial act of intercourse between the bride and groom following the marriage ceremony:

> The *cabaço* has to be delivered to the man after the ceremony. (Maria)

The "delivery" of the *cabaço* takes on an almost ritual importance which is hardly less significant than the marriage ceremony itself. It establishes the absolute control of the husband over the body of his new wife, and it transfers, at the same time, the question of *honra* from the central concern of her father and brothers to that of her husband.

Given the importance of the *cabaço* as a symbol of male control, it is hardly surprising that the *perda da virgindade,* the "loss of virginity," should focus upon it, and that this should be a highly problematic event capable of calling into question not simply the innocence of the fallen *virgem,* but the honor of her entire family:

> The woman who loses her *cabaço* outside of marriage isn't pure anymore . . .
> Now she's a whore! She dishonored her family . . . (João)

Speculation concerning a young woman's virginity is therefore extensive, particularly on the part of men, but among the women of the community as well:

> People often defame one another in Brazil . . . I think it's strange that where I lived . . . it was the kind of place that . . . a girl who loses herself, they debauch her life in such a way that the woman simply is transformed into almost nothing . . . She is a whore, she is shameless, she is a vagabond, a tramp, a prostitute . . . She dishonored the name of the family. Because to lose her virginity before marriage here in Brazil is to dishonor! (Antônio)

While terms such as *deflorar* or *desflorar* (deflower) are normally employed
to describe the husband's rightful possession of his virgin bride, the same
act, outside of wedlock, is invariably described in terms of loss, disgrace, or
dishonor. Through the intervention of men, and the initiation that they provide into the world of sexual experience, the *virgem* is transformed, in one
direction, into the *esposa* and *mãe*, the wife and mother, and in the other
direction, into the *piranha* or *puta*, the whore, who takes her place not
merely as an expression of male control, but as a threat to it.[8]

As in the case of the *viado* (who is in many ways a strangely analogous
figure), the effect the *puta* has upon the men around her varies depending
upon her own activities. In the case of the woman who accepts no fee yet
nonetheless gives herself up indiscriminately or unthinkingly, for example,
the *puta* clearly confirms the fundamental virility and masculinity of her
illicit partners. At the same time, however, she clearly denies control over
her sexual behavior to those men who should rightfully exercise it: her father and brothers or, if she has already married, her husband. She thus
undercuts the structure of power within which her sexual activities ought
to be deployed and which, within the proper order of things, her actions
ought ultimately to confirm. She emasculates the men of her family and
places horns upon her husband's head. In the case of the professional prostitute, even if family ties have been distanced or cut, one finds a structurally
analogous system. The *michê* (payment) which she receives from her cus-
tomers confirms their value rather than hers. And while control over her
sexual actions might be said, in some instances, to lie in the hands of her
gigolô (gigolo or pimp), his own financial dependence on her, his acceptance of the money she earns, and his willingness for her to engage in sexual
relations with other males, transforms him in the eyes of Brazilian society
into nothing more than a parasite—a *bicha* in the fullest sense of the term.

Once again, we find a configuration fraught with contradictions. Like
the *homem* who sleeps with the *viado*, the *homem* who sleeps with the *puta*
or *piranha* in no way jeopardizes his own moral standing. On the contrary,
in fulfilling his role as *machão*, in possessing her, however briefly, he confirms and even pronounces his own masculinity. For him, the *puta* can become a central object of desire reinforcing a particular vision of himself and
his place in the sexual universe. For her family, and for the other individuals
whose lives she touches, however, she is seen as an agent of destruction, as
the woman who "eats," who devours men, families, everything in her path:

> *Piranha* . . . This term was used because the fish from the Rio Amazonas de-
> voured, devour, the people or the animals so quickly . . . So, it's a term of
> destruction . . . The *piranha* destroys homes, the *piranha* transmits disease
> . . . the *piranha* takes the person off the path of virtue . . . (Luís, a thirty-five-
> year-old heterosexual male from the lower class)

She is as fundamentally destructive as the *mãe* is productive, and it is this destructiveness that makes possible an extension of the *puta*'s cultural meaning from the sexual to the nonsexual realm. Just as the term *viado* becomes an epithet used against a male engaged in virtually any form of socially unacceptable behavior, expressions such as *puta* and *filho* or *filha de uma puta* ("son" or "daughter of a whore," roughly equivalent to "son of a bitch" in English) are extended metaphorically as markers of social condemnation and forms of verbal attack:

> The *puta* lives by means of acts that are condemned by society. They live from sex. They make their work out of their bodies. It's because of this that you call a *puta* not just the woman who screws, but anyone who fucks over other people, who lives outside of the normal patterns of society. *Puta* is a pejorative name saying that the people are outside of the moral patterns, of religion or society . . . The *puta* is always doing something negative, something to fuck someone over—which doesn't mean to say that the *putas* who earn their price on the streetcorners of life are any less *filhas da puta* than a general who is acting as a dictator in a country or a boss who is making slaves out of his employees . . . they're both *filhos da puta*. (Jorge, a forty-five-year-old attorney, originally from northeastern Brazil but currently living in Rio)

Like the *viado,* then, the *puta* carries an especially strong, and especially ambiguous, meaning, which extends beyond the explicitly sexual. At one and the same time, she can both confirm the masculine identities of her partners and call into question the structure of power upon which those identities are founded. More forcefully than the *virgem,* she takes on a central role in constituting not only femininity, in and of itself, but its underlying and fundamentally threatening relationship to masculinity.

If from the point of view of the Brazilian male, the *piranha* represents the most threatening aspects of femininity, however, it is the *sapatão,* the "big shoes" or "dyke," the woman engaged in sexual relations with another woman, who embodies its most perplexing possibilities and departs most completely from the expected norms of feminine behavior. In terms such as *bota* (boot), *botão* (large boot), *coturno* (army boot), *lésbica* (lesbian), *machona* (macho woman), *mulher aranha* (spider woman), *mulher homem* (man woman), and *mulher macho* (male woman), emphasis is almost always given to the *sapatão*'s supposedly masculine character, and it is here that the symbol of the *sapato* (shoe) becomes central:

> The shoe has a connotation of the foot, that the man who has a large foot, he is good in bed and has a big prick . . . It's a popular proverb . . . So, women very . . . very . . . with movements that are very large, without feminine class, completely stereotyped like those of a man, are called *sapatão* or *sapato grande*. (João)

Thus not simply any shoe will do. It is the big shoe, the boot, or army boot:

> You can see that of all the terms for the dyke, "army boot" is the strongest . . .
> It's the symbol of the Brazilian army. So, it's the symbol of machismo, it's the
> symbol of the courageous man, it's the symbol of the strong man . . . He puts
> on those leather shoes, those boots that come up to here, a thing to step in the
> mud with, to go to battle, to go to war . . . So, it's very much a man's thing!
> Understand? So, the army boot is a shoe that stands up to everything and is
> strong. (Antônio)

At least initially, the *sapatão* is defined less in terms of her sexual behavior
than in terms of her fundamentally masculine style, and it is the shoe or
boot that serves as the concrete symbol of this style.

This initial emphasis on the masculine style or quality of the *sapatão*
contrasts sharply with the case of the *bicha* or *viado,* who is clearly characterized not merely in terms of his effeminized personal style (though this
too is noted and commented upon), but in terms of his apparently passive
role during sexual intercourse with another male. The lack of sexual emphasis in the case of the *sapatão* is understandable only if we realize that the
very idea of female sexual conduct outside of a context which is in some way
or another defined vis-à-vis male sexuality is almost unthinkable in traditional Brazilian life. The *sapatão* must somehow be situated within a male-
defined context:

> There's also the difference between *sapatão* and *sapatilha* (slipper). Because
> the *sapatão* is the active woman, the one who sucks, who puts the dildo in the
> other's cunt . . . And the *sapatilha* is the *mulher viada*—the one who screws
> with men, screws with women, the one who simply lays on the bed and lets
> the "macho" dominate. She's the one who plays the feminine role. It's because
> of this that you use the word *sapatilha,* because *sapatilha* is the shoe that
> ballerinas use. (José)

Thus, to be fully apprehended and managed both intellectually and emotionally, same-sex relations between two women must be structured along the
lines of opposite-sex relations—in terms of activity and passivity, penetration and being penetrated, dominance and submission.[9] From this perspective, a distinction between the *sapatão* and the *sapatilha* parallels the distinction between the *viado* and the *homem.* Just as the *homem* is able to
preserve his fundamentally masculine identity thanks to his performance of
the active role during sexual intercourse, the *sapatilha* holds onto her feminine identity through her performance of the properly passive role; and just
as the *viado* sacrifices his masculine identity in adopting a passive sexual
role, the *sapatão* sacrifices her femininity through her active dominance.
While the activity of the *homem* preserves his status in society, however, the
activity of the *sapatão* obviously does not. On the contrary, she emerges as

a woman out of control, a woman who has stepped—perhaps even more completely than the *puta*—outside of the patterns of accepted male and female conduct in Brazilian life, and whose presence thus calls into question the most deeply held assumptions of the Brazilian sexual universe.

Thus the oppositions that structure the general relationship between men and women operate as well within the more elaborate distinctions of the male and female domains.[10] The juxtaposition of oppositions at various levels of abstraction makes possible a degree of nuance in the construction of masculinity and femininity as cultural configurations which is far greater than might be expected. At the same time, it opens the wider ideological structure of this system to attack at its most vulnerable points, for just as the various "positive" and "negative" characters define the nature of culturally acceptable identities and behaviors, they simultaneously draw attention to the possibility of deviation from sanctioned patterns. It is against this nagging possibility, against the threat of internal contradiction and the potential for deviation, of course, that the system must somehow guard itself. More accurately, it is against the internal contradictions of the system of meanings in which they live that particular men and women must make their way, continually seeking to protect both themselves and those around them.

Sexual Socialization

The patriarchal tradition, the language of the body, and the system of sexual classifications discussed above clearly play a central role in structuring the experience of sexual life in contemporary Brazil. In dividing the sexual universe into two sharply opposed domains, as well as in blurring the exactness of this division, these symbolic forms map out the sexual terrain and suggest some of its potential traps or dangers. As is the case with all cultural systems, however, these structures are never apprehended immediately or entirely. On the contrary, they are internalized only gradually through a complex process of socialization beginning in the earliest moments of childhood. This process, while hardly invariable, is itself culturally determined and constituted. It not only produces and reproduces the structure of sexual relations in daily life, but becomes an integral part of the ideological system that it articulates.

In Brazil, as is almost universally the case in other cultures as well, responsibility for the care and education of children has tended to lie largely in the hands of women. Throughout early childhood, the *mãe* or some appropriate substitute (a female relative such as her own mother or sister, or if economic circumstances permit, a maid or nursemaid) is generally the child's constant companion; and the fundamentally feminine domain of the home, as opposed to the male-dominated world outside the home, typically marks the limits of the child's world. It is through the *mãe* or some female equivalent, such as the *babá* (nursemaid), that the child's earliest relation to reality is organized. It is through her breast that sustenance is first obtained and gratification first experienced. It is through her intervention that control over bodily functions and an understanding of bodily hygiene are gradually built up. It is through the toys and clothing that she selects, the songs and stories that she relates, that the traditions of the culture begin to be imparted. In short, while there have recently been a number of significant changes in these patterns, both nurture and education have been understood as essentially feminine functions, and children of both sexes have typically been relegated to this feminine domain. Whether boys or girls, their very earliest identifications, their first notions of self, as well as the images of them constructed in the eyes of others, have traditionally been built up within this context.

Because of this extremely close early association of both boys and girls with an undifferentiated world of women, however, a high degree of cultural attention seems to be focused on the importance of developing sharp distinctions between the two genders relatively early in childhood, and the path that each gender must follow in passing from childhood to maturity is understood as radically different. On the one hand, in the case of females, both sexual identity and sexual potential seem to be taken as givens. Identification with the feminine role is largely assured through continuous contact with the older women of the family, while the maturation of sexual potential is closely linked to the natural order of things through relatively concrete and observable physiognomic changes. Surging up out of nature, female sexual potential must be culturally molded, shaped, and most important, controlled—brought in line with the socially determined expectations of the traditional female role, with the passivity and submission that are the marks of femininity in Brazil. In contrast, male sexual identity is understood as problematic. Initially tied to the feminine world, to both the mother's breast and apron strings, and at least somewhat less marked than his sister by physiognomic changes as he matures, the boy's most fundamental sexual being is somehow more fragile. Threatened from the very start by an overly close association with the female domain, the virility and activity that are the key markers of masculinity in Brazilian life must quite literally be constructed, built from the group up through a process of masculinization capable of breaking the boy's initial ties with women and transforming him into a man.[11]

Throughout their early lives, young girls have traditionally remained sheltered within a women's world. They are quickly taught the skills that are most clearly associated with the woman's domestic role (whether in her own household or as a maid or employee in the households of others): cooking, cleaning, caring for children, and so on. The speed with which girls are taught these household skills contrasts radically, however, with the delays in and, in many instances, the complete lack of education on sexual matters. For girls, as well as for boys, early infancy tends to be seen as a time of relative innocence—a time when sex plays little role in the child's life. But by the age of five, and perhaps as early as three years, a pattern has set in which marks the culture's treatment of women throughout their lives. While any signs of unruly or unfeminine behavior are carefully corrected by the watchful parent, explanation and information concerning the girl's own sexual existence are studiously avoided, and the character and processes of her own body typically remain shrouded in a silence which becomes more absolute as time goes on.

The nature and extent of this silence is most evident in regard to the question of menstruation, for it is with the commencement of menarche that a *menina* (girl) is truly transformed into a *moça* (maiden), and that her sexual potential becomes unavoidably problematic. From this point forward, her essential femininity, far from being threatened by overly masculine behavior, is all too apparent. With this new physiological potential to *engravidar,* "to become pregnant"—and to thus bring shame on the honor of her family name—the underlying danger of her now fundamentally sexual being receives increasing attention and her body becomes increasingly marked as a locus of both mystery and filth. Menarche makes visible and real her sexual potential in its most concrete sense, and thus calls into action a complex set of processes aimed at circumventing, controlling, and even denying this new reality—at preserving virginity, enforcing chastity, and assuring passivity. It is a process which emphasizes the prohibition and repression of the *moça*'s natural potential, and which is characterized above all—at least from the *moça*'s own perspective—by an economy of silence or ignorance (see Alves et al. 1981). Menstruation is cited repeatedly by informants as a source of misunderstanding and trauma, fear and insecurity:

> I was one of those who didn't know about . . . menstruation . . . I remember the first time, when I saw that blood . . . I only saw it when I went to the bathroom. And I became afraid. I didn't know. And later, after I talked to my sisters, I became ashamed. (Sandra, a thirty-six-year-old housewife from an upper-middle-class family)
>
> I wound up discovering things, like this, through my girlfriends . . . But my mother herself, she was . . . she would twist things up a lot to talk to you . . . And after it happened she would come to ask, "How is it that you already knew?" I remember when she tried to talk about, you know, about this business (menstruation), "Ah, Telma, I have to talk to you about something . . . that every girl . . . I don't know, you're very young, you don't even imagine what it is . . ." And so then I said, "But tell me, Mother, what it is." And from there, my mother became ashamed, and said, "No, it isn't something that you

talk about." And this went on and on, and my mother never said anything. And one day, I was at school, and it happened, and I arrived at home crying . . . I thought that I was dying, you know. I had girlfriends at school who said to me, "No, it's this . . . ," and explained. But I arrived at home and wanted to talk to my mother. And she never really explained . . . She just said, "Ah, it was this that I wanted to tell you . . . it was this that I wanted to tell you." (Telma)

If menstruation seems to be especially significant and disturbing, however, it is hardly the only area where silence and ignorance are evident. On the contrary, in a society which speaks so much about sexual issues, an absence of speech and, when speech is in fact possible, the presence of conflicting explanations, characterize the early sexual education of young girls:

> Something funny . . . I remember that I didn't know how a woman becomes pregnant . . . my mother had never said anything . . . and I remember that I thought that the woman took some kind of pill . . . It was only at school, when I said, "How is it that it happens, does the woman take a pill, does she go to the doctor and take something, or what?" that my girlfriends explained, "No, it isn't that!" How they laughed at me. They explained, "No, it's a kind of a seed . . ." So I imagined, naturally, the kind of seed of an orange, of, I don't know, some kind of fruit. My God . . . I remember the day and the place. But how can it be! My mother never said anything! (Rose)

Just as the transformation from *menina* to *moça* that takes place with the beginning of menstruation is permeated with misunderstandings and silences, so too is the transformation from *moça* to *mulher* with the loss of virginity which marks the young woman's entry into full, adult, reproductive sexual life. Intercourse, pregnancy, and maternity—events extensively commented upon in other spheres of daily life—are remarkable by their absence from the early sexual education of the young women. While some information is inevitably obtained, of course, especially through the intervention of friends and schoolmates, it is almost always partial, fragmentary, and more often than not, contradictory. It must find its place within the wider context of misinformation and ignorance that has traditionally marked the early years of female existence in Brazilian society.

The extent to which such distortions mark off feminine reality in Brazil is understandable, of course, when situated within the hierarchical structure which it seeks to confirm and reproduce. Because femininity is understood as so inferior and yet, at the same time, so threatening, it must be rigidly controlled and regulated. The withholding of information is at least one means of achieving this control. Yet if this seems an especially effective strategy, it is but one of the possibilities that is open to the system as it seeks to perpetuate itself. Perhaps equally prominent is a strategy in which silence gives way to words, to the repeated *proibições* (prohibitions) that have traditionally restricted legitimate sexual expression on the part of women in Brazilian culture.

This is especially evident in the prohibitions pertaining to the *virgem*, which threaten her with the label *piranha* or *puta*. Following upon the silences of childhood and the transformations of adolescence (marked, of course, by the onset of menstruation), it is in active and vocal restrictions that female sexual life is delineated:

> It's like that, you know . . . Ever since I was young, I always heard these things, you know . . . that the woman has to get married, that she has to get married as a virgin, you know, and that if she isn't a virgin when she marries she isn't worth anything, she doesn't have any value . . . for the rest of her life she's, she's talked about by everyone. (Maria)
>
> I remember that one day I arrived home and I was complaining of a stomachache, and so on, and so on . . . And my father argued with my mother, because my father heard me complaining to my mother about the stomachache, you know. "You let your daughter go out with boys who you don't even know," and so on . . . He thought that I was pregnant, you know. So, he fought with my mother, and he told her to never let me go out by myself with a boy. (Telma)

Fraught with potential dangers, the freedom of movement of adolescent girls has tended to be sharply circumscribed, at least insofar as contact with young males is concerned. *Namorando* (courting) might well begin at a relatively early age, but always under the watchful eye of either adults or groups of peers theoretically large enough to ensure respectable conduct (see Willems 1953). And the delimitation of female sexual activity seems accepted by both boys and girls as the proper order of things, the only acceptable alternative:

> I wanted to be a virgin when I married. I thought that this was the right thing . . . A young girl can't permit certain things. (Vera, age twenty-four, originally from a very poor family in the state of Minas Gerais but currently living in Rio)
>
> I understand why a girl wants to stay a virgin . . . You know, she wants to be a proper girl . . . A girl is different from a guy, you understand? She has to act right . . . If she doesn't, who is going to want to marry her? (João)

If the figure of the *virgem* provides a focus for the values associated with femininity, female virginity (and the lack of sexual knowledge that it enforces) becomes a focus for the process of socialization which seeks to reproduce these values. It is a theme raised constantly by both males and females, and seems to take no less a hold upon the former than upon the latter, perpetuating, even today, many of the most fundamental assumptions of patriarchal sexual morality.

Just how strong a hold patriarchal structures continue to exercise in contemporary Brazilian life can be grasped by contrasting the silences, prohibitions, and repressions that characterize the socialization of females with the radically different sexual upbringing of males. If femininity is understood as a natural force that needs only to be controlled and disciplined, masculinity is seen as anything but certain. Constantly threatened, as we have seen, by forces impinging upon it from all sides, the virility that marks mature male sexuality must follow a tortuous and troublesome path in coming to be: it must be cultivated through a complex process of masculinization beginning in early childhood.

Perhaps because the boy's physical development is perceived to be so much less clearly marked by breaks than is the case with girls, his social development is more discontinuous. While the earliest years of a child's life, regardless of gender, seem to be focused around the activities of the household, in the case of boys, by the age of five or six this pattern begins to give way. Although the daughter's place will remain, in large measure, within the confines of the home, there is a strong (though not always explicitly stated) sense, on the part of both mothers and fathers, that the proper path for their sons to take will lead them increasingly away from this feminine domain. Boys must begin to make their way in the more public, masculine world outside the home. Individual histories vary, of course, depending largely on economic circumstances—the necessary contribution that some children must make to the family income, the availability of formal schooling, and the like—but from the age of five or six to the early teens when they begin to court, boys will spend increasing amounts of time with exclusively male company. In particular, they will take more part in the social life of groups of men such as the friends and associates of their fathers or older brothers, and these male groups will take over central responsibility for masculine socialization as well as sexual education and, often, initiation.

To impart to young boys the skills that will be necessary in their later life as *homens* seems to be a task taken largely for granted by older Brazilian males. It is rarely organized in advance. On the contrary, it takes place informally, in the general flow of daily life. Whether it is a question of teaching an economic craft, a sport such as swimming or *futebol* (soccer), or later, how to drive or repair an automobile, it is a task that older men both enjoy and take seriously. This is most true in the case of sexual education. After all, for the youth to become a true *homem,* a rigid set of behaviors must gradually be internalized and reproduced, and nothing is so central to this as a proper understanding of sexual life. The feminine ties of earlier life must be cut, and effeminate behavior must be eliminated. Properly masculine sexual techniques must be explained and assimilated. And it is within the context of male society that these goals can most effectively be accomplished.

Nothing is more important than the task of stamping out the vestiges of feminine passivity that may still mark even the least timid five-year-old. The chance that a boy might grow up to be a *viado* seems particularly troublesome, as one informant pointed out in recalling the conversation of a group of older men that took place when he was six or seven years old:

> There's a phrase that they used . . . especially the father . . . the phrase was this: "I prefer that my son be a bandit rather than a Zica or a sissy." "Zica" was a name that they gave in those days for *viado*. Therefore the father would prefer that his son died, that his son was a bandit, than that he be a *viado*. (Carlos, a twenty-seven-year-old bisexual man from the lower class in Rio)

Surrounded with an extremely strong emotional charge, the figure of the *viado* serves as a counterimage. He is what the true *homem* must never be and represents all that is unacceptable in the behavior of one's children. Expressions such as *você está agindo como uma bicha* (you are acting like a queer) or *você está agindo como maricas* (you are acting like a sissy) quickly meet the earliest signs of unacceptably feminine behavior and are in fact among the earliest sanctions employed in the socialization of gender among young males.

As important as the repression of unacceptably effeminate behavior clearly is in the formation of a fully masculine identity, however, the complete eclipse of feminine influence can only take place through the no less complete objectification of the *mulher* herself. As early as the fifth or sixth year of a boy's development, he may well be deemed old enough for at least some tentative direction in this regard on the part of either his father or some comparable adult (uncles, members of the father's friendship network, and so on). Since this direction often takes place in groups, it tends to provide not only a very real and impressive source of information for the boy himself, but simultaneously, a forum for the reaffirmation of masculine solidarity and the demonstration of sexual expertise on the part of the adult men:

> When I was maybe six years old, in groups of men, my father would say, "You have to fuck that one there . . . that one there is a woman . . . you have to fuck women . . . fuck cunt . . . you have to make her suck . . . you have to fuck her ass!" And the others, they would add on . . . They would give lectures. "Take off the bra first." "And when you're sucking her nipple, you take her hand and put it on your cock." "But you've got to have a hard-on, to show her that you're *macho*." And all those things. (João)

In a sense, then, through such exchanges, men define themselves not only individually, but as a group, in opposition to women. It is not enough that the boy should shed whatever vestiges of feminine influence might still linger on in his comportment. He must also begin to identify himself as a member of a wider male culture complete with its own esoteric and, in this case, erotic knowledge. And he must push even further in beginning to use this knowledge in opposing himself and his fellow males to the world of women, the subjects of his sexual will.

Older males have furthered this process of identification not merely through verbal instructions, but also by providing published sources of information, as well as, in some instances, arranging for sexual initiation itself. With the easing of censorship that accompanied political liberalization during the late 1970s, sexually explicit publications have become extremely common throughout urban Brazil, and are even found, though to a much lesser extent, in many rural communities. Sold openly at any newsstand, and purchased almost exclusively by men and boys, glossy magazines such as *Playboy, Fiesta,* and any number of others, have become a fixture of Brazilian male culture. But as early as the 1950s, far less refined publications known as *livrinhos* or *revistinhas de sacanagem* (dirty little magazines or booklets) had established themselves in male culture. Published either anonymously or under a pseudonym—the true identity of Carlos Zéfiro, by far the most popular author, for example, remains unknown even today—these booklets featured a wide variety of erotic stories, told principally, though not exclusively, from the male point of view, and were illustrated in almost cartoon fashion with a series of sexually explicit drawings or designs (see d'Assunção 1984, Marinho 1983, Da Matta 1983). While the influence of these more primitive publications has given way slightly before the onslaught of modern publishing, they are still widely available and, judging from the comments of informants, clearly have constituted a key element of the sexual heritage of a whole generation of Brazilian men:

My father used to buy dirty magazines and give them to me to read (and he liked to read them too, obviously). And I loved to see . . . I always liked dirty things . . . ever since I was young. And he loaned them to me to take to school, in order to show my friends, the other boys. Until the day that the principal of my school—an old lady principal, from an extremely conservative school—got my little booklets, with my folder full of dirty booklets . . . What happened? I was expelled from school! And my father and my mother . . . My mother gave me a scolding, but my father couldn't say anything . . . He had to put me in a more expensive school—something that I know he didn't like. Later, he scolded me, he yelled at me, he said that that wasn't something to take to school, that it was something for the street, that it was something that you look at behind the chicken coop, that it was something for, for . . . that you couldn't even bring it inside the house! But I was expelled from school . . . the woman kept all the dirty booklets, and my father got so pissed off at her that he went there and said, "I want the booklets of my son!" And she said, "Then it's you who . . ." "It's not me who gives them to him, no . . . Ask him." And I said no, obviously. And the woman said that she was going to open an investigation in order to find out where I got them, because she had to find a way to close down the source . . . For you to see the arithmetic progression of the thing. And my father said that he took responsibility for everything that I did, and that he didn't want me to continue any longer in that stinking school because the school was very bad and I had gotten horrible grades. And she said that this wasn't her fault: "It's not my fault that your son is so dumb." And my father became furious. My father hit the top of the woman's desk! And immediately the woman opened her drawer, the bottom drawer, where she must have put them so that she could look at them too . . . she opened the drawer, and got all of the booklets . . . There must have been eight or seven, I don't even remember any more . . . And she returned them to my father. And my father said, "Let's go home!" Real macho! To give a little respect, you know! He got to the car, put everything in my folder again, the booklets, and said, "Don't take this to the school!" (João)

If such booklets provided explicit sexual information, however, it is still doubtful that their impact has been as great as what remains the most important rite of passage within male culture in Brazil: sexual initiation arranged, often, by one's father, and carried out, no less often, by the *puta*, the paid prostitute (see also Willems 1953). Like the booklets, the brothel takes on a special significance for Brazilian males as part of a particular kind of sexual ritual, as a site for sexual exploration and discovery:

José: It was my father who took me to a bordello for the first time.

RP: How old were you, more or less?

José: Eleven years and three months. He took me to Três Rios.

RP: In Três Rios?

José: It's a city . . . a city in the mining triangle. He took me to this whorehouse where it was . . . like . . . it was the second most famous in Brazil . . . The first was Mangue in Rio de Janeiro and the second was Três Rios with the brothels. And all of the ranchers from the mining triangle had their businesses, their offices, in Três Rios . . .

RP: And he took you there alone, or with friends of his?

José: No, it was me, him, and a friend of his named Joaquim, who, by the way, is a very bad element. And I remember that he introduced me to Brigite. Brigite Bardô. She didn't have one of her teeth at the back. And her room was full of pictures of B.B., of Brigitte Bardot. Do you remember her? And she thought that she was the Brazilian Brigitte Bardot.

RP: She didn't have a tooth at the back?

José: No, one tooth was missing. I think that it was a blow that she received. And strange . . . She had a mark on her butt too that looked like the mark from a knife, from a knife or razor wound.

RP: Your father selected her?

José: That's right. Papa was the one who chose her because they said that Brigite was the hot one in the brothel. She was the one whose cunt was on fire. So there I went. And on arriving home, I stupidly said that I had been in

Três Rios. And my mother started to ask questions, in order to know . . . And I said, "Ah, I wasn't anyplace at all, no." But it was already too late, right. So, my father arrived at home, and said, "I took him to the whorehouse all right . . ." And so on . . . and so on . . . "He has to learn to be a man!" And my mother said, "You're crazy . . . You could cause your son to get a disease." She never said the names of the diseases . . . She just said "bad disease" or "disease from women." So, my father winked his eye at me and said that I used a condom, a rubber . . . "But he used a condom!" And he winked at me. I hadn't used anything at all because he hadn't given me anything. The only thing that he ordered me to do was: "When you fuck with a whore, afterward, piss, and wash your prick with coconut soap."

RP: And so what happened with your folks?

José: My God, there was a fight in the house . . .

RP: And after that, did your father take you to the brothel again?

José: He took me, yes.

RP: Many times?

José: No. Two or three more times. Later . . . later I learned the way, you know. Later I learned the way, and all the young guys who had a motorcycle or a car . . . my older cousins who were eighteen or nineteen years old, because at this time I was twelve or thirteen years old . . . I went with them too.

As yet another step in the boy's transition to manhood, the bordello, like the *livrinhos de sacanagem,* marks out the space of male sexual life. As these texts make clear, however, it is also apparent that this space is understood as a contested one—that a sharp distinction is built up not only between women and men, but also between types of women. On the one hand, as the photographic model or the prostitute, women emerge as sexual objects— the *mulher comível,* the "edible woman." On the other hand, as administrator or mother, as the *mulher respeitável* (respectable woman), women are agents of repression threatening to delimit or cut the free reign of masculine sexuality.

This duality, of course, is part and parcel of the double standard of sexual morality in modern Brazil. Recreating the same structures evident in patriarchal ideology, in the language of the body, and in the system of sexual classifications that we have examined, the processes of socialization focus upon (and, indeed, become part of) what Emílio Willems describes as the cult of virginity and the cult of virility (Willems 1953). On the one hand, female sexual life is defined by a set of rigid controls which make any and all sexual manifestations outside the structure of marriage (defined loosely, not necessarily as a legal or religious institution, but as a socially recognized relationship between husband and wife) absolutely unpardonable. Male sexual life, on the contrary, is almost incited. Early sexual activity is understood and encouraged as fundamentally positive and healthy, and the young

Brazilian male learns rather early on to structure his own self-esteem in terms of his sexual prowess. Marriage is expected to play relatively little role in channeling or restricting male sexual activities, and the patterns of sexual behavior established during adolescence (distinguishing, as they do, between certain types of women suitable for certain types of interactions) are expected to continue, for all practical purposes, throughout the sexual life of the adult male.

These cultural patterns are founded on an understanding of a fundamental difference in the sexual natures of males and females: a distinction in which the sexual potential of the female, dangerous and threatening as it is, follows its natural course through the clear-cut, physiological transformations that take place in her life while the sexual potential of the male is somehow inhibited by his early association with women, and must thus be coaxed and cultivated, built up and sustained against the constant threat of backsliding. Within the context of such different conceptions, then, the cultural treatment of female sexuality is quite clearly aimed at control and limitation. It is based upon a symbolic economy of silence and ignorance, repression and prohibition. The treatment of male sexuality, on the contrary, must be one of incitement and encouragement, an almost constant discourse about matters sexual within the confines of males groups and an ongoing and explicit sexual education offered by older males to younger ones. It is within the context of such socialization, within its terms and through the mechanisms that it relies upon, that the inequalities which have traditionally structured the Brazilian sexual universe can be continually reproduced, and no less important, that the contradictions which exist within the system itself, and which might thus call it into question, can be undercut.

The Gender Hierarchy

Ultimately the question of gender in Brazilian life must be apprehended as Brazilians themselves apprehend it. We can approach this question only through the labyrinth of cultural forms that define it and give it meaning in the flow of collective life. It is through these forms, as I have suggested at some length, that the perceived anatomical distinction between male and female is transformed, gradually, and not by any means unproblematically, into the more nuanced notions of man and woman, masculine and feminine, masculinity and femininity. And it is in terms of these distinctions that men and women build up what are clearly among their most significant and deeply felt understandings of themselves both as individuals and as members of a particular social order.

As we have seen, however, whether in the ideological structures of the patriarchal tradition, the language of the body and the system of sexual classifications which marks the flow of daily life, or the very patterns and processes of sexual socialization, these understandings are repeatedly linked to the question of power. They simultaneously give rise to and legitimize an elaborate hierarchical structure in which *homens* are distinguished in terms of their authority and dominance, while *mulheres* are distinguished according to their submission and subjugation. They underlie a no less dualistic sexual morality which offers the *homem,* at least within his culturally defined active role, almost complete sexual freedom, while sharply limiting the sexual life of the *mulher*—shrouding it in a world of mystery and misunderstanding. These same understandings both postulate the potentially dangerous forces that might call the hierarchical structure into question, and provide a set of highly specific (and often highly concrete) channels for the control of virtually anything that might threaten the unconscious acceptance of the established order.[12]

In its broadest outlines, of course, the structure of such a system might well strike us as commonplace. It certainly seems to parallel the structures found in the vast majority of human cultures currently available to us through the ethnographic record (see, for example, Rosaldo and Lamphere 1974, Reiter 1975, MacCormack and Strathern 1980; Ortner and Whitehead 1981). Yet what is most interesting about it is the contours of its uniqueness, the richness of its particularity. For if this system can be tied to the structure of gender relations in human life more generally, we must follow the Brazilians themselves in refusing to ignore its historical specificity—its existence as part of a highly complex and distinct historical reality. Indeed, if the structure of the gender hierarchy seems, in so many ways, to parallel the most general shape of those found around the world in an enormous variety of social and cultural settings, we must remember that it carries with it, as well, the remnants of its own historical baggage—its emergence in the clash of distinct social and cultural traditions, its development within the context of a slave-owning society structured around the absolutes of dominance and submission, and its more recent past as part of a rapidly changing social order in which the traditional structures of hierarchy and domination have suffered shocks from which they may well never recover.

The importance of situating this system historically becomes all the more evident, I think, if we refuse to take the question of gender (as anthropology has, more often than not, taken it) as an end in and of itself. If, on the contrary, we seek to link this system to the more general structure of sexual meanings in Brazilian life, a more complex and interesting picture begins to unfold. Approached in this way, the gender hierarchy takes shape less in absolute than in relative terms. It can be understood, as I have already suggested, as a cultural frame of reference which Brazilians have used, and which they continue to use, to both structure the nature of their sexual realities and interpret the meaning of their sexual practices. It is in terms of the distinctions which this frame of reference encodes—distinctions between masculinity and femininity, between activity and passivity, between domination and submission, and so on—that the most deeply significant understandings of sexual life in Brazil are built up. Yet as important as this frame of reference certainly is, it is in fact but one perspective among a number of possible alternatives in contemporary Brazilian culture, and its full significance can ultimately be understood only in its fundamentally historical relation to these additional possibilities.

Understood along these lines, then, not as an end in itself but as a culturally defined and articulated framework for thinking about the nature of sexual existence, the system of meanings built up around the hierarchy of gender has provided the most widely held view of sexual life in Brazilian society. As the work of writers such as Freyre has so forcefully suggested, its broad outlines can clearly be traced back through the expanse of Brazilian history to the formation of the Brazilian people. Even today, it holds almost absolute power among the most traditional segments of contemporary Brazilian society—in rural areas, in the larger cities of the more traditional North and Northeast, and among the lower classes in the large, heavily industrialized cities of southern Brazil. For that matter, among the most modernized segments of Brazilian society, the highly educated middle and upper classes, this same system continues to exercise a profound influence. While individuals from these groups will be more likely to question and, in some instances, to reject the most basic assumptions of the gender hierarchy as little more than tradition and superstition, they will in no instance be illiterate in its language—they will more or less implicitly understand the underlying principles which organize the system and will be capable, at least in certain circumstances, of functioning within its terms.[13]

Nevertheless, over the course of at least the past century, hand in hand with the development and differentiation of Brazilian society as a whole, there have emerged a number of alternative approaches to the whole question of sexual meanings. These coexist with the traditional gender hierarchy and increasingly offer contemporary Brazilians other possibilities for the constitution and interpretation of their sexual universe. The impact of these alternative perspectives has become so significant in recent years that the importance of the traditional gender hierarchy today can be fully understood only with reference to the other systems or subsystems which intertwine with or intersect it. It is in its relationship with these additional systems, these other perspectives, that the gender hierarchy acquires much of its current meaning in modern Brazilian life, and it is thus to an examination of these systems that we must now turn.

4

Norms and Perversions

As influential as the ideology of gender has been, it is but one among a number of possible perspectives available today for the organization of sexual life in Brazil. Throughout Brazilian history, and perhaps most clearly in the contemporary period, this relatively informal cultural system has consistently functioned alongside a set of more formal, rationalized discourses that have simultaneously confirmed it, extended it, and in some instances, transformed it. Whether in the early doctrines of organized religion, the slightly later discourses of social hygiene and medicine, or the more recent language of modern science, the sexual realm has also been the object of even more specialized interrogations and interdictions. While themselves characterized by certain fundamental differences in perspective, these interrogations nonetheless seem to offer a shift of emphasis from the question of gender to what would more accurately be described as sexuality (Rubin 1984). They are typified by a new preoccupation with sexual practices as external expressions of a distinct (and deeper) internal truth. The conceptualization of this truth has itself taken a number of different forms and has changed with the passage of time. In all of its guises, however, it has been focused on sexual experience not merely as a way of differentiating men from women and organizing them into a hierarchy of gender, but as somehow central to the meaning of individual existence, to the definition of the self (Foucault 1978). As subtle as this shift in emphasis might at first glance appear, it has nonetheless offered Brazilians a radically different frame of reference for organizing and understanding their sexual universe, and for constituting their own sexual realities within it.[1]

Sins of the Flesh

As was implicit in the discussion of gender, the Brazilian understanding of sexual reality can hardly be approached without reference to some form of

Catholicism. The division of the sexes, the structure of male domination, the importance of female virginity, and so on, can all be linked to a set of religious values that act both to legitimate and to reproduce the accepted order of the sexual universe. Within that frame of reference, however, such values are rarely stated explicitly. Drawn, as they are, from a kind of folk Catholicism rooted less in official doctrines than in the ideological structures of popular culture, they function informally, providing a backdrop for the sexual drama as it has traditionally been played out in Brazilian life. Throughout Brazilian history, however, this relatively informal, uncodified, religious backdrop has coexisted with a far more explicit and formal set of beliefs—the official doctrines of the Catholic church, with all its authority and institutional legitimacy—which, while perhaps less immediate in the course of daily life, have nonetheless exerted a profound influence on the nature of Brazilian reality.

At least since the early writings of Gilberto Freyre, it has been customary to emphasize the "sensual" character of the Catholic tradition inherited from Portugal—its festivals and village feasts in honor of the saints who protected the harvest and offered assistance in matters of love, its baroque processions marked by firecrackers and rockets, its remarkably relaxed sexual morality (see Bastide 1951, 334–35). This "softer" or "more human" Catholicism has been taken, by Brazilians themselves, both as an explanation for the success of the early Portuguese colonists in Brazil and as a key source for the unusual degree of sensuality that marks Brazilian life even today:

> To the advantages already pointed out that the Portuguese of the fifteenth century enjoyed over contemporary peoples who were also engaged in colonizing activity may be added their sexual morality, which was Mozarabic in character: Catholic morality rendered supple by contact with the Mohammedan, and more easy-going, more relaxed, than among the Northern peoples. Nor was their religion the hard and rigid system of the reformed countries of the north, or even the dramatic Catholicism of Castile itself; theirs was a liturgy social rather than religious, a softened, lyric Christianity with many phallic and animistic reminiscences of the pagan cults. The only thing that was lacking was for the saints and angels to take on fleshly form and step down from the altars on feast days to disport themselves with the populace. As it was, one might have seen oxen entering the churches to be blessed by the priests; mothers lulling their little ones with the same hymns of praise that were addressed to the Infant Jesus; sterile women with upraised petticoats rubbing themselves up against the legs of São Gonçalo do Amarante; married men, fearful of infidelity on the part of their wives, going to interrogate the "cuckold rocks," while marriagable young girls addressed themselves to the "marriage rocks"; and finally our Lady of Expectancy being worshipped in the guise of a pregnant woman. (Freyre 1956, 30)

It is this sensual, lyric Christianity inherited from the Portuguese, then, that has typically been taken as central to the formation of the Catholic tradition in Brazil. With its relaxed moral code and its emphasis less on the official doctrines of the Catholic church, or even on the priest as a mediator between man and God, than on the domestic liturgies of a cult of the saints tied to the life of the *casa-grande*, it has been seen as especially well suited to the early life of the colony and the tradition of patriarchal authority with its double standard of sexual morality (see, for example, Thales de Azevedo 1953, Bastide 1951, Forman 1975).

While the *fé* (faith) of folk belief has clearly been seen as the "cement" holding colonial society together (Freyre 1956, 41; Bastide 1951, 344), the influence of the Church as an institution has typically been minimized. Emphasis has been placed, instead, on the far more informal Catholicism of the plantations, symbolized not in the church or the cathedral, but in the *capela*, the "chapel" of the *casa-grande* (Freyre 1956, 192). Despite their recognition of the limited power of the Church in the face of this "familial Catholicism," however, writers such as Freyre have also pointed to the ongoing efforts of the Church to establish its authority in the New World as crucial to struggles for power that characterized the colonial period. They have thus portrayed a dualistic universe in which the sensual Catholicism of the *casa-grande* is contrasted to the more rigorous doctrines of the Catholic church as a competing system of belief, an alternative vision of religious life (Bastide 1951). Given the relaxed sexual morality that has defined the essential character of the patriarchal regime, it is hardly surprising that the question of sexual conduct should have become an especially important issue in the struggle for moral authority in early Brazilian life.

As Paulo Prado was quick to note in the opening pages of his *Retrato do Brazil*, the "immoral" character of life in colonial Brazil had become an almost constant source of concern for the Fathers of the Church during the sixteenth and seventeenth centuries. Nowhere was this concern more evident than in the activities of the Inquisition in Brazil at the end of the sixteenth century. While the question of sexual immorality was initially of less concern to the *Santo Ofício* (Holy Office) than was the problem of the *cristãos-novos* (the New-Christians, or converted Jews), it nonetheless became a central issue as the investigations of the Inquisition proceeded in Brazil (see Aufderheide 1973, Novinsky 1980, Siqueira 1978, Vainfas 1989):

> The Inquisition kept its enormous and watchful eye trained upon the intimate life of the colonial era, upon the bedrooms and the beds (usually, it would appear, made of leather) that creaked beneath the weight of adulteries and forbidden intercourse; upon the small chambers and the rooms occupied by the saints; upon the relations of the white masters with their slaves. . . . They enable us to behold the heresies of the new-Christians and . . . irregularities in the domestic and moral life of the Christian family: married men marrying a second time with mulatto women; others sinning against nature with effeminates of the country or from Guinea; still others committing with women the

lewd act that in modern scientific language as well as in the classics is known as *felatio,* and which the denunciations describe in minute detail; foul-mouthed individuals swearing by the "Virgin's muff"; mothers-in-law planning to poison their sons-in-law; new Christians placing crucifixes beneath the bodies of women at the moment of copulation or tossing them into urinals; lords of the manor having pregnant slave girls burned alive in the plantation ovens, the unborn offspring crackling in the heat of the flames. (Freyre 1956, xlv–xlvi)

For writers such as Prado and Freyre the records of the Inquisition have become essential to the whole task of knowing and understanding the most intimate (and scandalous) secrets of the Brazilian past. Yet this continued interest in the Inquisition clearly extends beyond the actual value of its documents as a historical record. Indeed, it seems somewhat incongruous given the fact that the activities of the Inquisitors were in reality limited both in time and space (see Aufderheide 1973). Arriving in Brazil only in 1591, the *Santo Ofício* would be active there for less than a century, and would limit its investigations almost entirely to a small number of coastal cities. It would focus its attentions neither on the very wealthy nor on the very poor—who together made up the vast majority of the colonial population—but on the far more limited middle sectors of these early commercial centers (ibid.). And yet, much like the patriarchal tradition itself, or even the myths of origin that we have already examined, the Inquisition continues to exert remarkable influence over contemporary readings of Brazilian history. It seems to have been interpreted as a paradigmatic event in the Brazilian narrative: the arrival, amid the chaos of colonial morality, of what João Silvério Trevisan has described as a *Deus punitivo,* a "punitive God" (Trevisan 1986, 58).

Ultimately, the Inquisition has acquired much of its continued significance as a model for the workings of religious authority in Brazil—a model focused, in no small part, on the response of religious authority to the permutations of sexual life. Although the activities of the Inquisition in Brazil have been interpreted, quite rightly, largely in relation to events taking place in Europe, they nonetheless served, as Trevisan has pointed out, the interests of a Church faced with an almost total lack of control over the moral character of colonial life. Indeed, it was only when Inquisitors made their way to Brazil at the end of the sixteenth and the beginning of the seventeenth centuries that the first widespread declaration of Church doctrines would take place in the colony: the *Editos de Fé e da Graça* (Edicts of faith and of grace), which were to be posted on the doors of all colonial churches. The posting of these edicts, in turn, would initiate an elaborate cultural performance in which the moral authority of the Church was to be made painfully evident to the colonial population. First, a period of grace was allowed in which individuals could freely confess to their crimes—and in which the colonists were obliged to denounce the crimes of their fellows. The accused were then brought before the authorities to answer the charges that had been brought against them. Finally, after an extended, and often difficult, hearing, the guilty faced a punishment determined by the Inquisitors to fit the specific nature of the crime or crimes:

> After the defendant had confessed and been interrogated, it was common practice in the Inquisition for the Visitor to prepare the accusation and to hear the defence procurator and the prosecution and defence testimony (which was always secret). If there were doubts during the trial, the Inquisitor could call for torture in order to define the extent of the confession. Only then did the Inquisitorial Tribunal give sentence, which varied according to whether the accused was considered *incompetent* (under age), *contumacious* (absent), *feigned* (pretending to repent), *persuaded* (continuing in error), *false* (confessing only to avoid penalty), *revocative* (contradicting oneself in the confession) or *relapsed* (recidivist, after having been resolved or reconciled with the Inquisition). The sentences were read out in the Tribunals or in public Autos-da-Fé which were held in the town square, with or without ceremony, and eagerly attended by the whole population. (Trevisan 1986, 58)

The entire event functioned as a ritual of discipline in which the official doctrines of the Church could be publicly displayed and transmitted to the general population in an especially powerful and immediate form. Because of their intensely dramatic quality, these rites of discipline have continued to exert remarkable influence on Brazilian thought, not merely as the object of historical research, but as a subject particularly well suited to the treatments of modern theater and drama (see, for example, Filho 1972).

In carrying out their investigations, the Inquisitors were able to draw upon predetermined lists outlining over seventy different offenses, which could be subdivided further in order to distinguish between up to two hundred types of offenders. The greatest number of cases clearly seem to have involved crimes against the faith, particularly on the part of the so-called New-Christians. The interests of the Inquisitors were hardly limited to the New-Christians, however. In addition to the crime of *judaísmo* (Judaism), the records of the Inquisition were dominated by the crimes of *feitiçeira* (witchcraft), *blasfêmia* (blasphemy), *sodomia* (sodomy), *bigamia* (bigamy), *solicitação* (solicitation), and *incesto* (incest). The question of sexual deviance was thus raised repeatedly, in relation to women as well as to men, and the language employed by the Inquisitors in order to speak of such sexual conduct was, as Trevisan has noted, both strangely oblique and circuitous, while at the same time detailed and elaborate:

> In the patronising language of the Catholic theologians, moralists and canonists of the time, varieties of the sexual act and the genitals were referred to by sometimes curious circumlocutions. The Inquisitors, of course, used the same

> artifice, which did not prevent detailed descriptions of the sexual sins from
> being noted down—sometimes even the opposite. Anal coitus was called "sod-
> omy," "dishonest touching," "vile touching," "abominable sin," "abominable
> work" or simply "abominable." The penis was called the "virile member," "na-
> ture," and "dishonest member" when used sinfully. "Nature" was also used to
> refer to the vulva, as was "natural passage" for the vagina. The anus/rectum
> was called the "rear passage" or "posterior part." "Embrace" and "kiss" were
> euphemistic variants for anal penetration, as "to sleep carnally from behind"
> and "put their natures together in front" were variations on position. "Agent"
> and "patient" meant the two partners in anal coitus while the one penetrated
> was also the one who "performed the female duty"; "*somitigo,*" "*sodomita*" or
> "*sodomítico*" referred to the masculine homosexual. "Dishonest touching"
> also applied to sinful sexual contact in general while feminine homosexual re-
> lations were called "abominable friendship" and "dishonest friendship." (Trevi-
> san 1986, 193–94)

Through such attention to the classification of sexual practices, and through
the remarkable detail used to describe the transgressions of the accused, the
Inquisition would provide colonial society not merely with a set of formal
prohibitions, but with a context in which the question of sexual conduct
would be raised for the first time at the level of public discourse. Indeed,
what is striking about the events of the Visitations is the extent to which
they forged a link between sexual behavior and language—the extent to
which, as Foucault might have put it, they incited sex to speak its name, and
ultimately defined it in relation to this speech (Foucault 1978). Whether in
its edicts, its lists of delicts and culprits, its denunciations and confessions,
or simply its remarkably detailed record keeping, the Inquisition not only
described the aberrations of sexual conduct in colonial life, but invested
them with meaning.

In the elaborate theater of the Inquisition, then, the interrogation of
sexual practices would be linked to the evaluation of moral virtue as central
to the project of the Church—a project which would continue to hold
meaning long after the events of the Inquisition had come to a close. Even
today, the significance of sexual conduct is often built up largely within the
terms of an essentially dualistic moral vision in which the notion of *carne*
(flesh) is diametrically opposed to that of *espírito* (spirit):

> The Catholic world is always divided between good and evil, light and dark-
> ness, spirit and flesh . . . Carnal life has always been opposed to spiritual life.
> The person has to transcend corporeal life. (Miriam, a twenty-six-year-old les-
> bian from the lower middle class)

And while notions such as sin and salvation have remained problematic, at
best, in folk belief, they have nonetheless been linked increasingly to the
question of sex focused upon by the Inquisitors. Indeed, it is very probably
in forging a relationship between sexual conduct and a concept of sin that
the official doctrines of the Church have most forcefully penetrated the bul-

warks of popular thought. While the notion of *pecado,* or "sin," is defined by
the Church in far more general terms as "the transgression of religious precept," it has been consistently invoked as a means of regulating sexual behavior:

> There are lots of sins of the flesh: gluttony, greed, avarice . . . But above all,
> the sins of the flesh refer to sex. In fact, when you speak of sin these days,
> everyone will think about sex. (Antônio)

What have been described as *os pecados da carne* (the sins of the flesh) have
clearly emerged as one of the primary threats to the life of the spirit and as
one of the major preoccupations of the Catholic church in its attempts to
regulate the beliefs and conduct of the faithful.

Sex, in and of itself, is profoundly problematic within this particular
vision of the world. Yet it is important to note just how complex and nuanced this vision is. A distinction is made between legitimate and illegitimate forms of sexual expression and is organized around at least three
interrelated notions: *casamento* (marriage), *monogamia* (monogamy), and
procriação (procreation). Sexual conduct which successfully combines
these three elements is understood as legitimate and accepted within the
Catholic vision of the world. Behavior which fails to link these three elements falls outside of the boundaries of the legitimate or virtuous. It is here
that the notion of *pecado* normally comes into play:

> In the Catholic vision, procreation within marriage is correct. But outside of
> this, sex is sin. Adultery, polygamy, prostitution, sodomy, incest, abortion . . .
> All this is sin. (Antônio)

Violating, in one way or another, the limitations of marriage, monogamy,
and procreation, each of the items on this list comes to define the *pecador*
(sinner) in the eyes of God and of the Church. The stain of sin need not be
permanent, of course; as in the model of the Inquisition, it can be removed
by the act of *confessão:*

> There is also the possibility of confessing . . . of going to the priest and con-
> fessing your sins. Even the sinner can save himself by confessing his errors.
> (Miriam)
>
> The priest is a person under God, and therefore has the right to absolve you
> (or not). It's like the time of the Inquisition—they had the power to take your
> life. The priest needs to know about your sins. You receive judgment . . . You
> get chewed out by the priest . . . You are given a series of prayers: Hail Marys,
> Our Fathers . . . You have to go to the church, give money to the church . . .
> Doing all of this, you are saved. (João)

But even here, in the possibility of atonement that the act of *confessão*
opens up, the constitution of legitimate and illegitimate sexual practices is
obviously quite different than in the traditional ideology of gender. No less

than in that ideology, the detailed classification of specific practices functions to regulate and control the conduct of sexual life. But the way in which this process is subjectively experienced is transformed in a number of quite significant ways.

Perhaps the most important point here is the extent to which this emphasis on *pecado* and *pecadores* is tied to a notion of *culpa* (guilt): indeed, it is only through the confession of sin that one can ever hope to rid oneself of the sense of guilt that attacks the soul and thus severely limits the freedom of sexual expression. At first glance, this notion of *culpa* parallels the sense of *vergonha* (shame) that plays such a key role in regulating the ideology of gender in Brazil. As has long been noted, however, the concept of sin in fact marks a fundamental shift in cultural emphasis. Not only does it emerge most clearly within an elaborate institutional structure (as opposed to the more open-ended flow of popular culture and daily life), but it also transfers the subjective locus of meaning from outside to in:

> I don't know . . . I think that the feeling of *culpa* is stronger than that of *vergonha*. You feel it more inside. It doesn't matter what other people think. What matters is that you feel guilty . . . you feel that you have done something wrong. (Antônio)

While *vergonha* seems to take place principally in relation to others, then, *culpa* turns in on the self: the opinions of others mean relatively little in comparison with one's own sense of failure and defilement. The sense of *culpa* is clearly internalized in a way that *vergonha* is not. And because the notion of *pecado* is so closely, and so consistently, tied to sexual behavior, the question of sex becomes unavoidably linked to the notion of guilt, to a sense of the self as *culpado*, "guilty":

> You feel guilty, like a criminal, doing things that are wrong. It's society that says it's a sin. It's you who feels guilty. (Nelson, a thirty-four-year-old heterosexual male from the middle class)

Sexual transgression becomes a kind of moral *crime* (crime), then, as opposed to a simple source of shame, and the subjective meaning of sexual practices is reconstructed at a very different level. The sinner is simultaneously a *criminoso*, a "criminal," a breaker of moral laws. And sex itself becomes a source of danger, of pollution, and even of evil that plays across the body but takes root within the soul.

The extent to which this configuration in fact dominates Brazilian life is clearly open to debate. If so many of the leading interpreters of religious life in Brazil are correct about the extent to which notions such as sin or salvation have actually been incorporated into the patterns of folk culture, than the impact of this system of meanings (like the actual impact of the Inquisition itself) on the lives of specific individuals may well be relatively limited. Yet the fact remains that it exists as an ever-present part of the sexual landscape in Brazil. Even for individuals who have only partially internalized its specific values in their own lives, it is a constant part of the cultural background within which they live. While it would be inaccurate to suggest that this system of beliefs had somehow superseded the traditional ideology of gender as a way of organizing the sexual universe, it would be equally incorrect to discount its significance. On the contrary, one can argue that this more formal system has superimposed itself on the foundation of folk belief that emerges in the ideology of gender. It has reasserted many of the most basic assumptions of that ideology, while at the same time transforming many of its meanings. Ultimately, this system of religious values has contributed to the development of yet another perspective that can be drawn upon both in generating and interpreting the significance of sexual experience, and it is perhaps along these lines, rather than in terms of its dominance in daily life, that its greatest importance lies.

The Health of the Population

If some form of religious authority has been present in Brazil since even the early colonial period, and has played an important role in organizing and regulating the sexual universe, since at least the mid nineteenth century the doctrines of organized religion have coexisted with a variety of other, equally formal, discourses that have also been influential in shaping the structure of sexual life. Disciplines such as social hygiene and, later, modern medicine, have gradually taken shape in Brazilian intellectual life over the course of the past century and have begun to exert increasing influence, especially among the upper class and the emerging middle class. Like the doctrines of the Catholic church, they offer a powerful framework for interpreting and understanding contemporary sexual life.

Marking the end of the colonial period and the gradual transition to a modern nation-state, the nineteenth century emerges as one of the most crucial periods of Brazilian history. Colonial life at the end of the eighteenth century was characterized by extreme decentralization—a society organized around the great patriarchal lineages and the declining sugar plantations of the Northeast, holding relatively little economic interest for the Portuguese crown, and thus left largely to its own political devices. Urban development had, for more than three centuries, been virtually nonexistent, and the center of both power and culture remained the rural *casa-grande*. While the Portuguese language and the Catholic religion provided at least some grounds for a common identity capable of bridging the gaps between one patriarchal island and the next, both ultimately looked back as much to Europe, to Lisbon and Rome, as to any particularly Brazilian reality. Within the first years after the turn of the century, however, the broad outlines of this picture were transformed, and a new set of historical processes began to change the character of economic, political, and social life.

From an economic perspective, radical changes had already been signaled in the mid eighteenth century with the advent of the gold rush in Minas Gerais. Gold resulted in a shift in economic activity from the North to the South as well as in Portugal's new economic interest in regulating and extracting wealth from the largest of her colonies. This southern shift would continue, however, even after the gold rush, with the emergence of coffee as Brazil's great export crop in the mid nineteenth century. It would carry Brazil, in the late nineteenth century, into the modern era, with the decline of slavery as a politically and economically viable institution and the subsequent constitution of a paid labor force to man not only the large coffee plantations of the rural South but also the increasingly significant commercial and industrial enterprises of expanding southern cities such as Rio and São Paulo (see Furtado 1963, Conrad 1972, Stein 1957, Toplin 1975).

Intertwined with these important economic developments, one finds a no less profound set of transformations in the political realm. By 1808, with Napoleon's invasion of Portugal and the flight of the court from Lisbon to Rio, the face of Brazilian history would be irrevocably changed. In many ways a strange historical accident, the arrival of the court set the stage for the declaration of Brazilian independence some fourteen years later—the peculiar experiment, from 1822 to 1889, of the New World's only self-declared empire, and finally, following 1889, the constitution of a republic modeled along Anglo-American lines. These political changes must be seen as part of, and as an influence upon, the economic life of the colony, as Brazilians struggled with the crucial issue of the day—the institution of slavery—and sought, first in 1850 through prohibiting the sale and importation of slaves, then in 1871 with the law of free birth, and finally in 1888 with the complete abolition of slavery, to take their place in the modern, liberal era (see Haring 1958, Conrad 1972, Toplin 1975).

Not surprisingly, social transformations were linked to these massive political and economic changes. Although Brazil would remain, for quite some time, a predominantly rural society, by the mid nineteenth century the urban population had begun to grow at an unprecedented rate as a result of the migration of both rural and foreign workers, and economic enterprises had begun to shift from commerce and services to manufacturing and industry. The presence of the monarchy and the declaration of independence brought about the construction of a centralized state and for the first time offered the possibility of a truly national identity. Taken together with the slow but persistent development of a capitalist economy, these changes signaled the decline of the rural oligarchy, of the classical patriarchal order, and the emergence of a relatively modern nation-state (see Freyre 1963, 1970; Morse 1978).

The Brazilian elite—the remnants of the patriarchal oligarchy and, perhaps more important, the emerging bourgeoisie concerned with solidifying its power in the face of past oligarchical domination—struggled to come to grips with both the practical and the theoretical dilemmas raised by the new order of an independent nation. While the problems they faced were obviously wide ranging and diverse, the most important converged, in one way or another, on the question of the changing Brazilian population (see Costa 1979, Skidmore 1974). Whether in relation to urban growth and the difficulties of organizing, controlling, and providing for the influx of new urban dwellers; to capitalist development, nascent industrialization and concerns about the productivity and reproductivity of the work force; or to political modernization and the well-being of an informed citizenry, the nature of the Brazilian population became a key focus of nineteenth-century Brazilian thought (see Costa 1979). Mirroring trends taking place at more or less the same time in Europe, it was in the nineteenth-century preoccupation with the nature, health, and reproduction of the Brazilian people that the system of folk beliefs about sexual life was most forcefully challenged and reinterpreted.

The ways in which Brazilians sought to confront the problems posed by this new concern with the population were various. Naturally, their responses were shaped by the unique characteristics of the Brazilian situation—in particular, by the legacy of slavery, the shock of emancipation, and the ongoing preoccupation with the racial composition of the population that achieved prominence in the extended debates concerning miscegenation (see Degler 1971, Haberly 1983, Skidmore 1974). Yet they proceeded, much as in Europe, through a reliance on the developments of modern science—through a positivist faith in scientific progress that seems to have been hardly less profound than the religious faith it threatened, at least in some instances, to replace (see Costa 1964). Whether in response to the racial question, out of concern for the well-being of the work force, or with regard to the vigor of the rising bourgeoisie itself, Brazilians turned to the most recent of scientific developments, in particular, to the discoveries of modern medicine (see Costa 1979, Machado et al. 1978, Stepan 1976).

It was during the nineteenth century—in response to the problems raised by a tropical climate and unchecked and unplanned urban growth, as well as troublesome racial intermixture—that the medical profession really began to assume its modern guise in Brazilian life. The medical gaze gradually shifted from the level of the individual to that of society, and the object of medicine began to shift from the simple curing of individual patients to the more far-reaching prevention of social ills (Costa 1979, Machado et al.

1978). Throughout the colonial period, the primary object of medicine in Brazil had been the struggle against *morte,* the struggle to cure the specific diseases responsible for death. In the nineteenth century, however, with the arrival of the court and a new influx of European medical thinking, this ongoing struggle against death began to give way to a new, and profoundly different, emphasis on the question of *saúde,* or "health" (Machado et al. 1978, 154).

This emphasis on health in turn provided an avenue for the increasing penetration of medicine in the life of society: the prevention of *doença* (disease) would rely upon the elaboration of new hygienic strategies aimed at preserving the health of the population as a whole (ibid., 155). Brazilian medicine became a kind of social science with concerns not unlike those of geography or demography, but with far deeper practical implications (see Costa 1979). It was here that medicine, armed with the corrective strategies of social hygiene, could come to play a central role in the organization and regulation of sexual life, in the classification of sexual practices, as well as in the definition of sexual desires, in terms of a new symbolic economy of sickness and health.

Central to this way of thinking was an essentially utilitarian approach to the whole question of sexual behavior, an emphasis on *reprodução* (reproduction) as the only really legitimate aim of sexual activity. At first glance, of course, this focus on reproduction might be understood as an extension of the stress placed upon procreation in the doctrines of the Church, or even of the importance of sexual potency within the patriarchal tradition. Yet within this new medical/scientific approach to sexual life, reproduction would be understood neither as an obligation to God nor as a sign of masculinity and the survival of the lineage. On the contrary, it would take shape as a responsibility owed by each individual to society, by the citizen to the state. In a sparsely populated society intent upon the goals of modernization and economic growth, the notion of reproduction would be tied, above all else, to the health and well-being of the people as a whole (see Costa 1979).

Energia sexual (sexual energy) that was responsibly channeled into reproductive relations, and which thus contributed to the growth of a healthy population and the advancement of the nation, could thus be contrasted with sexual energy expended or wasted solely in the pursuit of pleasure. However, while the Catholic tradition had condemned as sinful sexual activity outside of marriage and without regard for procreation, the moral discourse of medicine and science in the late nineteenth and early twentieth centuries would speak in terms of sickness. Just as in the doctrines of the Church, the monogamous conjugal couple would be taken as central to the structure of an accepted moral order (and would be contrasted, we might add, as the *saudável,* the "healthy," alternative to the syphilitic immorality of the patriarchal tradition as perceived by Freyre). While sin could only be confessed and forgiven, sickness might open itself up to understanding, treatment, and ultimately, cure.

Social hygiene, modern medicine, and scientific investigation were thus intimately tied to the question of sex in Brazil. As in Europe and the United States, *sexo* (sex) would become *sexualidade* (sexuality), an object of knowledge. A whole new set of sexual classifications would be developed which, although often paralleling the categories of the patriarchal tradition, would be aimed less at the articulation of a hierarchy of gender than at the analysis and treatment of sexual *anormalidades* (abnormalities) and *perversões* (perversions), at uncovering the roots of *promiscuidade* (promiscuity) and asserting the *normalidade* (normality) of reproductive sexuality. In focusing on the identification and analysis of those sexual behaviors that most clearly undercut the reproductive norm—on *onanismo* (onanism) or *masturbação* (masturbation), on *prostituição* (prostitution) and *libertinagem* (libertinism), *homossexualismo* or *homossexualidade* (homosexuality), and the like—this discourse would take up many of the problems that had dominated both the patriarchal and the Catholic traditions. But it would examine these problems from an increasingly rationalized perspective and would organize itself around its own distinct logic, thus offering yet another reading of the nature of sexual life.

Nowhere was this transition from the symbolism of sin to that of sickness evident earlier than in the case of onanism, or masturbation, already a focus of concern for social hygienists and medical doctors by the middle of the nineteenth century. No longer a simple transgression against the law of God, the practice of masturbation was reinterpreted as a source of sickness and danger, of physical and mental degeneration in both children and adults:

> Masturbation was taken as the cause of the most diverse illnesses . . . it hurt the *digestive* system (meteorism, vomiting, gastritises, gastralgias, diarrheas, constipations; imperfect intestinal absorption, etc.); *circulatory* system (hypertrophy of the cardiac muscles, strokes, apoplexies, etc.); *respiratory* system (difficult diction, stuttering, discordance in the sounds, weak voice, hoarseness, dry cough, thoracic anxiety, lack of development of the thorax, respiratory difficulty, suffocation, chronic colds, tuberculosis, etc.); *nervous* system (chorea, epilepsy, hysteria, nervousness, insomnia, hypochondria, hyperesthesia, vertigos, etc.). Without mentioning, naturally, all of the evils and deformities that it brought to the genital-urinary equipment. (Costa 1979, 187–88)

The struggle against onanism became a central component in the most modern theories of education. Defined, once again, as a kind of crime against the laws of nature and the preservation of one's own health, masturbation could be found at the root of even more serious and debilitating vices of the young:

> The primary and secondary schools, the boarding schools, the houses of education are, it cannot be denied, centers of moral contagion that extend themselves to the recently admitted of all ages; and if the endemic vice of the establishments spares the child, it will not be long until he succumbs to the spontaneous solicitations of the genital organs that awaken and create for him a new sense. Onanism reigns like a master among the youth of the schools and educational institutions. Indeed, the majority of boarding school students have reached the age of fourteen; the age of puberty has begun for them. The advent of virility causes them sadnesses and melancholies that make them seek solitude; and there, nature inspires in them desires that lead them often to discoveries which are as contrary to their health as they are to proper customs. With reclusion, the daily, and often almost continuous, instigation of the excitement continues, little by little, dulling their intellectual faculties, and their organic development fails to continue; there is even a halt in the general development of the organism, while that of the solicited organs is made with surprising precociousness. A vice almost as old as the world, practiced by all of the peoples of antiquity, is born of the isolation or of the life together of individuals of the same sex and of distinct kinship. It is pederasty, exhausting all of the functional energies through the exercise of a function that the novelty of the sensations invites to be put into practice, subjecting the young boys to the sicknesses dependent on this order of causes whose consequences will present themselves sooner or later. (Vasconcellos 1888; quoted in ibid., 191)

Wasteful and irresponsible, masturbation became a preoccupation of social hygiene and modern medicine because it so clearly violated the logic of a system of meanings focused on reproduction as the only legitimate form of sexual conduct, the only legitimate expression of the natural sexual energy that threatened the well-being not only of individuals, but of society itself.

If onanism seemed to pose a particularly clear threat to social order, however, it was nothing in comparison with the perceived danger of prostitution, libertinism, and homosexuality. While masturbation threatened the health of the young, these other ills struck at the very heart and soul of society, at the nuclear family, which was charged with the responsibility for the reproduction of a healthy population. The *prostituta* (prostitute), in particular, was blamed for the destruction of the family. In seducing her clients, she transformed them into *libertinos* (libertines) and was in the end responsible for the contamination of their wives and children as well:

> The *prostitutas* become the enemies of the hygienists principally because of the role that they supposedly had in the physical and moral degradation of the man, and, by extension, in the destruction of the children and the family. Contaminating the *libertinos* with their venereal diseases, they caused the production of children who are sick and damned to premature mortality. Se-

ducing the unwary with their depraved sensualities, they bring misery and un-
happiness to entire families. (Ibid., 265)

It was in relation to prostitution that an increasing concern with sexually
transmitted diseases began to emerge. The prominence given to syphilis in
the texts of writers such as Paulo Prado and Gilberto Freyre was foreshad-
owed by the medical interrogation of prostitution and libertinism during
the late nineteenth century:

The Academy and Faculty of Medicine turned to prostitution and showed how
it hurt the Brazilian population by directly affecting the family. Through the-
ses, memorandums, and sessions devoted to prostitution, the doctors pointed
to the deadly consequences of an unruly prostitution. The most important
sickness issuing from this situation is syphilis, a contagious, hereditary, and
powerful agent of disease. In the bed of prostitution, the man penetrates to the
interior of the "domicile" of syphilis. And from there he passes it to the bed of
his wife, transmitting to her a disease that will deform and kill her, transmitting to children created by him in a state of sickness the "brand of an insidious
and capricious disease." (Machado et al. 1978, 333)

And yet, at the same time that the dangers of prostitution were extensively
documented and explored, its existence was grudgingly conceded as a kind
of *mal necessário,* a "necessary evil." It was interpreted as an unfortunate
side effect of an uncontrollable *instinto sexual* (sexual instinct) that was part
of the organic constitution, if not of all women, then certainly of all men:

The man eager for venereal pleasure feels himself tormented by an irresistible,
imperious necessity, an astounding excitement vivifies his organism, a hot fire
consumes his organs, his arteries pulsate with excessive force, his humid eyes
ignite with supernatural brilliance, his face fills with color, his respiration becomes panting, his genital parts intumesce, fill up, and in them is experienced
the feeling of ardor and titillation. Thought no longer has force, will does not
dominate, all the faculties are concentrated in a fixed idea; the urgent appetite, that pursues the man robs him of other sensations concerning the objects
around him or the dangers that threaten him, and, delirious with the fever
that burns him, dragged by the necessity that impels him, carried off as if by a
demonic power, he is unresponsive to everything and only lives for the prosect
of the pleasures that he craves to enjoy: the most frightening obstacles do not
impede him, he fears nothing, everything disappears before the ardor of his
desire; only the organism rules; honor, virtue, duty, religion, and whatever
there is that is sacred above the earth are chimeras: only the desire that tor-
ments him, only the pleasure that fascinates him, are real. (Herédia de Sá
1845; quoted in ibid., 336–37)

Conceived as an uncontrollable drive, as a force of nature that could never
be fully harnessed by the moral strictures of society and culture, sex was an
ever-present danger. Because sex existed as a natural drive, vices such as
prostitution and libertinism could never be completely eliminated. Their

effects could be minimized, however, through the regulatory controls of social hygiene and modern medicine. By the end of the nineteenth century, at the same time that the growth of the urban population provided the context for an emerging underworld organized around the practice and profits of prostitution, attention had been focused on ways of reducing the potential social ills that it seemed to produce, for example, delimiting the locations where *prostitutas* could work, forcing them off of the streets and into *bordeis* (brothels) where their activities, and the state of their health, could be more easily regulated (see Costa 1979, Engel 1988, Machado et al. 1978).

If the dangers of onanism and the perils of prostitution and libertinism had become a concern for virtually all public officials by the late nineteenth century, none of these evils was as problematic as the notion of *homossexualismo* or *homessexualidade* that emerged at roughly the same time. No figure called into question the "naturalness" of reproduction and the family as did the *homossexual:*

> The *homossexual* was detested because his existence directly negated the paternal function, supposedly universal in the nature of the man. The manipulation of his life, in this case, served as an anti-norm to "normal life," assimilated to masculine heterosexual behavior. (Costa 1979, 247–48)

The fear of the *homossexual* could be tied back to the concerns with the care and upbringing of children and the problems posed by prostitution:

> *Homossexualismo,* it was said, exists because the young boys failed to exert themselves physically and became effeminate. Or because they weren't in the habit of working and became indolent, capricious, and weak. Attention was called to the lack of care with the morality of the boys in the schools and even in their families, which were unprepared to restrain their bad inclinations. On other occasions, the immoral atmosphere of society was itself criticized as being the instigator of homosexual practice. Along with this, proving that the frequency of homosexuality was greater among military men, artists and commercial employees, it was concluded that the causes of the vice were the high prices charged by prostitutes and the fear of syphilis. (Ibid., 248)

Perhaps the most far-reaching consequence of this concern with the origins of *homossexualismo,* and with its opposition to the norm of *heterossexualidade* (heterosexuality), was the creation of the *homossexual* as almost a distinct species or type: like the *masturbador,* the *prostituta,* and the *libertino,* a fundamentally new category for the classification of the sexual universe. Indeed, it is important to stress just how different this figure is in comparison to either the *viado* of popular culture or the *sodomita* of religious tradition. While the *viado* was defined by his passive role in same-sex intercourse, and the *sodomita* by his preference for anal intercourse, whether with the same or the opposite sex, the *homossexual* would come to be defined solely by his choice of his own gender as the object of sexual desire:

> *Homossexualidade* can, then, be studied in light of positive data verifying that
> it deals with an anomaly characterized by a group of modifications in the af-
> fective tendencies and tastes, accompanied by a special preference, from the
> sexual point of view, of diverse types and degrees, of a latent or declared na-
> ture, for intentions, words, attitudes, gestures or acts that an individual mani-
> fests in an active, passive, or mixed manner, for another of the same sex,
> whether man or woman. (Ribeiro 1949, 109)

The *homossexual* could thus be contrasted with the *heterossexual,* or in
some configurations of the problem, the *bissexual.* Indeed, perhaps more
forcefully than notions such as masturbation, prostitution, or libertinism,
concepts such as homosexuality, heterosexuality, and bisexuality would be
used to carve up the sexual universe in twentieth-century Brazil. Focused
not merely on particular sexual acts, but rather on essences, these new medical and scientific classifications went beyond the doctrines of the Catholic
church to define sexuality as lying at the core of one's existence, as constituting the truth of one's self.

Like the doctrines of the Catholic church, then, the medical/scientific
view of sexual life that began to emerge in the late nineteenth century placed
primary emphasis on a reproductive sexual norm. Even more than in Catholic thought, the conjugal couple became central to the notion of legitimate
sexual expression, and those practices that most clearly seemed to threaten
the existence of the nuclear family organized around the conjugal couple
would ultimately come to define *devassidão* (licentiousness or debauchery),
desvio (deviance), and *perversão* (perversion). Along with the emphasis on
the legitimate reproduction of the population, a whole new set of sexual
classifications came to problematize the nature of sexual life in Brazil. As in
Europe and the United States, though at a slightly later point, a concern
with the individual body and its various uses became intimately linked to a
preoccupation with the social body through the question of sex or sexuality—and modern medical science became increasingly important in exploring the roots of sexual abnormality and difference. Sexual deviance was
transformed into a sickness requiring a cure, and the sick themselves became the objects of whatever corrective strategies modern medicine could
muster.

Even today, in the very different world of the late twentieth century, few
symbolic configurations are as fundamental to the structure of Brazilian
sexual culture as this notion of *doença,* or sickness. The sense that certain
types of sexual behavior constitute forms of sickness, and that the individuals who take part in such practices are themselves *doente* (sick or ill), comes
up repeatedly in interviews with informants from all walks of life in contemporary Brazil. It clearly continues to serve as a general category for virtually
all forms of sexual conduct that are viewed as deviant, dangerous, or threatening:

> There are certain things that are . . . I don't know . . . that are really sick.
> People who want certain things. I'm very liberal, but there are things that I
> really don't accept. Like bestiality or incest. People talk about sexual diseases,
> like syphilis—but all of these perversions are the true diseases. People forget
> this these days. (Néstor, a twenty-eight-year-old heterosexual male from the
> working class in Rio)

And while the specific types of sexual behavior that are defined as sick may
vary slightly from one informant to another, they nonetheless tend to reproduce the basic structure of thought that took shape in the late nineteenth
century:

> Society creates rules . . . especially about sex. Sex is for reproduction, for hav-
> ing children. Any other type of sexual behavior is seen as a sickness, whether
> it's homosexuality, masturbation, sadomasochism, or whatever. (Roberto, a
> twenty-two-year-old homosexual male from an upper-middle-class family)

Sexual practices which violate the norms associated with reproduction, the
well-being of the family, or the health and fitness of children are thus, almost invariably, the focus of concern:

> In order to preserve the link between sex and reproduction, society punishes
> everyone who practices these acts. Sickness means deviance, and deviance
> must be controlled. (Roberto)

> You know, the list goes on almost without end. Incest, child abuse, violence
> against women . . . They're all sickness. People who do these things need to be
> treated by doctors, or psychologists, or the police. (Dulce, a forty-five-year-old
> heterosexual woman from the working class)

The concept of *doença*, has thus continued to function not simply as a way
of labeling the unacceptable, but as a way of regulating and controlling it.
The notion that certain sexual practices are fundamentally unhealthy, to the
individual as well as to society as a whole, has opened up an extremely important role for medical science in the care and treatment not merely of
sexually transmitted diseases, but of the moral sicknesses that are believed
to underlie various forms of sexual deviance.

The extent to which these developments have affected the thinking of
the vast majority of contemporary Brazilians is difficult to judge. There is
little doubt that the discourses of modern medicine and medical science
have had their greatest impact on the upper sectors of Brazilian society,
where access to education and information (particularly from abroad) has
been most significant. If nothing else, the texts of writers such as Paulo
Prado testify to the continued significance of these medical/scientific concerns for the elite. Except in a very general way, however, the impact of
these concerns has been more limited for the less educated sectors of society, where the patterns of thought associated with social hygiene, medical

science, and the like have hardly replaced the structures of popular culture. On the contrary, their impact on the lives of individuals in the lower sectors of Brazilian society has been partial and fragmentary.

Still, because the emergence of this medical/scientific perspective has been associated with the most powerful segments of society—and particularly with the rising bourgeoisie as it has tried, in the face of great difficulties, to wrest power from the decaying oligarchy—it would be unwise to underestimate the extent to which many of the general patterns of this system in fact have influenced the thinking of women and men from the lower sectors. Much like the official doctrines of the Church, which it seems both to contradict and complement, this more fully rationalized system of sexual meanings increasingly colors the drama of sexual life in contemporary Brazil. While it has not become as dominant as it appears to be in, say, the United States or the other countries of the fully industrialized Western world, it nonetheless adds an important element to the sexual universe in Brazil. As a frame of reference, it offers a powerful alternative to the traditional ideology of gender.

The Modernization of Sexual Life

Just as the developments of the nineteenth century have built upon the earlier foundation of religious doctrine, while at the same time going beyond it in elaborating a new set of hygienic and medical discourses, the twentieth century has been marked by a process of modernization in which the moral discourses of social hygiene and modern medicine have themselves been both extended and transformed. As in all periods of Brazilian history, these more recent developments have clearly been linked to a specific historical context, and have responded to a whole set of seemingly unrelated events— to the unpredictable swings from tenuous democratic governments to authoritarian regimes, the changing nature of the international marketplace, and the like. Perhaps nothing has been so important, however, as the ever increasing pace of urbanization, and the full range of social transformations that the processes of urbanization have unleashed (see, for example, Conniff 1981, Morse 1958).

By the mid twentieth century, a predominantly rural society had essentially given way to a society dominated by urban centers. While power and authority had been slipping out of the hands of the rural oligarchy since at least the mid nineteenth century, it was not until relatively late in the twentieth century that the real focus of Brazilian society came to rest in the cities. Even today, of course, that transformation is far from absolute, as the large landholders continue to wield considerable influence over all areas of Brazilian life. Still, it is hand in hand with the process of urban development that what might be described as the modernization of sexual life in Brazil has proceeded.

This process of modernization has clearly gone forward on a number of different fronts at the same time. Thanks in large part to the intellectual ferment of modern urban life, there has been an ongoing appropriation of ideas and values from Europe and the United States whose liberal character contrasts markedly with the more restrictive tendencies of the nineteenth century. New disciplines such as psychology, sociology, and even sexology have at least partially taken the place of hygiene and medicine in interrogating the sexual realm and shaping the contours of contemporary thinking about sexual problems. And, as in Europe and the United States, these disciplines have consistently pushed for a rationalized and reasonable treatment of sexual behavior—a treatment that would be free of the moralistic overtones of earlier discourses (but that would ultimately articulate its own set of moral values).

At the same time, the relative impersonality of urban life—as well as the receding significance of the extended family, traditional morality, and religious authority that have accompanied the processes of urbanization— has opened up new spaces in the fabric of society for the reorganization of sexual values and the reconstruction of sexual practices. Ongoing changes in the structure of the family have continued to undercut the force of patriarchal authority and have begun to affect the roles and statuses of women in Brazilian society. Indeed, among the more highly educated sectors in large cities such as Rio or São Paulo, the impact of the modern feminist movement has made a mark in recent years. While feminism has hardly achieved the status of a widespread, broadbased social movement, as seems to be the case in parts of Europe and North America, it has nonetheless played an important role in calling into question traditional understandings of gender and sexuality, and has thus contributed to an important rethinking of the Brazilian sexual universe (see, for example, Alves and Pitanguy 1983).

The same might be said of the homosexual movement, modeled on the gay liberation movements of Europe and the United States (see Fry and MacRae 1983, Míccolis and Daniel 1983, Trevisan 1986). While something resembling a subculture focused around same-sex desires and practices seems to have existed in the larger urban centers since the late nineteenth century (roughly coterminous, one might note, with the increasing medical interest in the *homossexual*), it is only in the very recent past that anything remotely similar to a "gay community" can be found in the most modern areas of some Brazilian cities, and even here, the notion that homosexuality might serve as the focus for a political movement is clearly limited to a very small segment of the elite. Still, the impact of the gay liberation movements of other Western nations has been seen in the creation of a number of political action groups and publications directed at the homosexual population, and these activities have played at least some role in challenging the certainty of many traditional moral values. While they have had little direct impact on the lives of most Brazilians, they have elicited certain changes in film, television, and the press—media dominated by the elite in Brazil, but clearly exerting an important influence over the lives of the popular sectors as well.

Thus a whole range of developments—again, more often than not, emanating from abroad and imported to Brazil by the highly educated urban elite—have played an important role in influencing a process of modernization in sexual life that has been linked to the modernization of Brazilian life more generally. Perhaps the single most striking aspect of this process has been the extent to which the subject of sex has come to dominate so much of the public discourse in contemporary Brazil. No longer relegated to the obscure tomes of medical doctors or the archaic doctrines of theologians, sex has come out of the back rooms and into parlors. In film, on radio and television, in both elite and popular newspapers and magazines, in bestselling books, indeed, in almost all areas of the modern communications industry, sex has become one of the favorite topics of discussion throughout Brazil. Columnists comment on it, popular psychologists build careers around it, social scientists study it and report about it, and through it all, a remarkably diverse public consumes it (see, for example, Inez 1983, Lima 1978, Suplicy 1983, Vasconcelos 1972).

This extensive discourse is characterized by the perceived importance of confronting ignorance with knowledge and information—a task which, as one leading sexologist has described it, depends on the undermining of *repressão* through a new emphasis on *expressão:*

> When speaking about sex we still have lewd laughter, scowls, playful or coarse jokes. It still isn't a subject that is discussed like any other. In treating sex, what we say is not as important as how we say it. . . . The first step in breaking down the generalized taboo against sexuality is to be able to speak about it openly. . . . The negative attitudes concerning sex have an importance that is greater than ignorance. . . . It is repression (*repressão*) that deforms the person's sexual and emotional life. . . . Just informing is not enough. In order to develop a positive attitude in relation to sex, the most important thing is to encourage the expression (*expressão*) of sexuality, from infancy on. It is this attitude that will encourage the growth of a capacity to relate emotionally with the other and enjoy the fruits of a sexual relation. (Suplicy 1983, 27)

In this profusion of discourse, then, modernity defines itself in relation to the false assumptions and superstitions of the past, and the function of the spokesperson for sexual modernization is to open up public debate about the true nature of sexual life, while at the same time acknowledging that this truth may be different for different individuals:

> I don't perceive my role, or that of any educator, as being that of imposing
> conformity to a determined pattern of behavior, but as being that of providing
> new understandings, stimulating the questioning of what is well-known, and
> bringing about an exchange of opinions that leads to individual decisions. In
> short, the goal is to provide for growth through the search for the truth. And
> the truth is not the same for everyone (Ibid., 29)

In short, the question of sex remains fundamentally linked to the question
of truth. But it has nonetheless become an object of public debate in a rather
new way. An earlier preoccupation with perversion seems to have given way
to a new sense of *diversidade* (diversity) in sexual life, and the discussion of
sexual diversity seems to have been focused less on the pronouncements of
moral authorities such as priests or doctors than on the varied opinions of a
somewhat wider (though still largely elite) public. In forming such opinions, however, information is crucial, and it is to this task of educating the
public that what we might describe as the modern science of sex has largely
dedicated itself.

Against the continued opposition of institutions such as the Church,
some form of systematic sex education has thus been seen as essential to the
modernization of sexual life in Brazil:

> Sexual Education, or the lack of it . . . is present in all of the aspects of our
> sexual behavior. . . . A cultural heritage that is not at all positive was be-
> queathed us in the area of knowledge about sex, and maintained through vio-
> lent repressions based upon a false moralism, it would not permit, in fact, a
> different situation. Sex is and will continue to be taboo in the family, in the
> school, in the society. (Lima 1978, 34)

As opposed to the haphazard and often inaccurate information acquired
from one's peers through the structures of popular culture, sexologists and
sex educators have sought to develop programs aimed at a rational, scientific understanding of sexual life. Focusing their attentions particularly on
the young, they have attempted to provide a fundamentally new understanding of the body and its functions, of its physiological development, and of its
role in both reproductive and nonreproductive practices.

The foundation for this new understanding of sexual life has been the
emphasis on the anatomy and the physiology of the human body: "If people
have a rational and objective understanding of their own body and its functions, perhaps they will like it as it is, care for it as well in a rational way and
come to experience their own sexuality and that of others in a natural and
positive fashion" (Mazín 1983a, 22). This "objective" understanding of the
body and its functions is obviously very different than the reading of the
body that has characterized the traditional ideology of gender. At some level,
it clearly reinforces the basic dichotomy established in this ideology. At another level, however, it restructures this dichotomy, focusing not simply on
the penis and the vagina, but on the far more complex distinctions necessary

for a fully scientific understanding of the body and its role in the reproduction of the species:

> The organs characteristic of one and the other sex are divided, for study, in external organs and internal organs. The sexual organs—also called genital or reproductive organs—are the following:
>
> **External organs**
>
> | *Masculine* | *Feminine* |
> |---|---|
> | Scrotum | Vulva |
> | Testicles | Labia Majora |
> | Penis | Labia Minora |
> | Epididymis | Clitoris |
> | Vas deferens | Vaginal opening |
>
> **Internal organs**
>
> | *Masculine* | *Feminine* |
> |---|---|
> | Seminal vesicles · | Vagina |
> | Prostate | Uterus |
> | Cowper's gland | Fallopian tubes |
> | | Ovaries |

> These different structures in one and the other sex appear as a form of biological specialization that contributes to the reproduction of the species. This biological dimension, interacting with society and culture, determines the expression of the sexuality of individuals of the human species. (Mazín 1983a, 25)

Within this more modern frame of reference, then, the body itself is reclassified and reinterpreted. Its structures are analyzed in far more elaborate fashion, and clearly take on new meaning. Their importance as markers of activity and passivity, dominance and submission, recedes from view, giving way to a highly rationalized understanding of their complementary roles in the physiology of reproduction.

Not surprisingly, with this new emphasis on replacing the silence and ignorance of the past with the objective knowledge of the present, a new set of controversies has been opened up around the problem of defining legitimate forms of sexual expression. The repression of masturbation, the taboo of virginity, and the severe restriction of sexual expression in traditional settings have all become subjects of intense debate within the more modern sectors of Brazilian society, as both individuals and institutions have struggled to construct a more rational, enlightened approach to sexual conduct. When confronted with the reasonable, scientific information of the present, even the most deeply held convictions from the past emerge as little more than contemptible superstitions:

> In the beginning of the twentieth century, in the time of our great-grandparents and grandparents, the act of masturbation was considered ex-

tremely dangerous, with consequences as serious as producing blindness, deafness, mental retardation, madness, and other derangements. In the time of our parents, masturbation still was responsible for pimples, impotence, and sterility. Today it is common to hear that the woman who masturbates will be impaired from having orgasm in sexual relations, since she has become "addicted," or some other foolishness of this type, and that the man who masturbates will become "weak" and impotent early on. As if impotence was something expected in old age principally for one who spent all his sperm in his youth. As if the person had a determined stock that would end definitively after having been used up. (Suplicy 1983, 97)

Far from being aberrations, practices such as masturbation are reinterpreted as the expression of truly natural sexuality, part of a complex cycle of psychosexual development, and a fundamentally healthy way to discharge excess sexual energy:

Today we know that masturbation has a specific role in the sexual evolution and the life cycle of the human being. Masturbation can be viewed as a rehearsal for adult sex. The person learns to relate sexually with himself, and this process of learning about the functioning of his body will be very important for his future fulfillment. This does not mean that masturbation is an immature activity that should be abandoned in adult life. Masturbation can occur from birth, increase at the beginning of puberty, decrease in adult life, and increase in old age. It depends very much on the individual needs of each person and the affective-emotional circumstances of that person in each period of his life. Even during marriage, masturbation can be utilized as a way of dealing with differences in the sexual desire of the conjugal couple, either because of the pleasure that is found in this particular form of stimulation or in order to confront moments of separation, the approach of childbirth, sickness, or divorce. It is recognized that a large number of individuals use masturbation in old age as a form of pleasure and a discharge of energy. (Suplicy 1983, 99)

Even masturbation serves its own highly utilitarian functions, then, and from this modern perspective, the problems associated with it lie not in one's sexual nature, but in the society that seeks to repress this nature. If sickness exists, it is not to be found in sex itself, but in the experience of shame and guilt that individuals must confront in the face of antiquated prejudices and prohibitions:

While students of the subject understand masturbation as part of a process of sexualization and sexual expression among human beings, society makes masturbation something ugly, dirty, sinful, and immature that should be prohibited for children and abandoned by adults upon becoming more mature. In fact, there is no relation between masturbation and sickness of any type. Generally, when negative consequences exist, they are related to the guilt and shame that stem from these prejudices, and not from masturbation itself. (Ibid., 100–101)

Thus, the very notion of sickness is turned on its head in these recent reformulations. Far from being situated in the bodies and practices of specific individuals, sickness is produced through the superstitions and repressions of society itself; and the road to health lies less in the diagnosis and treatment of specific patients than in the modernization of moral values.

Increasingly, this modernization of sexual morality has involved a rejection of the notion of social responsibility inherited from the discourses of organized religion or social hygiene, and a new emphasis on the fundamental importance of personal choice. Even the discussion of procreation has come to focus less on the duties owed by citizens to the state than on the importance of individual planning and choice. Debate has centered on the notions of *sexo fora do casamento* (sex outside of marriage) and *controle voluntário da reprodução* (voluntary control of reproduction), and procreation itself has begun to be seen as "manageable" through the techniques of modern science: traditional methods of contraception, such as coitus interruptus, have been augmented by more modern possibilities such as the birth control pill, tubal ligation, vasectomy, and so on. Indeed, the various problems associated with procreation and contraception dominate much of the contemporary discussion concerning the nature of sexual life, and the complex personal choices that are involved in controlling the processes of reproduction are central themes for modern sex educators:

> The decision to have or not to have a child, and when to have it, is a very
> personal choice of the couple involved. But this choice is affected by innumer
> able factors, ranging from family and social pressures to the economic condi
> tions necessary in order to raise children. At times people can wish to have
> children but haven't the financial situation for it. Other times, the couple
> thinks that it is still early to take on these responsibilities and prefers to wait a
> bit longer. A young single woman can want to be a mother but fear the gossip
> of others. There are many reasons, but what is important is that there is no
> right or wrong in these choices—they are personal to each individual. (Mazín
> 1983b, 54)

This marks a significant shift from the approaches advocated in religious doctrine, with its focus on procreation as a duty of the believer, as well as the discourse of social hygiene, with its focus on reproduction as a responsibility of the citizen. Still, this new emphasis on personal choice in reproductive matters is becoming increasingly widespread, particularly among the young from the more well-to-do, well-educated sectors of Brazilian society:

> Things are changing a lot nowadays—at least in the major urban centers.
> There is more choice. Women want to work. This doesn't mean that they don't
> want children. But they think more about family planning. Men too. At least
> the more modern men. (Cristina, a twenty-six-year-old heterosexual woman
> from the middle class)

The development of this perspective in turn has had an important impact in reducing the influence of traditional institutions such as the Catholic church. Indeed, notwithstanding the fervent opposition of the Church, even *aborto* (abortion) has been suggested as a viable alternative for individuals faced with the dilemmas of an unwanted pregnancy, and the debate concerning this issue has opened up new opportunities for questioning religious authority:

> Abortion has always existed, right . . . but these days people even discuss whether or not it should be legalized. It's very controversial. Most people are completely against abortion. And, really, nobody wants to abort a child. But there are also other considerations. Lack of money, the health of the mother, or some other thing. It isn't easy. Sometimes the pregnancy is a real tragedy. Abortion is prohibited by law and condemned by the Church, but even in the rural areas the number of abortions is rising. (Vilma, a thirty-two-year-old working-class woman)

It is clear that in the modern period sexuality, focused on reproduction, has become something to be managed not merely by the Catholic church or by the state, but by individuals themselves. Taking control over one's own body has become a rallying cry, especially for men and women from the relatively affluent and well-educated sectors of society, and the control of conception has been central to the modernization of sexual life in contemporary Brazil.

The emphasis on individual freedom and choice has made possible as well a fundamental rethinking of the distinction between *sexo normal* (normal sex) and *sexo anormal* (abnormal sex), at least among some segments of the educated elite. The absolute division between normal and abnormal sexuality has given way to a relativism focused on both the context of particular practices and the circumstances of particular cases:

> To speak of "normal" or "abnormal" in relation to sex is difficult. Studies in the area of sexuality have shown, increasingly, that sexual behavior is relative. It depends on the culture, the epoch, and the concept of "normality" of those who practice it. Depending on the angle from which the concept is analyzed—the social, the biological, the mental, or the ethical—the concept of "normal" differs. (Suplicy 1983, 287)

Given this breakdown of the distinction between notions of *normalidade* (normality) and *anormalidade* (abnormality), practices as diverse as homosexuality and bisexuality, fellatio and cunnilingus, anal intercourse, exhibitionism, fetishism, sadomasochism, and transvestism have all received more public attention as well as slightly more legitimacy as matters of personal preference rather than forms of sin or sickness. Classified as *comportamentos não-convencionais* (nonconventional behaviors), such practices continue to be contrasted to the norm of *comportamento convencional* (conventional behavior), but are nonetheless increasingly interpreted as relatively benign variations—as expressions of a natural diversity rather than a moral perversion. From this perspective, the problem is less the diversity of sexual behavior itself than the *preconceito* (prejudice) that condemns it as abnormal.

This attack on the prejudices of the past is especially evident in a rethinking of the problem of homosexuality. Not surprisingly, the popular prejudices and stereotypes of the traditional ideology of gender have been subjected to serious criticism from the more rationalized, scientific perspective. Even the inadequate analyses of earlier, less scientific science have come under attack as little more than extensions of popular prejudice:

> Even modern scientists have pointed to different routes for developing understandings of homosexuality that, nonetheless, are not always objective and not always convergent, for while some begin assuming that homosexuals are born with this form of sexual behavior already determined (biological determinism), others consider it an individual phenomenon, whether through initiation on the part of a corrupter, whether through the lack of an adequate paternal image or through the presence of a dominant mother, or even through the exaggerated or deficient functioning of their endocrine systems. . . . Obviously homosexuality can thus be regarded as a sickness, vice, maladjustment, or neurosis. (Mazín 1983c, 74)

In the face of such prejudices, contemporary sexologists have focused on the essentially natural roots of homosexuality and have reaffirmed the fundamental variability of human sexuality:

> The study of diverse cultures . . . has brought anthropologists to the conclusion that some type of homosexual activity is known in almost all societies. The attitudes in relation to these practices, however, are highly varied. . . . In our culture, which discourages homosexuality, the existence of this practice is common. To try to understand what causes the individual to be homosexual and to confront all this prejudice is a task that many have tried to respond to. . . . No single explanation, no "cause" has, up to the present, been considered as the determinant of homosexual behavior. It is understood, at least, that homosexuality has diverse and multiple roots, not determined by a single cause, such as hormones, genes, absent father and dominating mother, timidity, etc. (Suplicy 1983, 267–68)

Practices such as homosexuality can gradually begin to be reappropriated from the realm of perversion thanks to a more enlightened sexual science. And while the popular prejudices against such practices have hardly disappeared, the debate surrounding them has forced a fundamental rethinking of any number of so-called deviant forms of sexual conduct:

> Since the sixties, Brazil has changed a lot. At least in the large cities, everything is a lot more liberal. In the past, homosexuality was very repressed. But these days, homosexuals are everywhere. There are gay (*gay* or *guei*) beaches

in Copacabana and Ipanema. There are gay bars and nightclubs in Rio and São Paulo just like in New York or Paris. Even the transvestites, like Roberta Close, are on the covers of the magazines. Every year *Manchete* reports on "the *carnaval* of the dolls." This doesn't mean that homosexuality is totally accepted by society. But a lot has changed. (Antônio)

The prejudices of the past are irrational, whether it is prejudice against homo- sexuality or against the loss of virginity . . . Science shows that all this is fool- ishness. I think that each person is different. It isn't possible to speak of a morality that will serve for everyone. You have to respect individuality and discuss sexual variations rationally. (Rubens, a twenty-four-year-old hetero- sexual male from the upper middle class)

As scientific evidence is gathered to demonstrate their relative frequency, practices ranging from anal or oral intercourse to sadomasochism, transves- tism, and bestiality have emerged as topics for debate. While such practices have hardly been accepted (even by the most liberal and progressive) as le- gitimate forms of sexual expression, the absolute moral certainty with which they once would have been condemned has been seriously shaken. The fact that they have become the subject of relatively widespread discussion reveals the extent to which the structures of traditional morality have been under- cut in their confrontation with the forces of modernity.

In Brazil (as in many other societies, of course) many of these questions have taken on ever greater salience with the emergence of AIDS. Much like syphilis in an earlier period, AIDS has marked the discussion of sexual life in contemporary Brazil, providing a focus not only for medical investigation but also for moral discourse. The liberal trends of recent decades, and the apparent modernization of sexual morality, have once again been called into question—charged with responsibility for an epidemic that has rent the fab- ric of modern life. Both religious doctrine and modern medical authority have been reasserted in the face of AIDS, as accusations of sin and sickness have again merged in the discussion of a disease linked to sexual transmis- sion and unconventional behavior. Yet at the same time, by the end of the 1980s, the emerging AIDS epidemic had also given rise to a reassertion of more liberal doctrines. AIDS has increasingly become a focus for more pro- gressive politics, veterans of the feminist and homosexual movements have become leading AIDS activists, and the struggle against AIDS has given rise to a growing social movement committed to the modernization of sexual morality and the defense of sexual diversity. If questions related to sexuality had long been a focus for public debate, issues such as the importance of sex education, the diversity of homosexual lifestyles, and the complexity of sex- ual behavior have acquired a special urgency in the years since AIDS first became an issue in contemporary Brazilian life (see Parker 1990).

Even following the emergence of AIDS, then, while conventional sexual behavior continues to mark out an unmistakable norm in contemporary

Brazilian life, the possibilities of unconventional sexual behavior have been posed in a strikingly new way as questions of diversity rather than of perversity. As in the case of almost all of the more formal discourses we have examined, the impact of these developments has been limited. It has been associated almost entirely with an affluent, intellectual elite, and even among this elite, its impact has been far from widespread. But the change in orientation is clear. In books and magazines, on radio and television, in university lecture halls and chic cafés, a rethinking of sexual life has become part of the wider discourse of social life in contemporary Brazil, and the prejudices and stereotypes of the past have increasingly confronted the changing patterns of modern life. Complicated problems that were once discussed only in the privacy of the Catholic confessional or, later, in the writings of medical doctors have been taken up not only in the debates of sexologists or professional sex educators, but in the conversations of a much wider public. This highly rationalized interrogation of the sexual realm focuses on sex as a central truth of human existence, while opening up any number of fundamental doubts about the exact nature of this truth.

Gender and Sexuality

Whether in the doctrines of the Church, the discourses of social hygienists and medical doctors, or the discussions of modern sexologists and social scientists, the past century has been marked by the emergence of a fundamentally new way of speaking and thinking about the nature of sex in contemporary Brazil. The increasingly rationalized analysis of sexual practices has hardly supplanted what we described as the traditional ideology of gender as the cornerstone of the Brazil sexual universe; on the contrary, we have consistently stressed the extent to which its impact has been limited by any number of social and economic circumstances. It would be more accurate to suggest that, rather than replacing an earlier system of thought, this newer system has been superimposed on it, offering at least some members of Brazilian society another frame of reference for the construction of sexual meanings. In the emphasis on sexuality, as opposed to gender, sexual practices have taken on significance not simply as part of the construction of a hierarchy of men and women, but as a key to the nature of every individual. Yet if the hierarchy of gender has receded from view within the terms of this new frame of reference, the question of power clearly has not. Power is as profoundly involved in this modern discourse as in the ideology of gender. But in the invention of sexuality, the relationship between sex and power has been restructured: the hierarchy of gender has become what, following Gayle Rubin (1984), we can describe as a hierarchy of sex.

Within the ideology of gender, sexual acts have been less significant in and of themselves than through their specific relation to masculinity and femininity. They offered a way of organizing a hierarchy between men and women as well as between types of men and types of women. Yet it was always in relation to the perceived qualities of gender—in particular, in relation to male activity and female passivity—that their meaning was understood. Within the discourses of sexuality, on the other hand, sexual practices are linked far less to the question of gender than to the question of reproduction. Whether in the doctrines of the Church, the lectures of the doctors, or even the debates of the sex modernists, the meaning of specific sexual acts seems to be as important as the gender of the actors. Regardless of the many important differences which obviously separate these various perspectives, in all of them, the significance ascribed to the act itself is built up in relation to a logic of reproduction rather than a calculus of activity and passivity. As in Rubin's formulation, a hierarchical system of values is constructed in which reproductive, monogamous heterosexuality defines a norm from which all other forms of sexual practice clearly deviate (Rubin 1984, 279–82). Even in the debates of the sex modernists, who have questioned the absoluteness of this norm, it is in relation to it—in relation to the logic of reproduction—that discussions have been built up.

As Rubin has suggested in analyzing the traditions of Western Europe and the United States, the sex hierarchy maps out the range of possible sexual practices on a kind of continuum. At one end of this continuum, we find a sexuality that is defined as "good," "natural," or "normal": the norm of reproductive, monogamous, martial, noncommercial heterosexuality. Other sexual practices are defined as "evil," "unnatural," or "abnormal" and are pushed to the opposite end of the continuum—the bottom of the hierarchy. The reproductive norm has clearly dominated the discourse of sexuality in Brazil since at least the middle of the nineteenth century, and has been reinforced in a variety of relatively formal ways, ranging from the ideological strictures of received religion to those of modern science. The activities of any number of forces, such as the police in large urban centers, who have traditionally worked hand in hand with the priests, hygienists, and doctors in seeking to regulate sexual conduct, have not only confirmed this norm, but have sought to ensure it, often through the use of force or sanctions against those who have somehow deviated from it. Sex solely for pleasure, sexual promiscuity, prostitution, and homosexuality have all been the object not merely of stigma, but often of outright repression aimed at minimizing the threat that they pose to normal sexuality.

As in the system of gender, the specific practices mapped out on the sex hierarchy simultaneously define types of individuals. In the case of the various deviations that undercut the norm of reproductive heterosexuality, they ultimately define the pervert, who in turn can be classified more specifically: *sodomita, prostituta, onanista, homossexual, sadomasoquista, travesti.* Within this system, these figures function, as clearly as the *corno* or the *viado,* the *puta* or the *sapatão,* as negative images. They not only complete the hierarchy of sex, articulating its own distribution of power, and set out its negative limits, but reaffirm the reproductive norm. As in Europe and the United States, however, the lines separating these various figures, separating what Rubin has described as "good" sex from "bad," can be, and clearly have been, contested. While the norm of reproductive heterosexuality has been more or less constant, the definition of the perversions has been less clear. Particularly in the mid twentieth century, the modernization of sexual values has permitted a wider space between the extremes of the sex hierarchy for acceptable sexual diversity. Even for the most liberal sexologists and sex educators, practices such as sadomasochism, transvestism, and pedophilia have generally remained incurable abnormalities. Yet the line between the normal and the abnormal has been blurred as any number of practices, ranging from masturbation and homosexuality to contraception and even abortion, have been raised as possibilities. Such practices have hardly been accepted by the majority of Brazilians as right and proper, but they are nonetheless at least debatable.[2]

While this rethinking of sexual values has made possible a certain reorganization of the sex hierarchy, however, it has not essentially altered the process of rationalization that has characterized the changing shape of sexual life in Brazil for more than a century now. On the contrary, it has reconfirmed the fundamental importance of the reproductive norm in defining itself with central reference to this problem. More forcefully than either the Catholic tradition or the discourses of medical science, it has emphasized the profound significance of sexual meanings. Indeed, the liberalization of sexual diversity that has accompanied the modernization of Brazilian life has reconfirmed the central importance of sexuality as somehow a key to the very definition of the self. In so doing, even the most modern voices of the present have been linked to a system of power that functions, to follow Michel Foucault, not simply through the repression of deviance, but through its incorporation into wider structures and its investment with meaning. Sex has become both an object of knowledge and a source of truth. Whether in the doctrines of religion, the discourses of doctors and scientists, or the pedagogy of modern sex educators, sexuality itself has taken shape as a social and cultural frame, situated within and inseparable from a complex system of power. It has offered at least some Brazilians another way of building up the sexual universe that they live in, another way of interpreting its meaning and making sense of their own experience.

5

Bodies and Pleasures

As complex and varied as they are, the structures that define both the traditional hierarchies of gender and the more modern interpretations of sexuality do not exhaust the field of sexual meanings in Brazilian culture. On the contrary, we can point to at least one more perspective that both draws upon these discourses and situates itself in opposition to them. We might describe this cultural frame as an ideology of the erotic, organized in terms of a very different logic, and offering its own distinct reading of the sexual universe. Although elaborated with constant reference to the structures of both gender and sexuality, this system of erotic meanings has focused neither on the construction of hierarchies nor on the rationalized interrogation of inner truths. Instead, it examines the diverse possibilities for sexual pleasure that these other ways of conceptualizing sexual life have largely ignored or circumscribed. It has thus offered an alternative model of the sexual universe for Brazilians to draw upon in shaping and interpreting their sexual experience.[1]

Like the systems of gender and sexuality, or for that matter, the origin myths that have been built up around the symbolism of sexual life, the full development of this erotic frame of reference can also be situated historically. It can be linked to the same processes that have been responsible for the increasing rationalization of sexual meanings in Brazilian life: to the massive social dislocations that have taken place in Brazil since at least the early twentieth century as a result of the pace of industrialization, urbanization, and modernization. Its most elaborate articulation as a distinct cultural perspective can therefore be found in those sectors of Brazilian society where these interrelated processes have been carried furthest—where the changing nature of Brazilian life has increasingly undercut the legitimacy of social structures such as the family, the Church, and even the state. Indeed, as the institutions that have traditionally functioned as the chief regulators of sexual life have been called into question, new territory has been opened up for sexual exploration and experimentation.

However, it would be a mistake to interpret this ideology of the erotic as nothing more than an unintended consequence of modernity itself. Its relation to the central traditions of Brazilian culture is far more complicated and intimate. Although it seems to intersect at a number of points the self-conscious modernization of sexual life described above, it can also be linked in a variety of ways to the wider world of sexual meanings in Brazil. It can be found, for example, as a subversive undercurrent in the structure of the plantation economy and the patriarchal order. Indeed, throughout Brazilian history, while it has tended to escape or even overturn the boundaries of both gender and sexuality in its alternative reading of sexual life, this erotic frame of reference has nonetheless been unavoidably tied to these other systems. Through its relationship to these other systems, it has functioned to structure the nature of erotic experience, and only by examining it in relation to them will it be possible to interpret its own distinct logic and to understand the ways in which this logic transforms the meaning of sexual practice in Brazil. This, in turn, will enable us to explore the range of meanings associated with erotic life, and to examine erotic experience, not by reducing it to some other level of reality or additional set of explanatory principles, but by interpreting it as itself a cultural construct: a product of intersubjective symbolic forms, ideological structures, semantic configurations, and the like, which take on significance within the flow of social life.

Transgression

Whether implicitly or explicitly, the systems of gender and sexuality quite clearly articulate a repertoire of sexual practices, some defined as acceptable and others as prohibited. Yet they fail to limit this repertoire fully because the very notion of prohibition implies the possibility of transgression. Like a definition of the acceptable, a definition of the prohibited—and by extension, of the forms of transgression—has been central to the symbolic economies of both gender and sexuality in Brazil. It is through the negative images of sexual transgression, whether in concrete figures such as the cuckold or the whore or in abstract concepts such as sin, sickness, or abnormality, that the systems of gender and sexuality have been able to regulate and reproduce themselves. Yet because this is the case, because their internal order depends upon their ability to produce the very beliefs and practices that appear to subvert this order, both of these systems paradoxically open up a cultural space for an ideology of the erotic capable of contradicting their most basic assumptions.

Central to this ideology of the erotic in Brazil is a culturally defined distinction between public and private realms which is perhaps best captured in folk expressions such as *Em baixo do pano, tudo pode acontecer* (Beneath the sheets, anything can happen) or, even more common, *Entre quatro paredes, tudo pode acontecer* (Within four walls, anything can happen):

> There are so many phrases . . . "Beneath the sheet, anything can happen." Or "Within four walls, anything can happen." There is also "Within four walls everything is possible!" There are also sayings like "What would these four walls say?" or "The walls saw, but they can't talk." Because the only evidence that there is are the four walls. You understand? And the walls aren't going to talk. So, you can do everything. The woman doesn't just fuck with her legs open. She sucks cock, she gives her ass, she creates positions. Understand? And not just women. Men too. Women or men—really, these phrases don't refer to just one sex. (João)

> This is always said by people like this: it's a group that is always talking about sex, about sexual relations, and the people always say that "anything can happen within four walls" because the world doesn't matter. A woman full of inhibitions, a man full of inhibitions, the macho guys, or the superfemale—suddenly, they can be not so female or so macho within four walls. Because there isn't anybody watching, and only what happens inside is what matters. You understand? So, the people say, "Anything can happen within four walls." (Antônio)

Used in a variety of contexts that exhibit little sexual content, these interrelated expressions nonetheless derive their meaning principally from their sexual connotations and invariably play upon the same underlying semantic structure.[2] Whether "within four walls" or "beneath the sheets," the key is that one is somehow hidden from public view:

> It isn't important where you are . . . The point is that you are hidden! It can be at home, but it can also be on a deserted beach, at night, in the street, in an alley . . . (Katia)

In private, or when hidden, then, the character of sexual life is fundamentally transformed. Anything can happen. One encounters a freedom of sexual expression that would be strictly forbidden in the outside world, in the public world of daily life.

Thus, at the same time that these folk expressions articulate a clear distinction between the public and the private realms of sexual experience, they subvert this opposition by hinting at the unexpected possibilities of sexual pleasure. Through a series of symbolic inversions, they play rather freely upon a fundamental dichotomy in Brazilian culture, first noted by Gilberto Freyre and later elaborated by Roberto Da Matta: a separation of cultural domains which is given representation in spatial imagery, in an opposition between the *casa* (house) and the *rua* (street) as key to the organization of daily life (see Freyre 1963; Da Matta 1978, 1985). As we saw in examining the ideology of gender, the house tends to be linked to a whole set of notions related to femininity and the proper limits of female sexuality. It is normally understood as the domain of the family and of familial values. While it may be a world inhabited first and foremost by women, it is also associated with at least some form of traditional, patriarchic authority, and is obviously seen as the site of domestic (or domesticated), properly reproductive sexuality:

> The house is where the name of the family has to be respected . . . The morality of the family . . . It's the place of good conduct and exemplary morality. The preservation of the traditional family environment within the home is the duty of everyone: the mother and father, the children, the grandparents . . . (João)

The street, on the other hand, stands as a far more impersonal domain of work and struggle. It offers individual freedom as well as temptation and danger. It is a fundamentally male space, inhabited, perhaps, by whores and sinners, but certainly not by a proper wife or mother:

> The street is a platform for waging war, where, traditionally at least, the father, the head of the family, went to struggle—went to earn a living . . . The street is where you meet dangers and the house is the fortification where the family is protected. But in the street you also enjoy yourself . . . It's the place of the "life": of women who are in the life (*mulheres da vida*) rather than the morality of the family . . . (João)

In erotic ideology, however, the normal relationship, the sharp dichotomy, between these two domains can be at least temporarily inverted, as the sexual freedom (and the danger) of the street invades the secluded space of the house—or, for that matter, as the controlled sexual functions associated with the family life of the house escape its controls and play themselves out in the impersonal (and, hence, once again, dangerous) world of the street. The normally clear-cut distinctions between inside and outside, between private and public, suddenly dissolve, and the structures of daily life are overturned, relativized, and rearranged. In these moments, according to this ideology, anything can happen. Everything is possible (see Parker 1987, 1989a).

This notion of *tudo*, "everything," is pivotal. It is central, with its implied mixture of temptation and danger, to what Brazilians define as *sacanagem* (see Da Matta 1983; Parker 1987, 1989a). *Sacanagem* is in fact an extremely complex cultural category that has no exact English translation. Indeed, its meaning in Brazilian Portuguese is highly varied, contradictory, and constantly shifting. Traditionally, it seems to have carried a set of essentially negative connotations. It was used, most commonly, with reference to pederasty or homosexuality, and a person described as *sacana* was marked with the stigma of sexual deviance (see Almeida 1981). And while this meaning has become considerably less current, especially in more modern, urban settings, *sacanagem,* along with the verb, *sacanear,* is still widely used throughout Brazil to refer to "trickery" or "injustice" much as we, in English, might refer to having been "screwed over" or "fucked over" by someone or something:

> On the one hand, it means "to do bad" to someone: "Today I was screwed (*sacaneado*) by my boss" . . . I was fired, or something like that . . . "Today I got (*sacaneei*) that bastard" . . . I got revenge with someone who had screwed me over (*me sacaneado*), who had done me some wrong. (José)

But over the course of the past decade, the notion of *sacanagem* also seems to have acquired a number of more positive connotations. It now has a playful side as well, and it is often used to refer to the friendly "teasing" of one's colleagues or fellows:

> *Sacanear* also means to tease with a jest (*uma sacanagem*)—making a joke, doing a prank . . . "How I teased (*sacaneei*) my friend yesterday!" . . . How I kidded him! (José)

Nowhere is the ambiguity of *sacanagem* more evident than in contemporary usage as a general term referring to a whole range of things sexual—above all else, to those aspects of sex that are considered especially marginal, prohibited, or dangerous:

> *Sacanear* also means "having sex." At times, it has a negative meaning. A rape is a *sacanagem.* It links sex and evil or violence. But it also has a positive, exciting side . . . Making love isn't *sacanagem,* but you do *sacanagem* while making love when you do the uncommon: you go to a motel, you screw in a place that is public or dangerous, you suck, or fuck the ass instead of the cunt . . . In this sense, *sacanagem* is used playfully, speaking about breaking rules, and is seen positively. The *sacanagem* becomes an excitement. (José)

Ultimately, then, this concept of *sacanagem* links notions of aggression and hostility, play and amusement, sexual excitement and erotic practice in a single symbolic complex. Whether used positively or negatively, whether referring to injustice or violence, to joking, to teasing, to obscenities or sexual innuendos, to pornographic or erotic materials, or to specific sexual practices themselves, *sacanagem* focuses on breaking the rules of proper decorum—the rules that ought to control the flow of daily life. In almost all of its meanings, it implies at least some form of symbolic rebellion or transgression—overturning the restrictions which govern normal social interaction. It is in the sense of "doing everything" that would normally be prohibited that this transgression is most clearly manifest. In thinking about things sexual, it is the idea of doing everything that seems to lie at the heart of what a good many Brazilians would define as *boa,* or "good," *sacanagem* (see Parker 1987, 1989a).

Within the fundamentally marginal and rebellious world of *sacanagem,* sexual interactions acquire meaning, at least from the point of view of their participants, neither as an expression of the hierarchical relations that separate men from women nor as an external sign of some inner truth. On the contrary, they become an end in and of themselves, a realization of what Brazilians describe as *desejo* (desire) or, more commonly, *tesão* (potency, sexual excitement, hardening or arousal of the sexual organs), in the achievement of *prazer* (pleasure) and *paixão* (passion):

> What is important in *sacanagem* is excitement, pleasure. Coming doesn't matter that much. What matters is the excitement. What matters is doing the *sacanagem.* (João)

Within the context of this erotic frame of reference, however, excitement and pleasure are to be found in those sexual practices that, in the ideologies of gender and sexuality, would be considered most questionable:

> To have sex before marriage, to masturbate, to take a prick between your legs, to let the man suck your breasts, to give your tush. All these things are more exciting because they were said, ever since you were young, to be wrong. People come to be more interested in these things. They want to discover these things. (João)

> The things that are most prohibited are always the most exciting, you know ... It's like in that song by Caetano Veloso: in *sacanagem,* "it's prohibited to prohibit." Doing everything is what counts ... it's what gives the most pleasure. (Tereza, a twenty-year-old lesbian from a middle-class family in São Paulo)

Indeed, because certain practices seem to exceed the boundaries of good taste, they are seen as especially *excitante* (exciting). They open up a forbidden world—a world that is at once unknown and dangerous. The pleasures that can be found in this world become all the more profound because of the danger that one must confront in order to achieve them.

Focused on the transgression of those rules and regulations that would otherwise prohibit certain sexual practices, this frame of reference implies a very different interpretation of the nature of sexual life from that provided by either the ideology of gender or the discourse of sexuality. This interpretation is itself clearly immanent, of course, in the prohibitions that define these other systems. Yet within the context of these systems, the practices that break through the boundaries of good taste remain an affront to any proper sense of shame, a repository of sin, an undeniable sign of abnormality. Within the erotic frame of reference, however, their significance is radically different. It is fundamentally positive rather than negative. Indeed, in this model of the sexual universe, anything is possible, prohibition is itself prohibited, and even the most taboo desires and practices can be seen as especially exciting.

Within the terms of this alternative model, the significance of sexual life is reinterpreted. The desires and practices that provided the focus for interpretations of both gender and sexuality are no less central here, but the meanings associated with them—both socially and psychologically—are transformed. While perhaps never completely eclipsed, the hierarchical distinctions between men and women and the detailed classification of sexual normality and abnormality give way to a new understanding of sexuality—a symbolic economy which takes shape as an esthetic of excitement and desire, of the body and its potential for pleasure.

Excitement and Desire

As in both the popular ideology of gender and the more formal discourses of sexuality, sexual desire seems to be understood, in this erotic frame of reference, as a force or energy that is tied to life itself. Within these other systems, however, the status of sexual energy is ambiguous—positive in certain, limited situations, but profoundly negative in others. To draw on a distinction used long ago by Freud, the value of desire seems to lie in the object rather than the instinct or the drive (see Freud 1962b). Within the erotic frame of reference, however, it is desire itself, rather than its specific object or aim, that becomes the center of attention. Desire is seen as positive in and of itself, and the object of desire is less important than the physical sensations that it produces. Indeed, the very notion of desire as a kind of diffuse energy is itself constructed through a complex cultural symbolism that simultaneously defines it and links it to its concrete, physical manifestations in the human body—to sexual arousal. In keeping with the transgressive logic of erotic ideology, it is in the widest possible play of this energy that the positive value of desire is most evident.

Like the body, the notion of desire opens up a range of possible meanings and interpretations. Depending on the specific context, *um desejo* can be translated as "a desire," "a wish" or "a longing," "an aspiration," or even "an appetite." The verb *desejar* can be understood as "to desire," "to wish," or "to want." And these various meanings can be applied, as well, to a range of situations which carry no specifically sexual connotations:

> In a general sense, desire isn't exclusively sexual . . . It refers to anything that you are wanting: you can desire a good grade on an exam, or you can desire some kind of food, desire to be rich, that your samba school wins, or your soccer team . . . or you can desire a person. (João)

The key here would seem to be a general notion of lack, of being unsatisfied:

> It's the lack of something that creates desire. You want to satisfy your desire.
> (Antônio)

Satisfaction and desire are thus tied to one another through their mutual opposition. Regardless of what one desires, the experience of desire is a demand for satisfaction, for attainment, for completion.

Within this wider understanding of desire, sexual desire is something of a special case. While desire can be generalized and applied in almost any situation, sexual desire serves as a metaphor for all of the manifestations of desire, regardless of context:

> Still, it's true that sexual desire is strongest. When you speak of desire, you
> think principally of sexual desire. (Katia)

At some level, then, a general notion of desire and a specifically sexual desire become largely synonymous. And just as sexual desire serves as a model for the wider range of meanings, the notion of satisfaction becomes linked to that of pleasure. The human body itself becomes both the object of desire and the provider of satisfaction. It is a source of pleasure capable of satisfying desire.

The complex symbolic connections that are involved here become clearer in the more extensive language of desire that has been built up in popular culture—a language that links the largely mental connotations of desire to its more concrete manifestations in the arousal of the body itself. With this in mind, desire can be felt, for example, as a kind of *fome* (hunger):

> *Fome* is another word for desire too. When you are hungry, you want to eat
> something, right? It's the same with desire. You feel it in your body. (José)

Sexual desire is thus synonymous with sexual appetite: playing upon the notion of the sexual object as a kind of food, and the sexual act as an act of eating, an act of incorporation, sexual desire is linked to hunger, to appetite, to the desire for nourishment. Like hunger, however, desire can never be fully satisfied. No matter how sated one might momentarily feel, both hunger and desire inevitably return:

> You feel satisfied after eating, but you will always get hungry again. It's the
> nature of things. And it's the same thing with sex. You feel calmer after a good
> fling, but in a little while your desire will return. (José)

Yet even while focusing on the inevitable transience of sexual satisfaction, this symbolism of hunger links the experience of desire to a highly concrete notion of corporeal pleasure. Drawing on images that have been, from any other perspective, stripped of their sexual meaning, and incorporating them within the ideology of the erotic, it confronts, once again, the boundaries that have been built up to separate and compartmentalize experience. As in *sacanagem* itself, the established order of daily life is almost unexpectedly dissolved, and the dynamics of desire and excitement operate within this dissolution.

Reproducing the central meanings associated with desire, then, the notion of hunger is even more clearly situated in relation to the body itself. Mental desires, wishes seeking satisfaction, are tied to physical sensations, excitations. While this process is particularly obvious in the symbolism of hunger, it is developed as well in a whole set of images related to the temperature of the body and the physical transformations that are associated with sexual excitement. Notions of hot and cold are used extensively to speak about desire and to link it, in a variety of ways, to the arousal of the body. While slightly less common, the expression *Estou com calor* (I'm hot) can carry precisely the same sexual implications as *Estou com fome* (I'm hungry); the physical experience of sexual excitement is understood as an experience of heat. Sexual energy is *quente* (hot), and becoming aroused sexually is associated with *esquentando* (heating up), with a rising body temperature, a sense of physical warmth that is focused in the genital region yet diffused throughout the body:

> Sex is very alive. Heat . . . hot . . . excitement is something hot: the heat of
> sex. The ardor of sex is very great. Every moment that you feel more excite-
> ment, an increase of sex, the heat is greater. (Sérgio, a twenty-nine-year-old
> heterosexual male from a working-class background)

Not surprisingly, the notion of *fogo* (fire) is easily incorporated into this set of images as a particularly appropriate metaphor for both desire and excitement:

> Fire is something that burns. And it has a color that is alive. It's something
> that spreads very rapidly. So fire is a metaphor for talking about sex. It's that
> sexual voluptuousness that mounts up in you . . . a strange thing that you say
> is burning inside of you. (Sérgio)

The ambiguous associations are evident. Like desire, fire is tied to both life and death. Essential to culture, to cooking, to protection, it is at the same time a source of danger, a violent potential that can escape human control. It conjures up a whole set of religious images linking the sins of the flesh to the fires of hell, and is an especially apt extension of the transgressive logic of erotic ideology. Easily linked to the heat of sexual excitement, it becomes one of the most common ways of speaking about the sexual experience of the body:

> We have expressions like "fire in the cunt," "fire in the asshole," or "fire in the
> tail." You use this a lot for someone who is nervous or excited: "Damn, guy,

you have fire up your ass!" But it's like *sacanagem:* it has a sexual side too. Saying this sexually signifies the desire to have sex, to give your cunt or your ass. "You have fire in your cunt" or "You have fire in your ass" means "desire to do something." But it also means "that pleasure" when you are screwing . . . you have your prick inside, fucking, and you say, "You have fire in your cunt." When you're in that voluptuousness, that pleasure of fucking, you also talk about fire in the cunt. You understand? It's psychological and physical. (João)

An individual can also be defined using terms such as hot, fiery, or fire-cracker:

"Hot" is perhaps the most common. "She's a hot woman!" It means that she is very sexy, very sensual, ardent. "I'm hot!" means that I am sexy—or that I'm excited, that I have fire. It's this business of heat, of sexual fire. (Antônio)

Thus one's own experience of excitement can be described in terms of fire, and expressions such as *dar fogo em mim* (put fire in me) or *botar em brasa* (turn into live coal or ember) are not uncommon metaphors for sexual arousal. Like hunger, this notion of fire, tied as it is to the heat that one feels throughout one's body when sexually excited, becomes central to the language of desire. It is through such metaphors that one not only speaks of excitement and desire, but in fact experiences them.[3]

As important as images of hunger, heat, and fire may be in building up the experience of sexual desire, however, the play of arousal across and through the body is most fully captured in the notion of *tesão*—like *sacanagem,* a key category in Brazilian sexual culture that can be translated into English only through approximations. While more common than any of these other terms in popular usage, *tesão* shares their wide range of meanings. Indeed, if anything, it both expands and specifies their referents. At one and the same time, *tesão* can refer to desire, to any number of sexual or nonsexual excitements, and to the actual state of sexual arousal. It can apply, in some circumstances, to a sense of excitement that seems to have little or nothing to do with the nature of sexual experience:

It isn't always sexual. Any thing or activity that excites you, that animates you, is something that gives *tesão.* When you really like a class, or some piece of work that you are doing, then you speak like this: "I have *tesão.*" Because of the class. You understand? (Katia)

Yet even in such uses, it is the notion of *tesão* as fundamentally sexual in nature that serves as the basis for a metaphoric extension of its meaning:

Well yes, *tesão* has lots of meanings. But above all else is the meaning from *sacanagem. Tesão* is what you feel in *sacanagem.* What you feel in your body. That desire that you get. You know, *tesão* is *tesão*—and it's very good! (José Carlos)

It is here in the sexual realm that the vocabulary is most fully elaborated. In public, it becomes a mark of attractiveness and attraction: a particularly attractive person can be described using the noun *um tesão* (a *tesão*), or the exclamation *Que tesão!* (What a *tesão!*). This same character can be reproduced in private, as well, in speaking of one's lover as *meu tesão* (my *tesão*). Whatever the context, *tesão* serves as the key symbol for sexual desire and excitement:

> It's so many things. *Tesão* is the attraction that you feel seeing a beautiful, attractive person . . . It's the desire to fuck, the excitement. It is a common word, you understand? It's what the people say. (João)

Thus both the feeling of desire and the physical manifestations of arousal are labeled and classified in terms of *tesão*. As in the notion of hunger, though even more forcefully, mental image and physical experience merge into one another. As in almost all the imagery of desire that we have already examined, the notion of *tesão* breaks down the boundaries that have been built up around the erotic in the world of normal daily life, as sexual meaning becomes both a metaphor and a model for all forms of experience.

It is through this notion of *tesão,* more than any other single construct, that desire invests itself in the excitement of the body. Indeed, it is *tesão* that marks the physical arousal of the body itself. Like *sacanagem, tesão* seems to be at once diffuse and focused. It is felt throughout the body while at the same time drawing attention to the sexual organs. It describes the erection of the penis, clitoris, or nipples, and the moistening of the vagina:

> *Tesão* is what you feel in your body. It's the sexual emotion that puts your prick hard. It's that excitement. It's the voluptuousness. It's the desire that runs through or that happens in your body . . . It's the excitement that the woman feels in her vagina, what makes her nipples hard. People joke, they say, "She's got *tesão* . . . She's getting all wet!" But, really, it's exactly this that happens. (João)
>
> It's that desire that you get to have sexual relations—what you feel in your body. The transformations of your body. That heat. Excitement. Desire. All these things. (Jorge)

If *tesão* is focused first and foremost in the genital region, however, it is hardly limited to it. On the contrary, it seems to spread out throughout the body:

> You feel *tesão* everywhere. It's that vibration. A thing that's very alive. (Maria)
>
> *Tesão* shows up in all the parts of the body—like the ass, legs, arms, breasts . . . It's a generalized thing, not only in the genital organs, but in every part of the body. (Antônio)

In keeping with the playful logic of the erotic, the physical sensations of arousal become the subject of jokes and games:

People make jokes. When it's really cold, and the woman's nipples get hard, you know, because of the cold, the people tease (*sacaneam*) her. They say: "Hard nipples!" "She has *tesão!*" It's like in that rhyme for children: "Maria-zinha, of all the curves, nipple hard, cunt wet, the rooster crows, the prick rises, the cow bellows, the prick buries itself in" (*Mariazinha, do bole bole, peitinho duro, boceta mole, o galo canta, meu pau levanta, a vaca berra, o pau enterra*). (João)

Are you familiar with that square, in the shape of the letter T, that architecture or engineering students use? There is a joke. When they pass, in the street or some other place, then the people say: "You have *tesão!*" or "You have *tesão* in your hand!" Because ever since the word *tesão* appeared—I don't know exactly when, but it must have been in the sixties—there has been created the expression *tesão na mão* (*tesão* in your hand). It means "jacking off," "masturbating," or "desire to touch another person." You understand? So when the people pass with the T-square in their hands, there is a popular saying: "You have *tesão* in your hand!" (Antônio)

Once again, then, within the terms of this frame of reference, the significance of arousal is radically different than in the other systems that we have examined. The hardening and moistening of sexual arousal is interpreted neither as a sign of potency and activity nor of reproductive potential. On the contrary, it is understood in relation to pleasure. Its meaning is fundamentally playful, transgressive, and erotic, and it is through such intersubjective symbolism that the subjective experience of erotic meaning takes shape.

In all of these culturally constituted images, both desire and excitement emerge as much in specific symbolic forms as in the physical reality of the body itself. That is, the experience of the body is unavoidably merged with the cultural representations of that experience. The two are mutually implicated. Within their intersection, the subjective experience of the erotic can be located, and desire is most clearly linked to *fantasia* (fantasy). Even here, however, in the set of connections that link desire, excitement, and fantasy, it is essential to emphasize the extent to which the most private of erotic images are built up out of the possibilities offered by the wider cultural context. Fantasy takes shape as itself a cultural category. As understood in popular culture, of course, it has relatively little to do with the abstract, technical terminology of psychology or psychoanalysis. While its popular usage may lack some of the many-layered associations that are so central to psychoanalytic understanding, however, it nonetheless offers a remarkably similar understanding of the world.[4] It appears in *sonhos* (dreams), *imagens* (images), and *representações* (representations):

Fantasies are like dreams. They are dreams, really. They are made up of images, ideas, thoughts in your head. A sexual fantasy is an image, or the series of images, that you have about what you want to do sexually. (Katia)

Built up in thoughts and images, fantasy becomes the ideal expression of the underlying cultural logic that organizes the erotic. It dissolves the repressions and restrictions of *realidade* (reality). Like all erotic imagery, it focuses instead on the satisfaction of desire and the meaning of pleasure:

> In your fantasies, everything is possible. What causes people to have fantasies is the dissatisfaction or the desire to possess what they don't have. In fantasy, you can have it. You can do what you want. All your desires will be satisfied. It's the opposite of real life. (Katia)

The possible combinations, of course, are almost limitless—yet, once again, the key to the constitution of fantasy, like *sacanagem* and *tesão,* can be found in the logic of transgression:

> The most erotic fantasies are those that we think about, but can't do. The repression created by society is placed like a wall between us, our desires, and our realities. In fantasy, we can pass through this wall. (José Carlos)

> In fantasy, you can do everything that can't be done in reality. All your desires are realized. Obviously, even in fantasies, lots of people repress themselves. But it's the only place where you have at least the possibility of doing everything. There are no prohibitions in your fantasies. (Antônio)

In the transgression of rules and regulations, of prohibitions and taboos, desire plays itself out in fantasy. Fantasy, in turn, becomes a model for the erotic. Just as it is shaped by erotic ideology, it becomes the fullest expression of this ideology. Like *sacanagem,* it offers an alternative vision of the sexual universe—a universe dominated neither by a hierarchy of values nor by a utilitarian economy of energy, but by passions and pleasures.

Within this passionate world (a world in which desire and excitement take precedence over domination and subjugation), the erotic emerges as a kind of *jogo* (game) in which the cardinal rule is that the rules themselves must be broken. In some ways, it is less the history of one's actual sexual encounters than the world of fantasies and possibilities that is most deeply exciting. While often referring back to the memories (or memory traces) of pleasure that one has experienced in the past, desire in fact occurs *before* the pleasures of the present. It is an anticipation of satisfaction that, like fantasy, depends upon possibilities of transgression for its meaning and power. Desire is incited as much in the *caça* (hunt) as in the actual catch. Thus, because it undercuts the monogamous norm of a rationalized sexuality, *paquerando* or *fazendo pegação* (searching or getting—roughly equivalent to the English notions of "picking up" or "cruising") becomes exciting in and of itself:

> You know, sometimes it is better to search than to get. The excitement is in the search, in the seduction . . . (Paulo, a twenty-six-year-old heterosexual male from the middle class)

The act of *sedução* (seduction) is central not simply because, as in the ideology of gender, it implies a kind of *conquista* (conquest) or dominance, but because it overcomes some resistance or restriction. Indeed, seduction becomes all the more exciting when the object of desire is forbidden, when the *cantada* (a pass or erotic invitation, derived from the verb *cantar*, "to sing") must be disguised or secretive:

> People always want what is prohibited. And it's more exciting to make it with people who are prohibited too: a girl who is still a virgin, or a married women. Everything is more complicated. It's more exciting also. (Rose)

As in the images of fantasy, it is this search for what is lacking, for what is denied or prohibited, that defines desire. It takes on a playful character, as seduction becomes a kind of game, and excitement is built up within a radically restructured playing field. Anticipating the possibilities of pleasure that are understood as implicit in erotic practice, the symbols and meanings that mark out this new field of play offer a particular reading not merely of excitement and desire, but of the significance of sexual life as a whole.

Reproducing the transgressive logic of *sacanagem* itself, the play of desire is thus in some ways as much about transforming the range of erotic possibilities as it is about the actual reality of sexual behavior. Anticipating pleasure where it is most explicitly denied, notions such as *tesão* and fantasy become central to the ideology of the erotic in Brazilian culture. At the same time, they suggest a reinterpretation of the whole range of sexual meanings: of the human body and its sexual potential, the variety and structure of possible sexual practices, and so on. In order to understand the full implications of this reinterpretation, we must turn to the ways in which this erotic frame of reference reinvents the body as an object of desire and as a source of pleasure, as well as to the implications that this understanding of the body holds for sexual practice itself. It is in this erotic understanding of the body and its practices that excitement and desire are most fully realized. It is here, as well, that the qualities that distinguish the erotic from both the hierarchies of gender and the discourses of sexuality are most evident.

Bodies and Pleasures

No less than in the ideology of gender or the more rationalized interrogation of sexuality, a particular interpretation of the human body is central to the erotic frame of reference in Brazilian culture. As in these other systems, the body is never simply given: it is built up in the symbols and meanings that are used to conceptualize it. Within this erotic frame of reference, however, the body is constructed neither as a foundation for the hierarchy of gender nor as a physical site for the truth of the sexual subject, but as we have seen, as an object of desire and a source of pleasure. The cultural configurations that shape this erotic body characterize it in terms of its beauty and its sensuality, its erotic potential. And the ways in which Brazilians think and speak about this erotic potential are surely as important to their understanding of sexual life as are any of the conceptions that we have examined thus far.

Not surprisingly, erotic anatomy is dominated by the genitals. The meanings associated with the genitalia within the erotic frame of reference, however, are very different than the symbolism of the other conceptual systems. While the male and female genitals are taken, within the ideology of gender, as diametrically opposed anatomical and symbolic structures, and as functionally interrelated organs in the utilitarian analyses of sexuality, from an erotic perspective they are characterized by their complementarity as much as anything else—by their potential for mutual pleasure. The combative and the clinical languages of gender and sexuality give way to the essentially playful language of *sacanagem*. Terms such as *banana* (banana), *mango* (mango), *mangueira* (mango tree), *pepino* (cucumber), or *linguiça* (sausage) are ways of describing the penis, while *concha* (conch or shell), *fruta* (fruit), *pomba* (dove or pigeon), and *rosinha* (small rose) can be used to speak of the vulva or the vagina. Even the harsher language of gender opposition—weapons, snakes, and spiders—is transformed, recontextualized, in the playful world of the erotic. Indeed, in shifting frames of reference, such terms, labels, and metaphors can be invested with new meaning:

> The words are strong. But the context changes. When you say "cunt" in the street, it has a very negative meaning. But when you say the same thing with your wife or with your girlfriend, the meaning is totally different. It refers to the same thing, but it has a different meaning. (Jorge)

Thus the range of erotic meanings associated with the genitals is far different from either the ideology of gender or the discourse of sexuality. The vagina is no longer dark and dangerous, but warm and inviting, the penis no longer a violent weapon, but a source of pleasure and fulfillment. And the erotic elaboration of these meanings expands into a detailed description of the surrounding sensual landscape: the *lábios da buceta* (lips of the cunt) and the *grelo* (clitoris), the *membrana* or *pelinho* (foreskin) and the *cabeça do pau* (cock head), the *ovos* (eggs, i.e., balls, testicles) and the *saco* (sack, i.e., scrotum), all become important, not because of anatomical curiosity or reproductive function, but because of their erotic potential. In short, then, the meanings associated with the body—and, in particular, with the genital region—are contextual. Their significance is relative and constantly shifting. Within the erotic frame of reference, it is neither their hierarchical nor their functional character that matters. They are understood as instruments of pleasure rather than as markers of power.

This does not mean that the associations built up in other contexts evaporate within the realm of the erotic. On the contrary, the meanings of the erotic are superimposed on them, taking precedence over them within specific situations. Layers of meaning take shape and come to the fore in different ways, at different moments, for different individuals. Within this context, the notions of power, violence, danger, fertility, or potency else-where associated with the genitals may simply slip away. On the other hand, they may themselves be eroticized, becoming part of the configuration of pleasure. The implications of power or violence may therefore become part of the incitement of desire, or the meaning of fertility central to the config-uration of arousal, and so on. The point is that even these associations be-come linked to the construction of an erotic universe. They become essen-tial to the realization of sensual pleasure rather than serving simply as markers of masculinity and femininity or as tools for reproduction.

Just as the ideology of the erotic transforms the meaning of the sexual organs, it simultaneously transforms their absolute primacy within the symbolic economy of the body. While this primacy is never entirely under-cut or forgotten, the relationship between the genitals and the rest of the body is nonetheless reconstituted. The symbolism of gender and sexuality tends to narrow down, or to focus in, on the male and female genitalia, the reproductive organs; the language of the erotic, on the other hand, seems to expand out to all the limbs, members, and organs, which are themselves invested with erotic meaning:

> The whole body is important. The face, the eyes, the mouth, the breasts, the ass, the legs . . . The attraction is in the whole person. The best *sacanagem* is when you do everything: kiss her whole body, lick her ears, caress her legs, her ass, rub your cock between her thighs, between her breasts, suck her nip-ples . . . (Carlos)

While the erotic potential of the body may be centered in the genitals, it is realized in virtually every area of the body. The eyes, nose, hair, neck, back, arms, thighs, legs, and even hands and feet can all be invested, under the right circumstances, with erotic meaning. In short, any part of the body can be eroticized, or incorporated into a system of erotic meanings. Indeed, the emphasis placed on a number of key areas almost exceeds that placed on the genitalia themselves, and structures such as the *boca* (mouth), the *peito* (chest) or *peitos* (breasts), and in particular, the *bunda* (rump or ass) seem, at times, to rival the penis and the vagina in the construction of erotic ide-ology.

In keeping with the totalizing logic of *sacanagem*, the erotic emphasis on areas such as the mouth or anus explicitly overturns the limitations of reproductive sexuality. A woman's breasts are especially important within this frame of reference, for example, not because of their biological function, but because of their beauty, their shapeliness, the special color of their skin, the particular form of their nipples:

> Men are fascinated by breasts. I don't know why. I think that Freud explains it, right. But it's more than this. It's the form, the size . . . A woman with beautiful breasts is simply more attractive. (Rose)

The fact that the breasts have a role to play in the reproductive process is hardly lost within this cultural system. But as the reference to Freud might suggest, even this biological function is eroticized, with the verb *mamar* (literally, "to suckle or nurse") used to describe sucking or licking a lover's breasts and conjuring up, perhaps, the memory trace of a child's earliest source of pleasure, transposing the mother/child relationship into the erotic present:

> Mamão (papaw) is another word for the woman's breasts—it comes from *mama* (mammary gland). And *mamar* (to suckle) also. Do you know this word? It's what the baby does: sucking the breasts of the mother. You understand? But men also say, "I'm going to *mamar* that woman!" "I'm going to eat her!" "I'm going to fuck her!" And when you are licking her breasts, sucking her nipples, her teats, you also say that you are *mamando* (suckling). (João)

An even more complicated set of transformations is involved in linking the female breast to the male penis as the source (as we have seen) of a certain kind of *leite* (milk):

> When you want the woman to suck your cock, you say, "Come here! . . . *Mama* (suckle) here! . . . Drink my milk." Because cum is also called *leite* (milk) or *leitinho* (little milk). (Wilson, a fifty-two-year-old heterosexual from the working class)

The various parts of this erotic body thus become interchangeable. Symbolic associations are built up between them, and a whole range of highly charged connotations underlie them. The mother's breast becomes a lover's breast. The breast becomes the phallus—or the phallus, the breast. The boundaries between adult and child, between male and female, become blurred in the play of erotic meanings, while the nature of pleasure is built up in these symbolic forms as profoundly diffuse, multiplex, polymorphous.

Much the same set of symbolic processes can be found, as well, in the eroticization of the *boca* (mouth). The origin, as the use of the verb *mamar* indicates, of the individual's earliest notion of pleasure, the mouth is linked as well to the vagina (also described, as we have seen, as the *boca de baixo,* "mouth below"). Here, however, the connotations of this association are not threatening, but exciting. The *lábios* (lips) of the mouth are associated with the labia of the vagina, not primarily as a source of danger, but of pleasure. Common to both men and women, the *boca quente* (hot mouth) is taken as a sign of passion, the *língua* (tongue), no less than the lips, is understood as a sexual organ, and both *beijando* (kissing) and *chupando* (sucking) are seen as central to the structures of erotic practice.

Once again, then, this symbolic complex builds up an understanding of the sexual universe in which the utilitarian, reproductive functions of sexual behavior have relatively little meaning and the absolute, hierarchical divisions between males and females are increasingly difficult to maintain. On the contrary, drawing on much the same imagery of nourishment and satisfaction associated with the female breast, the language of the *boca* tends to tie the nature of erotic experience to a whole range of sensual pleasures. Building on the notion of desire as an insatiable hunger, the erotic takes shape in a language of the *gostos* (tastes), *cheiros* (smells), and *sabores* (flavors)—a language of culinary metaphors in which *chupando* the parts of the body is described, for example, as *chupando uma manga* (sucking a mango) or *chupando um picolé* (licking a popsicle, i.e., a penis). Perhaps more than any other single set of images, this language of tastes and smells, of food and eating, dominates erotic metaphor in Brazilian culture. Sexual pleasures are tied to the pleasures of the palate, and the definition of *sensualidade* (sensuality) is broadened and expanded.

The imagery of food and eating runs throughout Brazilian sexual culture. We have already seen the extent to which notions of *comendo* (eating) and *dando comida* (giving food), for instance, structure the hierarchy of gender. The symbolism of food or nourishment is central to the definition of masculinity and femininity: whether the mother's breast or the wife's culinary talents, the provision of nourishment and the preparation of food are explicitly tied to the female role in Brazil. They define it and articulate it. The kitchen is a female domain, and cooking is second only to the bearing of children in the functions associated with women in traditional culture. Because the pleasures of the palate can be tied, symbolically, to the pleasures of erotic experience, however, the symbolism of gender can also be transformed into the language of the erotic. Women (and even men in homosexual encounters) themselves become *comida* (food), and within this erotic perspective, even women can assume the dominant role of *comendo* (eating):

> The concept of fucking is that it's the man who always eats (*come*). But, in reality, the one who swallows the sausage is the woman with her mouth called *boceta*. It's the vagina that possesses the form of a mouth, not the prick . . . When the woman is on top of the man, and she's the one who makes the movement to the point of coming, then you say that the woman is eating (*comendo*), swallowing the dick. (João)

Here the symbolic violence that dominates the ideology of gender gives way to a very different set of meanings linked to the possibilities of erotic practice. The imagery of food and eating becomes a way of speaking about erotic attraction and sexual satisfaction. An attractive woman or man is described not only as *bonita* or *bonito* (pretty, handsome, good looking), but as *gostosa* or *gostoso* (tasty or tasteful). Someone who is not especially attractive physically, but who is still seen as in some way exciting or desirable, can be described as *comível* (edible). And a particularly pleasurable experience (whether sexual or not) is almost invariably described as *uma delícia* (a delight), *deliciosa* or *delicioso* (delicious):

> You analyze sexual pleasure like you analyze a good *feijoada* (black bean stew). When finished, you would say: "What a delight!" "It was delicious!" "It was tasty!" It gives the connotation of pleasure as much in food as in sex. (José)

Again it is the notion of pleasure that provides the symbolic focus within this frame of reference. Sexual pleasures become tied to a whole range of other corporeal experiences, and the so-called sins of the flesh take on fundamentally positive rather than negative connotations. Relativizing the interpretation of the body as a marker of gender or an object of science, the symbolism of the erotic recreates it in its own image—an image of flavors, tastes, and smells, in which the multiple possibilities of pleasure are constantly reaffirmed and restated in metaphoric language.

Like the symbolism of the breast, the emphasis placed on the mouth, and on a whole range of meanings associated with eating and nourishment, at least partially displaces the significance of the genital organs as the absolute center of erotic experience. More accurately, it integrates the genitals into a wider understanding of the body and its pleasures. Oral pleasure becomes as significant as genital pleasure. Indeed, within this imagery, the two are hardly separable. Each seems to implicate the other. Nowhere is this alternative understanding of the body and its pleasures more pronounced than in the remarkable emphasis that is placed on the *bunda*, the *rabo* (tail), the *popas* or *nádegas* (buttocks), and the *bundinha* or *cu* (asshole). Aside from the genitals themselves, there is nothing that so dominates the language of the body in Brazil:

> For the *bunda*? Let me think. There are so many words. "Tail" . . . "anus" or "rectum" . . . "hole" . . . "blind eye"—conception of Brazilians, isn't it, because it's a hole like the eye, but an eye that can't see . . . so it's a blind eye. You also talk about the "eye of the asshole." Also "smelly," "stinking thing," "farting thing," or "shitter" . . . "Behind" or "cunt behind." Mom never talks about the *bunda*—only about the "behind." My grandfather, too. He didn't speak about the *bunda* of a woman, but about the "behind." There is "rosette," that comes from the color pink, and "coubaril tree"—I don't know why, but it's a tree . . . "Ant hill" is another—it's where the ants live. "The *bunda* of that woman is an ant hill." It means that she is crazy to give (in anal intercourse). Another is "bottom" . . . or "perforation" . . . "Oven" also. It's that business of heat, of fire. (João)

Like the symbolism of food and eating, the *bunda* plays a key role in the ideology of gender. As we have already seen, it is essential in the verbal dueling and joking that establish relations of symbolic dominance in the course of daily life, and it is no less important to notions of masculinity than the symbolism of food is to femininity. Associated with *defecação* (defecation) and *sujeira* (filth) through its function in the body, words such as *bunda*, *rabo*, and *cu* are among the most highly charged obscenities in the Portuguese language:

> Antônio: I think that word (*cu*) is so ugly.
>
> RP: Why?
>
> Antônio: Oh, I don't know. It's something dirty. It gives the connotation of filth. It's a really strong word.
>
> RP: Do you use the word?
>
> Antônio: Only once in a while . . . Principally in the street, you know, you tell someone to stick it up their ass, or something like that.
>
> RP: And to speak about the body?
>
> Antônio: We talk more about the fanny (*bunda*). *Bunda* is less ugly.
>
> RP: Why?
>
> Antônio: I don't know. It's less negative. I think that it has less connotation of filth, of shit.

Because of its often overwhelmingly negative connotations the place of the anus within the erotic esthetic is perplexing. The metaphoric association of tastes and smells, culinary masterpieces, and the like, with sexual pleasures offers a relatively straightforward transposition of positively valued images from the world of daily life to the symbolism of the erotic. The primacy of the *bunda*, on the other hand, relies on a more complex set of symbolic transformations.

The fact that the sexual organs are also the organs for the excretion of waste from the body is constantly reaffirmed in the language of popular culture. The vagina is described, as we have seen, using terms such as *carne mijada* (urinated meat). *Xixi* (urine) and derivatives such as *xixim* or *xixita* can all be used, though not very commonly, as synonyms for the vulva. *Pipi* can refer not only to urine, but to the sexual organs of both boys and girls. The sexual organs of young boys and girls are clearly perceived as potentially sexual, but they are most often spoken of in relation to the act of urinating. And the child's *bundinha* (little fanny) is understood in even less overtly sexual terms. It is closely associated with defecation, with *fezes* (feces), or more commonly in the language of everyday life, with *fazendo cocozinho* ("going potty"), but hardly with sexual pleasure. The excretion of bodily waste products is understood as the central function of the child's genital organs and anus, and control over such functions is among the earliest demands that society makes upon both boys and girls:

> Children always have a little chamber pot, pink for the girls and blue for the boys, and always in a place that is visible to the child. The mother begins to teach him early on to use the infant toilet: the chamber pot. Or to call an adult to say that he needs to urinate or defecate. There is physical reprimand when the child forgets to speak about his physiological necessities. When the child pees or poops in his diapers and doesn't tell his mother that he needed to do this, the mother reprimands the child by spanking his buttocks. This is a form of educating the child to use the toilet and not to do his necessities in his clothing. (Dulce)

As a focus for attention and restriction on the part of the wider society, it is not altogether surprising that these same functions should also offer a certain kind of physical pleasure for adults as well as for children—that they should be perceived as a form of release from the discipline imposed upon the body:

> It's a kind of pleasure, having a good pee or a good shit. I think that you tense up so much in order to control your body. Afterward, you can relax yourself. (Néstor)

This release may be only temporary, but its significance is more long-lasting. It is in this undercutting of social restrictions that erotic ideology locates the most exciting pleasures of later life, and the early experience of the child serves not only as a foundation for the construction of the erotic, but plays a key role in relativizing the meanings that are associated with the physiological processes of the body. No less than the imagery of food and eating, this association between urination, defecation, and pleasure celebrates the material existence of the body, even in the face of society's severest reservations and restrictions.

With the physical changes that accompany adolescence, the explicitly sexual—as opposed to urinary—functions of the genitals come to the fore. The role of the genitalia in sexual intercourse, and as a source of sexual pleasure, soon takes precedence over the earlier meanings associated with them. Yet these earlier meanings never really disappear. On the contrary, the taboos associated with the excretory functions of the genitals and the anus become linked, by analogy, to the repressions associated with their sexual potential, and by extension, the pleasures associated with urination and defecation as a release from the controls of social existence come to be tied to sex itself:

> When we are children, we learn that filth is to play or mess with shit or piss. But when we begin to get to a certain age, where the sexual emotions are in force, then we come to hear and have to learn that sex is part of the filth of

life. Now, it is no longer just unwashed hands that are dirty, but our minds.
(João)

Like the excretion of waste products, sex comes to be understood as simultaneously liberating and pleasurable yet dirty, and nowhere are these connections more evident than in relation to the *bunda:*

> The penetration of a prick in an asshole is really known as dirty sex, not just because it's the asshole that defecates . . . It's the conception of the social structure. This type of incorporation of filth is placed in all the meanings of things that are done outside of the taboos of society. (Roberto)

Because of such complicated associations, by the time of early adolescence, the *bunda* seems to have taken on a meaning especially well suited to the transgressive logic of the erotic. The changing shape of the developing girl's *bunda* is, if anything, even more noticed and commented on than are her enlarged breasts. The fact that the *bunda* (like the *boca*) can serve as a substitute for, or an alternative to, the vagina is constantly reaffirmed. Particularly for males, there is a kind of fetishization of the *bunda* as a sexual object which envelopes and transforms its earlier association with defecation. Control of the sphincter, which is primary in the disciplining of the body through the self-regulation of defecation, is transformed into a sexual practice and a source of pleasure. Like the mouth and the vagina, the anus is far more than just an orifice; it becomes central to the erotic techniques of the body:

> The asshole isn't just a hole. It can be tightened, contracted, relaxed . . . It has to be relaxed to let the prick enter. Then it can be tightened to hold on to it. It's like the cunt, or a mouth . . . you have to know how to use them.
> (Néstor)

Within this ideology of the erotic, then, the *bunda* can become a focus for sexual pleasure. Because of its especially negative connotations in the everyday world—its associations with *excremento* (excrement), with *bosta* or *merda* (shit)—it has a unique role to play within the erotic economy of the body. Intimately linked to notions of *sujeira* (filth), it is especially well suited to the undermining of social norms and proper decorum that is fundamental to the constitution of erotic experience.

The *bunda* both complements and completes the erotic images that we have already examined. Like the genital organs, the breast of the nursing mother, and the suckling/sucking mouth, the anus becomes a point of contact between the body and the world around it. As much as the incorporation of food and drink, the subsequent excretion of waste links the material body to this wider world. Like sex itself, both of these processes break down the barriers of individuality, presenting the body as integrated and united rather than separate and distinct. For this reason, the symbolism of *sujeira,* so profoundly negative in the world of daily life, can be inverted and transformed in the world of erotic meanings.

Rooted in images of excrement, the use of *sujeira* as a metaphor is normally taken as an indictment of the immoral and the unacceptable. In the play of the erotic, however, this set of meanings is overturned. Just as the defecating anus is transformed into a sexual organ and an object of desire, *sujeira* takes on a positive connotation. Within this frame of reference, to call a lover *sujo* or *suja* (dirty) can imply that he or she is especially exciting. To playfully suggest performing *uma sujeira* (a filthy act) can be the invitation to a *sacanagem* which is all the more arousing because it breaks the rules of proper decorum:

> Outside of *sacanagem*, the word *sujeira* is used in a thousand different forms. But when we refer to *sujeira* with *sacanagem*, it is just as possible to find a good connotation as a bad one. For example: "Let's do a really dirty (*suja*) *sacanagem*." It isn't negative. It doesn't mean dirty sex—dirty because of people's hang ups. Here, the really dirty *sacanagem* means that everything that is possible sexually will be done. It's what carries us to total pleasure. It's the so-called sex without hang ups—without restriction. (Antônio)

While the value of actual physical cleanliness is never disputed (on the contrary, it is constantly described by informants as essential to erotic appeal), the use of *sujeira* as a metaphor follows the underlying logic of *sacanagem* itself. It inverts the meanings of daily life, stands them on their head, and offers a radically different reading of the significance of sexual practice. *Sujeira* thus becomes another component in an erotic vocabulary—a vocabulary that reconstructs the body as a source of pleasure and integrates it fully, through its sensuality, with the physical world around it.

This constant emphasis on the sensuality of the body clearly marks the construction of erotic meanings in Brazilian culture. Just as a notion of sensuality typifies the Brazilian interpretation of their own character as a people and invests itself in their understanding of the social body, so too it becomes absolutely central to their understanding of the physical, individual body. Tying together a variety of disparate—indeed, sometimes highly contradictory—images, this understanding of the body extends the notions of *sacanagem, tesão,* and the like, that structure an ideology of the erotic. It provides an alternative reading of the sexual universe in which the body becomes significant not as a marker of gender differences or as a vehicle for reproduction, but as a source of sensual pleasure. Linked, as it is, to sensuality, the notion of pleasure in turn permeates the meaning of sexual life, and the very experience of pleasure as a physical reality is itself built up through the cultural symbolism that structures the erotic universe. Within this frame of reference, the body itself is reinvented. The primacy of the genitals to sexual life is never undercut, yet it is at least partially displaced.

Almost any part of this sensual body can be eroticized—treated, for a variety of reasons, as especially pleasurable and exciting. Indeed, the body as a whole is approached in almost esthetic terms, and it is in its totality, its completeness, that its *beleza* (beauty) lies.

Ultimately, then, this erotic reading of the body is inextricably linked to the dynamics of sexual desire and excitement in Brazilian culture. The most diverse parts of the body become sources for the sensation of sexual pleasure. At the same time, however, they are also transformed into images and symbols which, through any number of complex psychic processes, incite desire and excitement.[5] Because desire and arousal are not simply natural impulses experienced as essentially the same for all human beings regardless of their social or cultural circumstances, the highly specific cultural forms that map out these domains of erotic experience become linked to the no less specific imagery of an erotic body. Together, they form an elaborate system of meanings that contrasts markedly with the systems of gender and sexuality. It is within the context of this particular system and its polymorphous, open-ended understanding of both desire and pleasure, that what we might describe as the culturally constituted structures of erotic practice take shape.

The Structures of Erotic Practice

It has often been suggested that while the meanings associated with sexual practices cross-culturally are almost infinite, the actual practices themselves are in fact rather limited—conditioned by the limitations of the body, with its finite number of convex and concave surfaces (see, for example, Gagnon 1977). While there may be some truth to such an assertion, because the body and its possibilities are themselves culturally constructed, sexual practices can never be treated as somehow simply given in nature or, for that matter, limited *by* nature. What one society may conceive of as sexually possible, another may not, and the experimentations that might open up the widest range of imaginable sexual practices are rarely initiated entirely by individuals. On the contrary, it is the cultural construction of potential practices that allows individuals to imagine them, and in Brazil at least, it is within this erotic frame of reference that the possibilities of sexual practice are formulated.

Given the emphasis that this ideology places on the transgression of sexual prohibitions in the constitution of meaningful (exciting) erotic experience, it is hardly surprising that the structure of erotic practice, like the body itself, should be characterized by what we might describe, following Freud, as a remarkable polymorphous perversity (Freud 1962b). In Brazilian culture, however, the polymorphous character of sexual pleasures is hardly limited, as in the traditional psychoanalytic framework, to the experience of infants and then gradually suppressed through the child's entry into the world of culture. Instead, at the same time that the restrictions which circumscribe the growing child's erotic life become evident, so too do the practices which circumvent these restrictions. It is this full range of sexual possibilities, then, rather than some more delimited segment of it, that becomes meaningful even to adults within the erotic frame of reference. And it is the full range of meaningful possibilities suggested by this frame of reference that particular individuals can in turn draw upon in shaping their own erotic meanings.

This way of construing the erotic universe once again undercuts and transforms both the ideology of gender and the discourses of sexuality in Brazilian culture. In both of these systems, primary emphasis seems to have been given to some form of genital (hetero)sexuality as the only really legitimate form of sexual expression. Other sexual practices are certainly articulated: anal intercourse, masturbation, bisexuality and homosexuality, and so on. But in every instance, these practices are defined in negative terms; as negative examples of prohibited conducts, they serve to define and legitimize the normal, the conventional. In the constitution of the erotic, however, these prohibited practices acquire positive value. From early childhood on, masturbation, oral eroticism, and anal eroticism, as well as same-sex relations and any number of other deviations, emerge alongside the genital sexual norm as alternatives for the structuring of erotic practice—alternatives which may or may not be realized in the conduct of any given individual, but which are at least imaginable within the ideology of the erotic. Indeed, in keeping with the transgressive logic of *sacanagem* itself, these otherwise marginal sexual practices become absolutely central to what we might describe as the erotic scripts produced in Brazilian culture.[6]

Masturbation is among the earliest of sexual practices to take on an explicitly erotic meaning. As in the case of so many other significant domains of sexual experience, the vocabulary that can be drawn on in order to speak of masturbation is itself an indication of its significance. While the verb *masturbar-se* (to masturbate oneself) is frequently used, particularly to speak in public or in polite company about issues related to masturbation, it is a fairly technical term with rather formal or even medical overtones. Far more common, in popular speech, are expressions such as *tocar punheta* for males or *tocar siririca* for females. The verb *tocar* is used in Portuguese to mean both "to touch" and "to play (an instrument)," and this combination of touching while at the same time mastering a pleasurable technique is clearly pivotal in any number of expressions, as is the playful, joking quality that characterizes the world of the erotic generally:

> *Tocar punheta,* for men, and *tocar siririca,* for women, are the most common expressions. For *tocar punheta* there is also *tocar flautim de cabo* (to play a

handle-shaped flute) and *tocar trombone de vara* (to play a pole-shaped trombone)—it's because these instruments have the form of a prick. There are various jokes. When someone asks, "Do you play some musical instrument?" you respond, "Yes!" The person is going to ask which instrument it is. And you tease (*sacanea*) him, saying "handle-shaped flute" . . . There are other really common expressions as well . . . *carinho de mão* (tenderness by the hand), *depenar o frango* ("to pluck the chicken") . . . you understand . . . it's because you're jacking off your dick, and it's like taking out the feathers of the chicken . . . There is also *vício solitário* (solitary vice). This is strong. You should write about solitary vice. (João)

Regardless of the nuances that can be found in these various expressions, a common thread ties them to the wider structure of erotic ideology. While they play upon a range of associations and meanings, they all focus on erotic pleasure as an end in and of itself. Indeed, within this frame of reference, masturbation is understood, not as a threat to procreation, but as a source of pleasure that is all the more exciting because it is repressed.

It is thus hardly surprising that masturbation should be intimately linked to fantasy. Much like fantasy, it is in some ways an erotic ideal, as it offers a stage for the fullest realization of the transgression that underwrites the play of erotic desires. In masturbatory fantasy it is possible, however momentarily, to construct one's own sexual dramas with a freedom more absolute than anything one will ever experience in the course of daily life:

> Beating off is better than fucking . . . With *punheta,* and in any place or any time, you can get whatever you desire. You just have to think and develop your imagination, and the climax of coming will give you satisfaction. (José Carlos)

Once again, however, such erotic possibilities are hardly "natural." They must be learned. They are dependent on a whole set of meanings that are commonly transmitted during childhood or early adolescence by one's friends and associates:

> I began to masturbate behind the water tank with a friend who was two years older than me. He wanted to compete with me in everything, but I always won the contests. But with jacking off (*punheta*) and hair around the prick he beat me because he was older. (João)
>
> The games and championships of jerking off were important rituals in the day to day life of my youth. Every day, after school, we had reunions of the whankers, some with big cocks for their age, and others in the phase of development. Whoever shot first became the stud of the group. The reunions took place in ruined old houses or in the middle of groves of banana trees. The ritual became almost a religion, and you couldn't let on about this secret, principally because we lived in a society that was extremely repressive and Catholic. But

there was always someone who got upset or frustrated in the group and who opened his mouth like Judas Iscariot. We received beatings from our families, but we didn't take long to start up our mutual competition again, because the solitary jacking off (*punheta*) did not cease to exist at our homes or in the bathrooms of the schools. The funny thing is that our fathers punished us, but they had also passed through the same jack-off club (*clube de punheta*). (Antônio)

Given the divisions of gender, the learning of masturbation is tied to a setting which carries a whole range of bisexual or homosexual connotations as well. The transgressive logic of masturbation itself becomes linked to the context of transgression in which it is learned, and while the structures of fantasy that are built up in relation to masturbation may, at one level, serve to confirm or reaffirm the accepted norms of heterosexual desire, they can also function, on another level, to undercut the distinctions between homosexuality and heterosexuality that have been established in the discourses of daily life. Within the reality of erotic practice, then, the meanings of gender and sexuality can be rearranged and transformed, and this process can be seen with particular clarity in the transgressive play of desire that becomes linked to masturbatory practice.

While masturbation is most commonly understood as a form of autoeroticism, it is important to understand the extent to which it is also integrated into a wider structure of sexual interactions. Because of the prohibitions that have been built up in the ideology of gender and the discourses of sexuality, masturbation can become central to early sexual explorations with others as well as alone. The same-sex settings which serve as the context for learning about the sexual meanings associated with masturbatory practice can easily be transformed, and mutual masturbation becomes a key sexual interaction in more private same-sex explorations as well:

> I remember that for a few years during my adolescence I had a number of friends who were my partners for good times. We always went out in pairs to hunt for girls. We passed through bars, parties, streets, plazas, alleys, and clubs, but at the end of the night we hadn't gotten what we really wanted. Sometimes we would pick up hookers to fuck with us. The price was agreed upon for serving the two of us. But there were nights when we didn't get anyone and we went to sleep in one of our houses. We slept in the same bed. We talked about everything and everyone. We got into erotic conversations, and the cock started to get excited. We looked at porno magazines (*revistas de sacanagem*) and put our hands to work. Everything started out really slow, because nobody wanted to be accused of being a *bicha*. But after talking a while, we wound up jacking one another off. (João)

Indeed, given the continued significance of virginity, as well as the desire to avoid unwanted pregnancy, masturbatory practices are also an important part of the sexual scripts of young males and females:

Marly was a virgin (or is even until today), but she liked to see my prick hard beneath my jeans. This is when we were in her parent's house. I rubbed against her so much that I chafed my dick and came in my pants. The good times were camping where we had a tent for just two people. There, with lots of difficulty, I got all her clothes off. I pushed my dick against her belly. "One palm above the vagina." (It's almost a popular saying.) One palm, so that jism doesn't fall and make her pregnant. You understand? I was always very cautious about pregnancy. I always came jacking off (*tocando uma punheta*) between her breasts, and then I passed my finger in her cunt, giving her a good rub (*tocando uma boa siririca*). She would grab my prick and start to jack it off again—especially at the moment when she was coming. (Roberto)

And perhaps especially in keeping with the wider logic of *sacanagem,* masturbation can also serve as the only effective form of sexual contact in certain public settings where the danger of being discovered prohibits interactions involving more extensive disrobing or intertwining:

My boyfriend really likes to stir me up, especially in public. He gets excited almost anywhere. On the bus, he always stands behind me in order to protect me from inappropriate pushes—but he always rubs against my behind. At the beach, we go to swim and in the water he is after me right away with his finger. He really likes to masturbate me. I like it too. When there isn't a possibility of a more comfortable place, I like this game with the hands. One day I was almost caught in the act by my mother, who, in spite of not having complete certainty about what was happening, was still suspicious. (Rose)

In almost all of its manifestations, then, masturbation quite consciously undercuts the utilitarian logic of reproductive sexuality. In all of its meanings, it seems to reproduce consistently the basic structure of the erotic in Brazilian culture—to articulate, once again, a radically distinct vision of at least one aspect of the sexual universe in Brazil.

This same vision can certainly be found, as well, in the elaboration of oral sexuality and oral intercourse. If the mouth is clearly associated with a variety of sensual pleasures going back to early infancy, during childhood and early adolescence it is increasingly invested with meaning as central to the scripting of erotic behavior. Even for very young children, the romantic *beijos* (kisses) that pass across the screens in movie theaters or on television are among the earliest models for structuring sexual conduct:

When I was seven or eight years old, or maybe one or two years earlier, I already tried to portray a kiss on my lips. I didn't know just how to do it, but I had the idea of rubbing lips against lips—this was already enough to reproduce what I had seen at the matinée in the cinema. One of the things that I waited for most was the final kiss in every film with the word "END" representing eternal happiness. On Sunday itself, I didn't have the opportunity to practice my fantasies with the community of female cousins that lived around me—but on Monday, after school, there we went behind the chicken coops or in the area of the water spouts, the place where our mothers washed clothes and passed around the gossip of the day. But after four o'clock, you only heard the falling of the water in the large wooden troughs . . . There was the school of kisses. We passed hours and hours with our lips stuck together—without opening the mouth, only lips. Until the day that an older cousin learned that, along with the lips, the tongue had to be used. The party was complete and the psychological confusion was formed, because the mixture of lips, tongues, and saliva gave us the sensation of something filthy. But in spite of the Sunday Masses with teachings of sin, of flesh, and so on, it didn't take much time to develop the true meaning of the kiss. Sometimes I was surprised by an adult, and then the confusion took shape with blows and punishments—especially without the films on Sundays, and with dominical confessions with the priest of the parish. I prayed ten Our Fathers, ten Hail Marys, and other prayers as well, in order to purify my soul and deliver myself from the sin of the flesh. But when the punishment ended, there I went again to the lessons and practices with the kisses. (João)

While this school of kisses may focus, initially, on imitating the practices of matinée idols, with their sensual lips and their long, dramatic kisses, the fact that the *beijo* can be applied to any part of the body is quickly perceived as well: to kiss not only the lips, but the genitals, is a common enough extension of the early sexual play of children. As children grow older, it is a relatively easy step to the notion that kissing everywhere, even remote recesses of the body, is especially exciting and erotic. And the eroticization of the mouth, in turn, is incorporated into the imagery of food and eating. Verbs such as *lamber* (to lick), *chupar* (to suck), and *sugar* (to suck up) are all invested with erotic meanings. Just as it can be kissed, any part of the body can be licked and sucked:

There are verbs like "to suck," "to lick," or "to suck up" . . . It doesn't mean that it's only sexual. You can suck a candy, you can suck a finger, an ice cream, a fruit. It has various meanings. But it's sexual too: "suck cunt," "suck cock." "To suck up" too. "To suck up" is like "to suck." It's very sexual. "I'm going to suck up all the liquid from your cunt!" You understand? And not only the cunt. The entire body. You suck the breasts, the fingers, the toes . . . You lick the belly, the fanny, the balls . . . It really excites me when someone licks my balls, my groin, and my prick. (José Carlos)

A *banho de gato* (cat's bath) refers to the thorough licking of even the most inaccessible places, and a *chupão* (hicky), to the mark left on the skin from prolonged sucking or kissing. Although the intricacies of such practices can perhaps be fully discovered only through one's interactions with others, the fact that they constitute significant forms of sexual conduct is constantly reaffirmed in the language of popular culture.

As in the case of masturbation, notions of licking and sucking are central to the early sexual explorations of adolescence. Like masturbation, the importance of oral sex (especially for males) is often learned in the context of same-sex interactions—with members of one's peer group, for example, or from older males—and can sometimes be integrated with homosexual play or experimentation:

> My older male cousins began to teach me *sacanagem* by making me suck their dicks. They told me that to be a man I needed to suck and to give (*dar*) to them. The first time that my cousin, Cênio, put his prick in my mouth, I almost died from nausea. But I went to look for a boy younger than me and I did the same thing, telling him that in order to be a man he had to suck my prick. (Sérgio)

Also like masturbation, oral sex can offer young couples an important alternative to vaginal intercourse that can be used extensively to circumvent the restrictions placed on sexual conduct. Indeed, its practice is often taught to young females by their male partners, and it can come to play a leading role in the sexual scripts of both males and females in the early explorations of adolescents:

> I played around a lot with my girlfriends in my room behind the mirrored door of my clothes closet. It was an extremely safe place for them to suck me, because my mother never suspected. I put my prick out without taking off my pants. My girlfriend sat on the edge of the shelf inside my clothes closet. She sucked me looking at the mirror. The door to my room stayed open and nobody suspected what was happening. At the same time that she sucked me, I spoke, in a loud voice, about angelic things, and it was all done like that . . . (Sérgio)

Perhaps even more than masturbation, then, oral sex is often especially important in early sexual exchanges with others, regardless of gender. The erotic possibilities of the tongue and the mouth are intimately linked to the notion of *sacanagem:* to the idea of sexual practices which escape the regulations of conventional life, and which are exciting in proportion to the prohibitions which inscribe them.

It is probably this early association with transgression, coupled with, or superimposed upon, an understanding of the body and the sources of pleasure, that lies behind the importance of oral sexuality in the construction of erotic life. As primary as oral eroticism may be, however, it hardly compares with anal eroticism and anal intercourse in the erotic. Just as the emphasis on the *bunda* seems to exceed the emphasis given to even the *boca* in the erotic esthetics of the body, the importance of anal intercourse in the structures of erotic practice is more powerfully evident than any other single aspect of erotic ideology. Along with both masturbation and oral sex, anal eroticism has a key role in early sexual play. For boys, it is the focus of same-sex explorations such as *fazendo meia* (literally, "doing half") or *troca-troca* (again, literally, "exchange-exchange"), games in which partners are said to take turns masturbating, fellating, or most commonly, penetrating one another:

> *Fazer meia* or *troca-troca* is a game that every group of young guys at the age of puberty plays. It's simply one guy jacking off another, or sometimes one sticks it in the other and then an exchange is done. (José)

Although often an egalitarian transaction in which active and passive positions and roles are exchanged and the partners view one another as equals, *meia* or *troca-troca* would seem to function as well as a kind of transgressive underside to the highly conscious cultivation of heterosexual masculinity that defines the interactions of male groups. Just as older males instruct younger ones in the intricacies and techniques of lovemaking with women, and often even arrange for heterosexual initiation, in *meia or troca-troca* the older males offer an initiation into homosexual practices by symbolically feminizing their partners. As one frequently cited expression puts it, *Homem, para ser homem, tem que dar primeiro*—in other words, "A man, in order to be a man, has to give (to take the passive role in anal intercourse) first." Older or stronger partners thus assert their own dominant masculinity in *troca-troca* by slyly manipulating the situation in order to penetrate their partners before finding some excuse to leave the game. What ostensibly begins as an egalitarian exchange can thus quickly be transformed into a problematic competition as the many different meanings of *sacanagem* are brought together:

> Sometimes one gives (*dá*) first, or sucks or jacks off the other, and then when it is the turn of the one who received pleasure first, he doesn't want to do it for the other. There are sometimes when this same first person goes about telling others that the second did this or that with him. The connotation of activity and passivity. The active defames the passive, giving rise to fights and shame, if not blows and serious punishments coming from family members. The game can sometimes get complicated. (José)

Emasculating young boys in order to create men, then, *troca-troca* (or any playful sexual interaction along the same lines) seems to reproduce the logic of *sacanagem*. It provides younger males with a wide range of information about same-sex practices and initiates them, at one and the same time, to the hierarchical structure of domination associated with activity and passivity, as well as to the transgressive logic which overturns the restrictions and repressions of daily life.

While anal eroticism is clearly important, in a number of complicated ways, in the early transactions of males with other males, like forms of masturbation and oral eroticism, it is also common in interactions between males and females. Like both masturbation and oral eroticism, it is often used to avoid the loss of virginity (embodied in the hymen) or the dangers of unwanted pregnancy. And because it is thought to parallel most closely the practice of vaginal intercourse—which is culturally elaborated both as a desirable ideal and, for the young, as a prohibited taboo—anal intercourse would seem to offer a far more satisfying alternative than any of the other possible practices:

> Especially for adolescents, fucking ass (*comendo bunda*) is an act of substituting for vaginal coitus. Fucking ass begins early in the start of puberty. In giving or eating an ass, the pleasure is heightened in comparison to sucking or jacking off. Some people say that it's better to screw an ass than a stretched-out or overused cunt. (Antônio)

Anal intercourse may have special importance for young people, but its significance is hardly less evident even later in life, when the problems associated with virginity and (more problematically) pregnancy give way, and vaginal intercourse becomes common and expected. On the contrary, particularly for men, but also, it would seem, for many women as well, anal eroticism continues to be associated with the transgression of taboo. Indeed, because one's earliest transgressions are invested with a surplus of meaning and are thus remembered as especially exciting and pleasurable, anal intercourse continues to be central to the structure and significance of erotic practice:

> Anal sex is my favorite. When we're young, we learn that it is condemned by the Bible, by the teachings of the Church. The sense of sin is very great. But we also learn that fucking an ass is very pleasurable (*gostosa*), very exciting. There is the desire mixed with a sense of prohibition, of sin . . . When they get older, people remember these emotions. For many people, the ass can even become a fixation. (Jorge)

Anal intercourse is thus linked to masturbation and oral sex as key elements within an erotic vocabulary in Brazil. Invested with erotic meaning through the sexual scripts learned during childhood and adolescence, these practices maintain their significance during adulthood. Because of the numerous prohibitions surrounding them, they fit perfectly into the transgressive structure of the erotic. They are not simply a dark underside of perverse pleasures which somehow escape the controls of culture, for they are themselves culturally constituted in relation to the notion of control.

Given these facts, it might be tempting to downplay the importance of vaginal intercourse and genital sexuality within the world of the erotic. Nothing, however, would be more inaccurate. Genital practices are very much a positive ideal. The point is not that the genital is downplayed in erotic ideology, but that it is integrated equally within a wider set of practices rather than set above these practices as somehow more valuable or correct. The significance or meaning of genital sexuality is thus transformed within this erotic frame of reference, with its emphasis on the polymorphous nature of pleasure, and Brazilians often joke about the limitations of what they call *papai-e-mamãe* (literally, "daddy-and-mommy"), or what in English is sometimes referred to as "the missionary position": heterosexual genital intercourse with the female partner beneath the male. While *papai-e-mamãe* fits perfectly into the ideology of gender, with its symbolic domination played out in the structure of sexual practice, as well as in the discourses of sexuality, focused on what is perceived as the "natural" form of intercourse or copulation, it is hardly suited to the cultural logic of the erotic. On the contrary, within the erotic frame of reference, emphasis is placed upon the extensive variety of possible sexual positions:

> We Brazilians like to vary positions. Doing the same thing every day becomes monotonous. I prefer to screw my wife "on all fours" (*de quatro*). I like to feel her ass banging against my dick. I also like "fried chicken" (*frango assado*): having her lie down, with her legs spread way out. The fried chicken that I like is to put my prick in her ass and then to take it out and put it in her pussy. There are various books that they sell on the newsstands teaching the 600 or 700 different sexual positions. (José Carlos)

The point is that the positions for genital intercourse merge with a whole range of possibilities that are quite clearly focused on other combinations:

> *Papai-e-mamãe* gets boring really quickly, right. It's that same position of in and out and come. This served for the previous century, or for women who are full of restrictions. (Rose)

> Positions like fried chicken, sixty-nine, or fucking on all fours get away from the rule of the taboo about fucking only the cunt. These positions can be used for other types of *sacanagem* . . . you know . . . sucking, or screwing someone's ass. (José Carlos)

Ultimately, then, within this erotic perspective, the primacy of genital intercourse tends to dissolve. Traditional vaginal intercourse is integrated into a more extensive set of practices—and variety is clearly emphasized as the spice of life.

Some sense of this transformation can be found in an understanding of the extent to which genital intercourse can help define a wider notion of *transando*, from the verb, *transar*. *Transar*, like *sacanagem* and *tesão*, links a set of apparently unlikely meanings and can be rendered into English only with some difficulty, using the verb "to transact." On the one hand, *transar* can refer to economic exchanges, to having financial dealings with someone, to selling or dealing a product, and so on. *Uma transação* is "an economic transaction," and *a transa* refers to "a deal," "an agreement," or "an arrangement." At the same time, however, *transar* is perhaps the most commonly used term for speaking of a sexual interaction or, perhaps better, transaction. *Uma transação* refers to "a sexual affair" or "fling" or even to the person with whom one had sex. *Uma transa* refers to "the sexual trans-action" itself, to the sexual act:

> *Transar,* in the sense of negotiations, is the complete opposite of *transar* doing *sacanagem.* In the first, it's organizing a business deal. This means that everything has to be arranged before arriving at the end of the planned negoti-ation: *transar* an exchange of cars, houses, magazines, and so on. The sense of sexual realization is completely absent in the word when it's used for business purposes. There are also sentences like, "Let's *transar* well!" It can mean so many things: "let's dance," "let's take some drugs," "let's have a good conver-sation," or "let's have sex," "let's fuck." Maybe it comes from prostitution, where there is the financial *transa* before the sexual *transa*—the prostitute negotiates (*transa*) the price with the john before they trick (*transa*), screw, or fuck. But these days, *transar* isn't just used for the act of prostitution, no. It is used for a tasty (*gostosa*) screw, a terrific screw. (José)

Transar can thus be used as a synonym for verbs such as *foder* or *trepar* in order to describe vaginal intercourse. But it includes even more than this. While it may refer to genital sex, it need not necessarily include it. A trans-action limited to mutual masturbation is still *uma transa,* and in the right circumstances, transgressive and dangerous, it can be far more exciting than *uma transa* that culminates in intercourse:

> A good, erotic *transa* doesn't mean just sticking it in. It's doing everything, you understand? It's doing *roça-roça* (literally, "rub-rub"), kissing the whole body, sucking . . . A good *sacanagem* is a lot more than just fucking. (João)

In the end, the priority of coitus is part of a far wider understanding of sexual practice. The pleasures of genital sexuality are integrated with a fuller range of sexual practices rather than being set off against them. Indeed, once again, the boundaries between the public and the private, the utilitar-ian and the pleasurable, are subverted, as the economic *transações* of daily life merge with the sexual *transações* of erotic life. The distinctions charac-teristic of the perspectives of gender and sexuality give way, again, to a to-talizing vision of the world which transforms their impact, and the subjec-tive meaning of erotic experience is built up through this vision.

This same process plays itself out even in what one might expect to be as much the final goal of erotic interactions as it is of sexual intercourse within the ideologies of gender or of sexuality: in the experience of orgasm or, in popular terminology, *gozo* (perhaps best translated into English as "coming"). The notion of *gozo* is obviously central within this erotic frame of reference. It is understood as the most absolute form of pleasure that exists—and thus as the fullest realization of erotic potential:

> *Gozo* is one of the popular words for "sexual orgasm." It comes from the verb *gozar* (to enjoy, experience pleasure). It's the act of ejaculating. You say it

when you arrive at the climax of the screw—women as well as men—like: "I'm going to come" or "Wait to come with me." (Antônio)

Yet while the notion of *gozo* refers to the moment of orgasm, and to the release of sexual fluids associated with this moment, it is also broadened to include the whole experience of pleasure. Indeed, it is even extended to the nonsexual pleasures of daily life: the verb *gozar* can be used not only to speak of the pleasurable release of tension that accompanies orgasm, but of any number of other pleasures. It can describe the pleasure of eating a particularly enjoyable dish, of playing a game, or becoming involved in an exciting project. It is often used to speak of the kind of playful teasing that is so much a part of *sacanagem* itself:

> *Gozo* is used popularly also to express satisfaction and pleasure (*gozação*), jokes that are in good taste or bad taste. For example, "She lived fully (*gozo a vida*) until her death"; "Stop jerking me around (*gozar na minha cara*)" or "playing around with me (*gozar com a minha cara*)"; "The joking (*a gozação*) was widespread." There are also the double meanings: "The *gozada* (joke, orgasm) of the girl was well done" or "Let's *gozar* (enjoy ourselves, come) all night long." (Antônio)

Once again, as is so often the case within this frame of reference, the well-defined boundaries built up to separate distinct domains of experience are broken down. The pleasures of sexual intercourse merge with the pleasures of other forms of *divertimento* (amusement). And while *gozando* (coming) never really loses its primacy in the structures of erotic practice, it is certainly not the sole objective that it seems to be when viewed from the perspectives of gender or sexuality. *Sacanagem* need not end in *gozo* in order to be satisfactory or fulfilling. Within the erotic universe, it is the way one proceeds, rather than the predetermined end, that defines the quality of the experience, and thus even the conceptualization of *gozo* seems to reproduce the transgressive logic of erotic ideology. The pleasures of *gozo* can be found not only in genital intercourse, but in masturbation, in oral intercourse, in anal intercourse, and in a whole range of other frictions and fantasies. *Gozo* is not limited to the end result of orgasm; it encompasses the pleasure of transgression itself. It is in this emphasis on the widest possible range of sexual pleasures that the erotic defines itself in relation to the other perspectives that structure the sexual universe in contemporary Brazilian life.

Thus the structures of sexual practice, the acts that individuals perform, or think about performing, whether alone or with partners, emerge less as products of nature than as constructs of culture. While the physiology of the body may place certain limits on the possibilities that can be encoded in cultural symbols and played out in social action, these limitations, whatever they might be, are actually far less important than the systems of meaning which construct the body and its pleasures in any given social and cultural context. What particular individuals can or cannot imagine is shaped, as much in the sexual realm as in any other, by the intersubjective symbols and meanings of the world in which they live.[7]

Gender, Sexuality, and Eroticism

As in the cases of both the ideology of gender and the discourses of sexuality, the question of just how great or wide-spread an impact this erotic system of meanings in fact has in contemporary Brazilian life remains difficult to answer. The question is all the more elusive because the erotic frame of reference really cannot be linked, in any direct way, to the kinds of social institutions that have played an important role in our discussions of gender and sexuality: to the family, the Church, the medical profession, and so on. On the contrary, it is almost through a negative relation to these sorts of social institutions that the erotic presents itself—in their absence or decay it asserts itself most strongly. In the moral space opened up by the disintegration of the family and the declining influence of the Church, in the largest, most impersonal urban areas, in the marginalized subcultures tied to prostitution or homosexuality, in the social circles of self-styled bohemians and the alternative cultures of the young, the erotic system of meanings that we have described is as significant as any of the meanings associated with either the ideology of gender or that of sexuality. In this sense, we might easily point to the essentially historical relationship between the ideology of the erotic and these other cultural systems: to the increasing importance of the erotic at those points at which these other systems seem to recede.

Yet just as it would be incorrect to argue that the formal doctrines and discourses of sexuality have managed to supplant the traditional ideology of gender in Brazilian life, it would also be incorrect to suggest that the erotic has somehow displaced either of these other frames of reference. This would ignore the fact that the relationship between these various frames of reference is not only historical but structural as well. Because of its emphasis on transgression, the ideology of the erotic is unavoidably tied to these other systems and their elaborate prohibitions. It is built up through constant reference to the hierarchical and utilitarian structures that regulate sexual practice in normal daily life: the structures of gender and sexuality. Clearly relativizing the significance of these structures, erotic ideology seems to open up a whole new of possibilities for the organization of sexual life. It reinterprets the meanings associated with the body, with sexual excitement and desire, and with sexual practices themselves; and above all else, it focuses on the pleasures that these other frames of reference so often deny as the most important goal of sexual life. Yet if it calls into question the structures of both gender and sexuality, the fact remains that it exists only in relation to them.

It would also be a mistake to think that the erotic escapes the intimate relations with power that characterize these other systems. Because the erotic must be understood as a social and cultural construct, rather than as a force of nature unlimited by the conventions of social life, it is linked to the structures of power that permeate all social experience. The relationship between power and eroticism can only be understood, however, by situating the erotic in relation to the other systems that we have examined. We must understand it not only in and of itself, but as a kind of alternative to these other systems. If both gender and sexuality are defined (though, obviously, in their own ways) through differentiation, distinction, and hierarchy, the erotic overturns their order. Breaking down the separations of daily life in the fleeting moments of desire, pleasure, and passion, the erotic offers an anarchic alternative to the established order of the sexual universe: an alternative in which the only absolute rule is the transgression of prohibitions.

Because of this emphasis on transgressing the established order of daily life, of course, even the structures of power can themselves be eroticized within this frame of reference. The social inequalities separating individuals from different classes or different races can be invested, as we saw in examining the texts of writers such as Prado and Freyre, with a heightened erotic value. The sexual interactions of a white male and dark-skinned female, of an upper-middle-class married man and a lower-class transvestite prostitute, of a middle-aged woman and her teenage lover, for example, take on a special significance because they violate the differentiations that, it is thought, should order the sexual universe. No less than same-sex interactions, extramarital affairs, masturbation, or anal intercourse, they become especially erotic because they destroy the hierarchical values of the everyday world. As in the cases of gender and sexuality, then, the relation between eroticism and power must be understood not by seeking to reduce one to the other, but by examining the ways in which each takes shape through the other. The symbols and meanings that structure the world of erotic experience cannot be explained away by dissolving them into an underlying system of power, any more than the structures of power can be interpreted as somehow dependent upon or derived from the force or energy of the libido. That is, the workings of power must be understood through the cultural forms and meanings of the erotic, and the symbolism of the erotic must be interpreted through the structures of power and its capacity transform them.

Organized around a distinct cultural logic and possessing its own particular relation to power, then, this ideology of the erotic can be situated in relation to the systems of gender and sexuality. Like these other frames of reference, it cannot be altogether separated from the rest of Brazilian life, as if it had no meaning outside of the speechless walls or the cover of darkness that mark out its context. If erotic experience its built up in opposition to the world of convention, it simultaneously spills out to invest any number of other social and cultural forms with erotic meaning. Nowhere is this more true than in the case of *carnaval,* which has come, over the years, to stand as a symbol for the unique character of Brazilian life. While *sacanagem* has been described by Roberto Da Matta as a kind of "carnivalization" of the world of daily life (Da Matta 1983), the world of *carnaval* might just as easily be examined as a kind of large-scale "ritualization" of what we have described as the transgressive play of *sacanagem.* Yet if *carnaval* is somehow especially linked to the world of erotic meanings, it is also unavoidably tied to structures of sexuality and gender, and even, as we shall see, to the myths of origin that provided us with a point of departure for this examination of the Brazilian sexual universe. In closing, then, it is worth turning to the *carnaval,* and to the key role that it plays in the construction of sexual meanings in contemporary Brazilian life.

6

The Carnivalization of the World

Sin, the saying goes, does not exist beneath the equator. It is an idea that has been traced as far back as the writings of the austere Dutch historian Gaspar von Barlaeus, in his seventeenth-century chronicle *Rerum per Octennium in Brasilien* (Barlaeus 1980). First published in 1660, Barlaeus's work would become a classic document of the Dutch occupation of northeast Brazil (see Freyre 1956, Boxer 1957). For all its historical importance, however, its greatest impact has been as an example of the perplexed northern European mind confronted with the almost intangible reality of tropical Brazil:

> All wickedness was amusement and play, making known among the worst the epiphany: "—On the other side of the equinoctial line there is no sinning"—, as if morality did not pertain to all places and peoples, but only to the northerners, and as if the line that divides the world separated as well virtue from vice. (Barlaeus 1980, 49)

No less than the writings of Pero Vaz de Caminha, Vespucci, Thevet, Léry, Soares de Sousa, or Staden, Barlaeus's chronicle seems to have marked Brazil out as somehow unique and problematic: hardly, in this instance, a tropical Eden, but rather a land of sin and wickedness, whose inhabitants seemed to believe that the universal laws of morality and virtue did not apply to them. With his northern severity, Barlaeus, of course, could only scoff at such a misguided notion before going on to outline the renewed sense of order that Dutch rule had gradually been able to enforce upon the chaotic existence of the tropics. Surely he could not have imagined the impact that his own words would later have in shaping a very different understanding of the world.

136

In the early 1970s, at the height of the military dictatorship that lasted from 1964 until the return to civilian rule in 1984, the poet and novelist Lêdo Ivo published his prize-winning political allegory *Ninho de Cobras* (Snakes' nest), set in the provincial port city of Maceió, in the northeastern state of Alagoas, during World War II (see Ivo 1981). Exploring the underside of social and political life in Maceió, Ivo focused on the often conflicting perceptions of reality that result as much from political as from psychological repression. The almost mythical power of the past in the present reappears throughout his text. It is most evident, however, in a chapter entitled *A Festa* (the Portuguese term for both "party" and "festival"), following the description of a night-long party held by members of the local elite at Dina's, one of Maceió's leading houses of prostitution, when Ivo echoes the words of Barlaeus for his own purposes:

> "Beyond the Equator sin does not exist," Barlaeus had noted when writing the chronicle of the Dutch period. Then that landscape had been part of New Holland and through the rows of crooked streets and warehouses bursting with sugar passed the worst scum of the earth. Besides the Portuguese, there were Dutch, French, Scots, Englishmen, Jews, and Germans who, sought after or hunted by the Inquisition and other tribunals which foreshadowed the eve of the stake or the gallows, had arrived there with their dreams and vices. . . . "Beyond the Equator, sin does not exist," they alleged in word or in thought; and they killed Indians and Blacks and their own white companions. They sacked plantations, robbed warehouses and ravaged women, depositing in them, in their burning Indian or Negro cunts, the seeds of the green or blue eyes of those red-haired and white-featured Northeasterners of today. This permissive code has crossed the centuries. And today, in Maceió's turbulent brothels, when somebody shouts "everybody naked," or wild orgies splash creek or ocean waters awakened by man's lasciviousness, a hidden tradition surfaces once again. It is a tradition of creatures faithful to the life of the flesh and the senses and suffocated by the Church and the State. . . . It is as if the Alagoans momentarily remembered those remote times when everything was permitted. (Ivo 1981, 113–15)

What is most striking about this narrative is its suggestion about the ways the collective memory of this past breaks through, at certain moments, to structure the experience of the present. In the face of centuries of social development and repression, the vision of a past in which, as Ivo puts it, "everything was permitted" continues to interrupt the flow of social action. What Ivo describes as a "hidden tradition" surfaces to give meaning to contemporary life. In short, the vision of wickedness and lasciviousness that Barlaeus abhorred seems to have been recreated and transformed as a cultural tradition that plays an important part in contemporary Brazilian life— that momentarily breaks through the repressions and prohibitions of modern life to offer up a vision of the world in which anything is possible.

Here, in the present, however, what is most striking about this "hidden tradition" is the degree to which it has been recreated in positive, rather than negative, terms. A vision of evil and wickedness has given way to a kind of playful celebration of the most fundamental possibilities of life. This quality has been captured by Chico Buarque de Hollanda in *Não Existe Pecado ao Sul do Equador* ("Sin Doesn't Exist to the South of the Equator"), his reinvention of Barlaeus, and one of the most successful songs of the past two decades of Brazilian popular music:

> *Não existe pecado*
> *do lado de baixo do Equador.*
> *Vamos fazer um pecado*
> *rasgado, suado, à todo vapor.*
> *Me deixa ser teu escracho capacho,*
> *teu cacho diacho, riacho de amor.*
> *Quando é a lição de esculacho,*
> *olha aí, sai de baixo, eu sou professor.*
> *Deixa tristeza prá lá,*
> *Vem comer, me jantar,*
> *sarapatel, caruru, tucupi tacacá,*
> *Vê se me usa, me abusa, lambuza,*
> *que a tua cafusa não pode esperar.*
> *Deixa tristeza prá lá,*
> *Vem comer, me jantar,*
> *sarapatel, caruru, tucupi tacacá,*
> *Vê se me esgota, me bota na mesa,*
> *que a tua holandesa não pode esperar.*

> Sin doesn't exist
> on the side beneath the equator.
> Let us commit a sin
> spread open, sweaty, all steamy.
> Let me be your depraved doormat,
> your devilish bouquet, stream of love.
> When it's a lesson of disorder,
> look out, get out from under, I'm the professor.
> Leave sadness aside,
> Come to eat, dine on me,
> *sarapatel, caruru, tucupi tacacá,*
> See if you can use me, abuse me, soil me,
> Because your mixed-blooded woman can't wait.
> Leave sadness aside,
> Come to eat, dine on me,
> *sarapatel, caruru, tucupi tacacá,*
> See if you can exhaust me, put me on your table,
> Because your Dutchwoman can't wait.[1]

Playing on the double entendre of the human body as a world unto itself, and the waist as an equatorial line dividing north from south, *Não Existe Pecado ao Sul do Equador* takes Lêdo Ivo's text one step further, suggesting that if sin exists, it is only in the mind. True to the transgressive logic of erotic ideology, beneath the waist is a world of pleasures and passions, of tastes and flavors, that would be unimaginable in Barlaeus's northern reality. Subverting the established moral order in a poetic voice reminiscent of Oswald de Andrade's cannibalistic modernism—or, perhaps more accurately, the "tropicalist" movement in Brazilian music during the late 1960s and 1970s—it offers the vivid sensuality of Brazilian life.[2]

Once again, then, what emerges from these various texts, fragmentary as they are, is a vision of a world divided, split into two sharply opposed modes of being or forms of experience. The seriousness and severity of daily life, which is made possible only through the repression of desires and the prohibition of pleasures, is contrasted with a rebellious world of sensuality and satisfaction in which the pleasures of the body can escape the restrictions imposed by an oppressive social order. It is a vision of a world free from sin and given over to the sensuality of the body, and it is most fully realized today in the experience of *carnaval,* the annual pre-Lenten festival that has existed in the West since the early days of Christianity but that has taken its most elaborate form in contemporary Brazilian culture.

Always understood as a festival of laughter and license preceding the severe restrictions of Lent, *carnaval* has become much more than this in the complicated scheme of Brazilian life. Like the myths of origin that tell of the formation of a uniquely sexual people in an exotic land, the carnivalesque tradition has taken on new meaning, beneath the equator, as somehow definitive of the peculiar character of Brazilian reality (see Da Matta 1978). For Brazilians and foreigners alike, the *carnaval* has become almost synonymous with Brazil itself. Like Brazil, it defies the possibility of any single reading or interpretation (see, for example, Da Matta 1973, 1978, 1981; Ortiz 1976, 1978; Queiroz 1981; Risério 1981; Sebe 1986). Yet even if it were nothing else, *carnaval* would still be the clearest example in contemporary Brazilian life of those peculiar moments when a hidden tradition comes out of hiding and an entire society discovers and reinvents itself—when, for a few brief days, myths of origin take shape in cultural performance, the past invades the present, and the sensuality of the body defies sin. It is a time when everything is permitted, when anything is possible.

Celebrating the Flesh

The carnivalesque tradition has, of course, already been described and analyzed extensively by any number of writers (see, for example, Bakhtin 1968,

Baroja 1979, Burke 1978, Gaignebet and Florentin 1974, Ladurie 1979, Toschi 1955). It has been interpreted, through its essential opposition to the world of daily life, as a kind of ritual of reversal or rebellion in which social life is turned on its head and time played back to front (Davis 1975, Leach 1961, Turner 1969). It has been seen as a world of laughter, of madness and play, in which the established order of daily life dissolves in the face of an almost utopian anarchy, in which all hierarchical structures are overturned and the fundamental equality of all human beings is proclaimed. Above all else, it has been understood as a celebration of the flesh in which the repressions and prohibitions of normal life cease to exist and every form of pleasure is suddenly possible (Bakhtin 1968). Indeed, even the name of the festival itself has been interpreted as meaning "a farewell to flesh" (from the Latin *carnis* or "flesh" and *vale* or "farewell")—a kind of final triumph of sensuality before Lent (Leach 1972). And although there has been at least some awareness of the specific manifestations of this celebration of sensuality across both time and space, of the concrete symbolisms that are present in different historical periods and different cultural contexts, the basic formal unity of this carnivalesque tradition has been an underlying assumption of almost all of the significant work that has been carried out (see Burke 1978).

The outlines of this structure are as distinct in contemporary Brazil as in any other part of the world today (see, for example, Da Matta 1978, Sebe 1986). Indeed, the sensuality of the carnivalesque tradition is nowhere more evident than in Brazilian *carnaval,* which is arguably the most elaborate, widespread recreation of the logic of the festival anywhere in the contemporary world. No less than the traditional carnival of medieval Europe, the modern Brazilian *carnaval* embodies a single overriding ethic: the conviction that in spite of all the evidence to the contrary, there still exists a time and place where complete freedom is possible. If the carnivalesque tradition has taken root in Brazil, however, it has hardly remained stagnant. On the contrary, it has clearly continued to change and grow in response to the specific circumstances of Brazilian life, merging with the "hidden tradition" of the Brazilian past that is essential to the understandings that Brazilians have built up of themselves as a people. In other words, the *carnaval* itself has been "Brazilianized" and has itself become a kind of metaphor with its own highly complicated set of meanings.

Once again, some sense of what all of this means on the ground, of how it is experienced and understood by the people who participate in it, can best be approached through the language that they use to make sense of it. The world of *carnaval,* like the world of *sacanagem* more generally, is a world of diverse pleasures. As Nancy Scheper-Hughes has noted, one of the key metaphors structuring the Brazilian perception of reality is the notion of normal daily life (as opposed to the world created by the *carnaval*) as a kind of *luta,* "struggle" (Scheper-Hughes 1988). This *luta* takes many forms and is played out on a number of different levels, but it clearly characterizes the nature of day-to-day existence, filled, as it is, with *trabalho* (work) and *sofrimento* (suffering). The life of any given individual is conceived, in essentially linear terms, as a constant uphill battle, a struggle that must constantly be waged in order to produce and reproduce even the most minimal conditions of one's existence:

> You talk about life as a "struggle." It's the metaphor of the verb "to struggle." The meaning of this is that life, survival, is an eternal war. The struggle for our daily bread . . . The struggle for a miserable salary . . . The struggle because of a lack of hope . . . In itself, everything in order to arrive at the end is simply a total struggle to the death. (Antônio)

This linear (and ultimately tragic) trajectory of one's life is interrupted each year by the cyclical rhythm of the seasons, by the time outside of time, during *carnaval,* when the work and suffering of daily life give way to a world of *risos* (laughter). Here, in this world of laughter, the normal conditions of human existence, marked as they are by an almost overwhelming *tristeza* (sadness), are transformed in the *felicidade* (happiness) and *alegria* (joy or elation) of the festival:

> It's like in that song from the film *Black Orpheus: Tristeza não tem fim, felicidade sim* (Sadness has no end, but happiness ends). Leaving sadness, the struggle of day-to-day life, forgotten inside an imaginary drawer, the people allow themselves to be carried away by the reality of fantasy (*uma fantasia real*) in the three days of *carnaval.* They are three days of merrymaking, sweat, and beer, but everything comes to an end on Shrove Tuesday. (João)

In these fleeting moments of happiness, the daily struggle of life is reinvented, transformed into *brincadeira* (play, fun, amusement, joking, etc.). No longer the deadly serious battle for existence, the playful struggles of the *carnaval* take on an altogether different form in the chaotic battles of the traditional *entrudo* (a ritualized street fighting in which the participants pelt one another with filth, garbage, mud, excrement, or urine); the somewhat tamer jests and jokes of *foliões* (literally, "merrymakers" or "revellers," but derived from the French terms for madness and madmen); the *brincando* (playing) with water pistols, clubs, or similar weapons in the street; or even the playful *campeonatos* (championships) of the great *escolas de samba* (samba schools) that are a focus today for the *carnaval* of Rio de Janeiro.

The use of the verb *brincar* (to play) is instructive, for it is especially here, in this notion, that the sexual meanings in the symbolic structure of the festival are most evident. *Brincando* (playing) can take shape on any number of different levels. On the one hand, it refers to the apparently innocent play of children, the _brinquedos_ (toys) and _brincadeiras_ (fun and games) that everyone remembers from their childhood:

> In the life of a child, the word _brincar_ is perhaps one of the most frequently used, not to mention "to eat" and "to drink." This word is heard all the time in the life of the child, not only from the child himself, but from everyone around him. There are examples like: "Go and play little boy (or little girl)"; "Today you will not play"; "Let's play hide-and-seek, doll, car, tag, ring-around-a-rosy, and so on . . ." The child believes that life will be one long game. He won't wake up to reality until a certain age when he has to start to struggle for a livelihood. It will be a huge change from the world of toys and games to a real, a degrading, world. (Rose)

At the same time, however, there is the less innocent play of early adolescence and even adulthood—the _brincadeiras sexuais_ (sexual play) that, as we have seen, has such an important place in the formation of the erotic universe:

> The _brincadeiras sexuais_ in the life of a child around the age of puberty pass from the material toys (_brinquedos_) to the playthings (_brinquedos_) of the sexual organs . . . The doll and the toy car are left aside, or almost totally forgotten, in order to give room for the so-called _brincadeiras_ of discovery of the body in transition to adulthood. The child, or the adolescent, will pass through a phase that is more daring . . . and sexually active. (Rose)

It is this notion of play as not only pleasurable, but also profoundly sexual in nature, that shapes the fully adult use of _brincar_ as a synonym for both sexual intercourse itself and erotic play more generally:

> The verb _brincar_ is also used. "I want to play (_brincar_) with you" or "I want to play (_brincar_) in your cunt (or your ass, or your mouth)." "Let's play a good game (_brincadeira_)." "I have a toy (_brinquedo_) here that you will like." "Can I put my toy (_brinquedo_) in your garage?" It's a word that is used often in _sacanagem_. (João)

Linking the play of children to that of adults, then, and true to the totalizing and transgressive logic of erotic ideology, the use of _brincar_ in the world of _sacanagem_ breaks down the kinds of hierarchical categories and distinctions that normally order daily life. It builds up another, very different, understanding of human experience, in which enjoyment and pleasure become the focus of attention, the most important reason for being.

It is in this world of play, of course, that sadness most clearly gives way to joy and happiness, that _gozo_ and _gozação_ escape the serious struggle of life. It is hardly surprising, then, that _brincar_ should be used as well as the verb for "doing _carnaval_":

> _Brincar_ is used also for the _carnaval_. You say that you are going "to play" (_brincar_) the _carnaval_. "Let's play (_brincar_) the _carnaval_." This verb was cho-

sen because of giving adults the liberty to let everything out during these three days of merrymaking and paganism for the Christians. To play (*brincar*) the *carnaval* is to dance, to drink, to fuck, to get high, to kill, and to die. They are days to let out your emotions like a child—but the adult, when he plays (*brinca*) the *carnaval*, these are perhaps the only days of the year that he can really be himself and not some jester from everyday life. (João)

Through the notion of play, then, the experience of *carnaval* is linked, simultaneously, to the innocent and carefree play of children and to the sexual play of adults. In the playful space that *carnaval* opens up, the normally marginal experience of children comes to the center of the social universe, and for a few brief moments, adults are able to let go of their worries and responsibilities to enter into a world of play as if they were children once again.

The past that is recreated in the carnivalesque present is at once social and individual: the hidden tradition of an unruly and sensual historical past and the repressed freedom of childhood. Linking the pleasurable experiences of infancy to the erotic pleasures of adulthood, oral symbolism abounds. For young and old alike, the oversized *chupeta* (pacifier) is among the most common *brinquedos* used during the *carnaval*, and since its original recording in 1937, *Mamãe Eu Quero* ("Mommy I Want"), with all of its possible meanings, has continued as perhaps the most popular of all *carnaval* songs:[3]

> *Mamãe eu quero,*
> *Mamãe eu quero,*
> *Mamãe eu quero mamar.*
> *Dá a chupeta,*
> *Dá a chupeta,*
> *Dá a chupeta,*
> *Pro bebé não chorar.*
>
> Mommy I want,
> Mommy I want,
> Mommy I want to suckle.
> Give me the pacifier,
> Give me the pacifier,
> Give me the pacifier,
> So that the baby won't cry.

Recreating a world outside of time, a world where wishes and desires can always be satisfied, this emphasis on sucking and suckling breaks down the lines that separate children from adults and the divisions that separate one individual body from another. Like the structures of erotic ideology, it opens up the possibility of a union or unity that is at once maternal and erotic, and it presents this possibility in almost ritualized form in the playful games and music of the *carnaval*.

This emphasis on union, on the fundamentally erotic merging of the body with other bodies, is especially evident in the experience of the carnivalesque crowd—the _massa_ (mass) of revelers playing _carnaval_ (see Bakhtin 1968). Pressing up against other bodies in the crowd, feeling the physical contact, being pulled along by the flow of the group, the individual body merges with the collective body:

> During the _carnaval_ you stop being the master of your own body. The mass becomes master . . . (Alexandre, a twenty-seven-year-old homosexual male from the lower middle class)

Losing control, losing mastery, over one's body and merging with the bodies of others, the individual finds himself integrated into the masses, or perhaps more accurately, the _povo_ (people). The _povo_ in turn is offered a new and different awareness of its sensuality, its material unity and community. For a few brief moments, hierarchy and patronage collapse, and the masses rule the streets.

Within this unruly crowd, bodies not only rub up against one another and, at least in symbolic terms, merge into one: they can be exchanged and transformed. The _carnaval_ proposes that fantasy should become reality, and _fantasia,_ the very term used to describe the mental images of psychic fantasy, is also used for the costumes of _carnaval._ Through _fantasias_ and masks, individual reality is transformed and the fantastic reality of _carnaval_ is created:

> It's the representation of a transfigured reality. The costumes and masks that people use in the _carnaval_ are the mirrors and reflections of their own lives . . . You put on glitter and happy, bright colors in order to disguise and conceal the tragedy that society itself is going through. (Katia)

The diversity and complexity of the _carnaval_ costumes defies description, ranging from clownlike fools and Chaplinesque tramps to grotesque monsters, anthropomorphic animals, skeletons, and ghostlike representations of death. While many of these fantastic disguises might just as likely be found today in the carnivals of Europe or the Caribbean, and obviously draw on a carnivalesque tradition that subsumes the Brazilian _carnaval,_ it is not surprising that just as many have taken a particularly Brazilian turn. The characters of a number of imaginary figures, such as Zé Pereira, from carnivals of the past, are recreated and become popular motifs in the present. _Pretos-Velhos_ (Old Blacks, who are among the principal _guias,_ or "guides," in ecstatic trance religions such as _Umbanda_) and any number of other figures from the world of the Afro-Brazilian religious cults, are common in the world of _carnaval._ And while indigenous peoples have been driven further and further into decay and extinction, costumed _grupos de índios_ (groups of

Indians) have become a special focus in carnival celebrations throughout Brazil.

Marginalized and oppressed in contemporary life, in the world of *carnaval,* these figures come to the center of attention. They call up a violent Brazilian past, yet they integrate it into a form derived originally from Europe. Indeed, in properly cannibalistic fashion, they almost devour that form: they ingest it, digest it, and spit it out again in what is somehow a distinctly Brazilian shape. Calling up the hidden tradition of a past in which everything was permitted and sin ceased to exist, they create a present that is clearly part of a broader carnivalesque tradition, while at the same time uniquely Brazilian—the quintessential expression of the Brazilian spirit.

Given both the obvious presence of sexual symbolism in the carnivalesque tradition and the importance of sexual meanings in the Brazilians' interpretation of their own reality, it is not surprising that the playful manipulation of sexual images dominates this world of masks and costumes. Joking clowns adopt enormous, clublike phalluses that can be used to beat upon the bodies of other merrymakers. Grotesque, diabolical, or monstrous figures combine the body parts of male and female in order to create ambiguous *andróginos* (androgynes). Men transform themselves into women, and women (though somewhat less commonly) into men. Indeed, no symbolic form dominates the symbolism of the festival as completely as transvestism:

> Transvestism during *carnaval* is one of the most common things in Brazil. Since childhood the Brazilian learns to cross-dress in the carnivalesque period . . . The girl dresses herself as a man, with masks made of pillowcases and with large shirts, suit coats, and men's pants, wearing a hat and masculine shoes. The boy dresses himself as a woman, using dresses, purses, jewels, wigs and masks made of pillowcases as well. (Rose)

This gender-crossing is to be expected in a festival that plays all social life back to front, reversing or inverting the established order in relatively systematic ways. Yet even here, emphasis must be placed less on some assumed or predetermined formal unity than on the fundamental multiplicity that the *carnaval* seems to open up. The transvestism of the festival is anything but a single, structural phenomenon. On the contrary, it is multiple and varied. There are the comic *blocos de sujos* (groups of filthy ones), for example, whose gender-crossing is relatively balanced between male and female, and whose tone is largely comic or absurd:

> In the 1950s, 1960s, and even the 1970s, it was common for children to cross-dress and go out asking for coins . . . The girls would put on, and put on even today, large asses, and with their faces hidden they can play (*brincar*) and say improper things to people or flirt with the guys that they are after. They liberate themselves a little more than normal. The boys put on large false breasts and let people play with their boobs and with asses made out of pillows. This

transvestism starts very early. Parents help to make the costumes, and sometimes the whole family goes out together cross-dressed, or in large groups
called *blocos de sujos*—which may or may not use masks, but with heavy
makeup and extravagant feminine clothes . . . The joke of the large asses,
pregnant bellies, and large breasts is one of the most common things in the
blocos de sujos. Signs and dolls are used by the merrymakers who cross-dress
as pregnant mothers or single women with one child already in their arms and
another in their wombs. (João)

While the *blocos de sujos* often seem to focus on the mundane and ordinary—maids, housewives, and the like—in building up their comic transformations, there are also far more stylized and serious performances.
Young adolescent males from the lower sectors dress as high-class whores
and call themselves *piranhas*. Homosexually identified males from the more
modern middle sectors choose low-cut gowns exposing their masculine
chests, make use of an exaggerated makeup, and sprinkle glitter in their
beards or mustaches in a carnivalesque version of what has been described
in English as "gender-fuck" (Read 1980, 17–18). And most ubiquitous, the
travestis (transvestites) who usually work the shadowy streets of almost all
major Brazilian cities during daily life become absolute centers of attention
with their elaborate gowns and stylized performances:

The true *travestis* that already live the entire year in their costumes (*fantasia-
dos*), these let themselves go in the best possible way. In the extravagance of
their clothes, makeup, and gestures, they seek the best way to appear within a
society that in one way or another repudiates them. In the *carnaval*, where
everything is really permitted, the true *travesti* lets out all his capacity to appear as extremely exotic and extravagant characters. (José)

What at first glance appears to be a unified symbolic inversion takes shape,
upon closer inspection, then, as a set of transformations as diverse as the
sexual universe more generally. Celebrating confusion and ambiguity, but
building up subjective meanings as varied as their subjects, these multiple
transvestisms push and pull at the seams of any system of meanings that
would seek to separate the world into two distinct, opposed, and hierarchically related categories, in order to organize the better part of collective life
around this separation.[4]

As the emphasis on transvestism obviously suggests, the sexual universe that the *carnaval* opens up is altogether different from the world of
daily life. Just as the meanings associated with *sacanagem* offer an almost
carnivalesque incursion of pleasure into the established patterns and
rhythms of a world in which prohibitions and repressions *do* exist, and
everything is quite explicitly *not* permitted, the festival creates a special
time and space, opposed to this everyday life, when the silent, and sometimes perverse, pleasures that occur "within four walls" escape their bound-

aries and create a fully public world in which, like the private world of erotic ideology, anything is possible. The two seem to reinforce one another, each providing a kind of model for the other, and even in the cyclical passage of time, they are intimately tied together:

> The sexual rhythm of the year gets faster during the summer, principally with the arrival of *carnaval*. With the heat of the summer, people have more energy for everything . . . Libertine *sacanagem* becomes especially active during this period of the year. Everyone tries to find the sun, and the beaches become super-full with sweaty and golden bodies. Clothes become a key for the exhibitionism and display of the body, of the gifts of nature. Everything is very seminude, especially in cities where there are beaches. The nights are exhilarating, and there is no place where there aren't people. They are hot nights, propitious for love, sex, freedom of the body. In the summer, nothing is a sin (*nada é pecado*), principally with the arrival of *carnaval* mixing with the summer and tropicalism of this country. Everything comes to a climax in the *carnaval* . . . This is the key that closes the psychological summer of the Brazilians. After the *carnaval,* the sun is still there for a few months, but the interior heat and the hope don't generate so much excitement as in the summer that comes before *carnaval.* (Antônio)

Linking notions about the sensuality of *sol* (sun), *suar* (sweat), *praia* (beach), and *verão* (summer) to the practice of *sacanagem,* then, the *carnaval* embodies a "tropical" vision of the world. Quite literally "beneath the equator," the place of the festival within the annual cycle is transformed: coming not at the end of winter and the beginning of spring, but at the end of the tropical summer, the festival takes shape as part of a somewhat different rhythm. Perhaps less the traditional fertility rite looking to the coming of spring, it is more an orgiastic climax capping the long, hot summer. At the same time, however, because it is not self-contained, because its impact spills over into the world of daily life, like the carnivals of the northern hemisphere, this *carnaval,* too, offers a vision of the future: a utopian vision of the possibilities of life in a tropical paradise, somewhere south of the equator, where the struggles, suffering, and sadness of normal human existence have been destroyed by pleasure and passion. In the *carnaval,* everything is permitted, as it would be in the best of all possible worlds. The polymorphous pleasures of erotic ideology become the norm, rather than the transgression of the established order, and the fullest possibilities of sexual life take concrete form in the play of human bodies:

> During the *carnaval* everything is permitted in terms of sex or drugs. The *carnaval* balls are, in certain places, a true orgy. Everything is permitted. You understand? There is no censorship, and the unrestrained exhibitionism and the desire to expose oneself are very common in the carnivalesque atmosphere. During this period, sex is present everywhere. There is no place where we don't encounter a sexuality linked to grotesque sex. The interesting thing

> is that it isn't the sex that is grotesque but the people who make it grotesque. Within a society full of ups and downs, the permissiveness of the *carnaval* is not interrupted by anything, and bodies, souls, and semen are left at their will, giving to everyone the freedom to do what they really desire. It is a good period for prostitution and the buyers of pleasure. Everything is sold, everything is bought, everything is given, everything is received with a lewd and inviting smile on the face. Beaches, corners, bars, bathrooms, parks, buses, trains, and other places are stages for sensuality and sex. The streets become completely given over to the beat of *samba* and the frenzy of sweaty bodies having sex. (João)

Impersonal sex between strangers who may never see one another again, sex in groups, sex in the streets or on the beach, sex in public, in full view rather than hidden within four walls—all become part and parcel of the play of *carnaval*. Sexual transactions that cross the lines of class, age, and race, lesbian and homosexual interactions, exhibitionism, and any number of other marginal pleasures become possible in a world where repression and oppression cease to exist. Playing, pressing up against other bodies (and ultimately losing one's own) in the crowd, entering the bodies of unknown partners, their faces hidden behind masks or beneath makeup—anything is possible in a world where sin ceases to exist. Freeing the imagination from the seemingly interminable struggles that are inevitably one's lot in life, it offers a better world, a world of pleasure and satisfaction, of joy and happiness. Even if these few moments of pleasure and joy must always come to an end on the morning of *Quarta-Feira de Cinzas* (Ash Wednesday), they nonetheless hold out the possibility of something better than the endless sadness of daily life. They offer *esperança* (hope), and they root it in the pleasures and passions of the people as a whole.[5]

In the Wheel of Samba

If the *carnaval* recreates a more long-standing and widely distributed carnivalesque tradition, then, it does so in specifically Brazilian terms. For all the formal similarities that one might point to, *carnaval* in Rio de Janeiro, Recife, or Salvador is not just a somewhat more contemporary version of the traditional carnivals of Venice, Madrid, or Lisbon. It has not merely responded to, but has in fact fully integrated, a distinctly Brazilian reality into its symbolic structure. Through a kind of cannibalism that the modernists of the 1920s and 1930s could not help but admire, the contemporary Brazilian *carnaval* seems to have fed upon a traditional European form in order to invest it with a particularly Brazilian content. And because of this, just as sexuality has been seen as the concrete mechanism of the racial mixture that is understood as fundamental to the formation of the Brazilian people, the *carnaval,* with its symbolism of sexuality, and its own mixture of European, Amerindian, and African cultural traits, has increasingly been offered up as the most authentic expression of the underlying ethos of Brazilian life.

That the *carnaval* should have provided fertile ground for the elaboration of both indigenous and African cultural traditions is hardly surprising. Because the festival creates a space outside of the normal social order, outside of the structures necessary for *civilização* (civilization), it takes shape as something somehow *primitivo* (primitive) and *selvagem* (savage). It is understood as a time when the most "primitive" and "savage" urges of the individual unconscious rise up and play themselves out on an elaborate stage, and it is a simple step from this understanding to a more global view of the festival as a time when the civilized structures of European tradition give way to the "savage" or "primitive" configurations of African and Amerindian cultures. Indeed, to many early observers, there was really little difference between the pagan excesses of *carnaval* and the excessive ceremonies of the pagans. The grotesque anthropophagous ceremonies of the native Brazilians and the orgiastic dances of the African slaves seemed to flow into and merge with the obscene celebration of the flesh during *carnaval,* and it is not unexpected that the symbolism of these "savage" performances should have been incorporated into the festival (Sebe 1986).

Given all of the sexual and sensual connotations of the act of eating in Brazilian culture, the symbolism of anthropophagy is especially well suited to the semantic structure of the *carnaval.* The transgression of a food taboo can easily be linked to the transgression of sexual taboos in a symbolic construct focused on devouring the flesh of another human body in order to incorporate it within one's own. As a symbol of incorporation, then, anthropophagy can be invested with layers of meaning ranging from cannibalism itself, to the act of sexual intercourse, to the mixture of races and cultures that is taken as definitive of Brazilian reality. In the persons of the *blocos de índios,* the use of masks and costumes harking back to the totemism of the native Brazilian tribes, and the altogether unruly and chaotic incorporation of "savage" imagery (ranging from the use of colored feathers and headdresses to bows and arrows), the symbolism of the *carnaval* not only overturns the order of daily life, but offers an interpretation of Brazilian reality as less modern and civilized than savage and primitive (see ibid., 48–53).

As important as this configuration focused on indigenous culture has obviously been, however, the distinctly Brazilian character of *carnaval* has been most clearly asserted in the music and dance derived from the African cultures of a slave-holding society. The *batucadas* (the rhythmic beating of percussion instruments) and *sambas* (both a style of dance and a specific type of music) that dominate the contemporary *carnaval* are interpreted in terms of their African roots, and their perceived sensuality is linked to the milieu from which they emerged. Not surprisingly, given the significance of

Afro-Brazilian religious traditions even today, there has been relatively widespread agreement on the importance of religious ritual as a focus for the preservation and transmission of African traditions within the oppressive setting of a society organized around the institution of slavery. African music and dance have been seen, in turn, as closely associated secular expressions of African culture that were originally derived from the context of religious ritual, but that took on new meaning, at least in part, because of the encouragement of the slaveowners themselves, who viewed them in erotic terms and saw them as useful in increasing the size of their herds:

> The *samba* dance was introduced in Brazil by the Africans. In the slave quarters, and in their rituals, the dance began to take on great force. It was seen, even by the masters, as an erotic dance—a kind of aphrodisiac. You understand? The slaves spent their days at forced labor on the plantations. At night, they got together in circles, and with the palms of their hands and a few primitive drums began to sing and dance *samba*. The ritualization of the *mulata* woman's walk and the agile grace of the feet of the *mulato* man began to spread in Brazilian culture. From the most remote and marginalized places, it was gradually introduced into the general culture, and now it is not known as just a part of black culture, but is generalized and known worldwide. (Sérgio)

While there were numerous differences, themselves reflecting differences in the African origins of the slaves, from one region to another, dances such as *batuque, caxambú,* or *umbigada* (named after the *umbigo,* or "navel," and characterized by the touching of *ventres,* or "bellies," a symbol for sexual intercourse between the partners that would be a prelude to actual intercourse following the dance) are taken as predecessors of the modern *samba* (Carneiro 1982).[6] Following the freed slaves from the rural plantations to the cities, and up into the hills and *favelas* of Rio de Janeiro and Salvador, *rodas de samba* (wheels or circles of *samba*) sung and danced to the beating rhythms of the *batucada* situated themselves at the margins of Brazilian society—in the shantytowns where even the police were unwilling to venture, in the Afro-Brazilian religious cults with their perceived emphasis on witchcraft and sorcery, in the bohemian bars associated with crime and prostitution. Yet like the *sambistas* (*samba* composers or dancers) who invented them, they come down from the hills each year for *carnaval,* when the most marginal elements of Brazilian society come to the center of the social universe and create a world of fantasy and happiness.

Like the symbolism of anthropophagy, the symbolic associations of the *samba* are particularly well fitted to the world of *carnaval.* Recreating the festival in Brazilian terms, *samba* simultaneously reproduces the erotic focus of carnivalesque symbolism. In its rhythms and movements, as much as in its lyrics, it reinvents the body, freeing it (as on the plantations) from the discipline of work, and opening it up to the experience of pleasure:

> The first thing that is important for the *samba,* in order for you to really dance the *samba,* is that you have to let your body go free. You have to be light, to have free movements. The second thing is to make it charming. And to get across the grace of the *samba,* you have to smile, to let out energy with your face. It's the happiness (*felicidade*) of *carnaval.* The third thing is to place the *samba* principally in the arms, in the belly, in this part here . . . The *samba* is divided between the head, the torso, and the limbs. With the head, it's the movement that announces the *samba.* With the smile, with singing, with the music . . . You understand? With the torso, you give lascivious movements, sexual movements. With the feet, you give the rhythm and the movement of the *samba.* If you have a good foot, if you know how to move with your feet, your body will go along in the swaying movement also. (João)

Like the carnivalesque symbolism of the body more generally, *samba* focuses less on distinctions of right and left than on those of upper and lower. The waist becomes a kind of equatorial line separating the upper body (and especially the head, where the reason and repression that must be overcome by the ecstasy of the *carnaval* are located) from the lower body (the torso or pelvis, where sin, of course, no longer exists, and the feet, that feel the madness of the music and rhythm):

> The rhythm, the movement that comes from the feet, fills the whole body with the shake-shake (*mexe-mexe*) of the *samba.* The belly, the ass, the thighs, the belly-button . . . These are the most important parts of the body for the lasciviousness of the *samba.* The ass, where you stir, emphasizing the swinging hips of the black woman or the *mulata* . . . The thighs, where you control the sexuality of the body in the swinging of the hips, in the dips, when you go all the way to the ground . . . The movements are well defined with the movements of sex. (João)

Rising up from the feet and filling the entire body with life, the movement of the *samba* opens out, like the outstretched arms that are among the most characteristic gestures of the *carnaval,* to *abraçar* (embrace) the world. *Balançando* (swinging or rocking) and *mexendo* (stirring or wriggling) different parts of the body in response to the polyrhythmic structures produced by the *batucada,* the *samba* dancer descends to the ground and rises up again, stopping abruptly, but momentarily, only to begin again, demonstrating control and balance while at the same time offering up an impression of complete abandon:

> The light and graceful movements of the arms are combined with symmetric and rapid steps, with abrupt and balanced stops, giving a special touch to the *samba,* drops to the ground, giving or showing the capacity to take this dance all the way to the level of the ground . . . You have to swing your body, stir your body. (João)

Reproducing the strangely controlled madness that has always been associated with the *carnaval*, but giving it a specifically Brazilian cast, *samba* frees the body from the daily constraints imposed upon it, defying sadness and suffering within the space of the festival. Like the symbolism of *carnaval* more generally, it celebrates the flesh. It focuses on the sensuality of the body. It offers a vision of the world given over to pleasure and passion, joy and ecstasy.

At the same time that it reproduces the logic of carnivalesque pleasures in a specifically Brazilian language, the role of *samba* in the *carnaval* also plays into the wider system of inversions that bring the most marginalized sectors of Brazilian society to the center of the festive world. Just as *samba* descends from the *favelas*, so too do the *sambistas*—the poorest (and darkest) segments of urban society, whose struggles and suffering in an oppressive economic and social system cannot be stated strongly enough, become the focus of the *carnaval*. Freed, momentarily, from misery and oppression, they are disguised as kings and queens, wealthy and powerful men and women who exert influence and draw attention that would be unthinkable in the world of daily life:

> In the *carnaval*, the poorest *sambista* goes out to play (*brincar*) costumed (*fantasiado*) as a king of France or Portugal. In daily life he has no importance within the society. But on the avenue, he's the professor. (Sérgio)

If the poor and the powerless can become kings and queens, however, this carnivalesque inversion is hardly the only way in which the *sambista* comes down from the hills in order to take center stage during the festival. The symbolism of *carnaval* works as much through intensification as through inversion, and it is perhaps in the figures of the *malandro* (translated, at best, as a "rogue" or a "scoundrel") and the *mulata* (a dark-skinned, mulatto woman) that the marginalized reality of the *favela* is most clearly enacted in carnivalesque performance.

Treated normally as a "bad element," a dangerous good-for-nothing who is likely to be a criminal, a racketeer, or a thief, in the carnivalization of the world, the *malandro* becomes a kind of culture hero—a trickster, really, known for his ability to circumvent the rules and regulations of the established order:

> The *malandro* always likes to "put something over on" or "rob" other people. He's a man who is looking for freedom—freedom of expression and financial freedom . . . Society labels him as an assailant or a thief. It treats being a *malandro* as if it were like being a bum, an easy and dangerous life . . . (Jorge)

If it is the mark of the *malandro* that he is able to find a way around the structures of authority, it is no less clear that he lives not for hard work or struggle, but for pleasure and sensuality:

> The *malandro* is a poet, an artist of life. Most times, he doesn't like to work. He waits for everything to fall from the sky. He lives for pleasure, for *sacanagem, carnaval*, all these things . . . (José)

Like *carnaval* itself, then, *malandragem* (the way of being that characterizes the *malandro*) seems to merge with *sacanagem*, to become part of a single configuration in which the rules of convention cease to exist and a world of pleasures and passions opens up. It is a way of surviving and of finding meaning and enjoyment in life—an affirmation of sensual pleasures in the face of the most severe difficulties. It is a style of life, a mode of being, that is defined as distinctly Brazilian, and that finds its fullest realization in the *carnaval*.[7]

Like the *malandro*, the *mulata* is given a key role in the symbolic universe of the *carnaval*. Defined, ever since the days of slavery (as the writings of Gilberto Freyre made so evident), as an erotic ideal in Brazilian culture, the *mulata* is perceived as the perfect embodiment of the heat and sensuality of the tropics (see Sant'Anna 1984). The living expression of racial mixture, she possesses a charm and attractiveness unimaginable in any other woman anywhere else in the world:

> The *mulata* is the black goddess of Brazilian culture. She is a symbol of sexuality and fertility, and is known as one of the most beautiful women in the world. She possesses movements and gestures that no other kind of woman possesses. Like the way she walks, talks, smiles, makes love . . . Her voluptuous way of moving her body is imitated by many, but only the *mulata* has such grace in moving her behind. (João)

Yet if the *mulata* appears as an ideal of female attraction, it is an ideal that exists within the paradoxes of Brazilian life, within the double standard of a patriarchal tradition developed in a slaveholding society. Perhaps best captured in a proverb cited by Freyre, the *mulata* has been held up as a sexual, rather than social ideal: *Branca para casar, mulata para foder, negra para trabalhar* (White woman for marrying, *mulata* woman for fucking, black woman for working) (Freyre 1983, 10). In the most sensual of celebrations, however, the *mulata*, perhaps even more forcefully than the *malandro*, comes to the center of attention:

> The *mulata* is known as a sexual symbol of the *carnaval*. It's the *mulata* who knows how to stir things up, who knows how to *samba* and play. She is the symbol of the attractive woman, the Brazilian woman. (Wilson)

In the elaborate theater of the *carnaval*, the *mulata* thus emerges as the most concrete symbol of a much broader ethos. Embodying an entire ideology, she becomes a representation of Brazil itself—of the Brazilian people, formed from the mixture of three races and cultures, somehow marginal and distant (beneath the equator) from the world's great centers of wealth and power, yet possessing a seductive charm that sets them apart from any other people anywhere on the face of the earth.

If much of the sexual symbolism of *carnaval* seems to undercut the certainty of established classifications, relativizing and destroying them through grotesque combinations or elaborate transvestisms, then in a strange way this world of *samba* that has been integrated into the structure of Brazilian *carnaval* seems to display them in an intensified or exaggerated form. *Samba* itself, at least in its most popular manifestations, is created within a fundamentally male space: the popular bars where the predominantly male composers spend their free time, and where women who wish to avoid being labeled as *putas* or *piranhas* are unlikely to venture. Even the language, the poetry, of *samba* is a kind of male discourse, which often focuses on the suffering and injustice imposed, it is claimed, upon men by women. These distinctions are even more obvious in the movements and gestures of *samba* dancers, with their strikingly sexual choreography, their pelvic thrusts, their grinding hips, their elaborately simulated transactions. If the transvestite seems to terrorize the normal distinctions of gender and sexuality, then the *malandro* and the *mulata* loudly proclaim them.

Even here, however, as everywhere in the world of *carnaval*, things are not always all that they seem to be—or, perhaps more accurately, things are often *more* than they seem to be. If the symbolism of the *samba* displays the hierarchy of gender in particularly stark form, it simultaneously calls into question the neatly ordered structures of bourgeois sexual morality. It offers up a sexuality that is at once primitive, savage, and tropical. Reckless and unruly, it is a sexuality that rises up from beneath the equator, that takes shape in the rhythms of tribal ritual and plays itself out in the symbolism of *carnaval*. Situating itself within a structure of fantasies that is perhaps as old as the first European contact with the non-European world, it plays on a whole set of white images about black sexuality and sensuality. Transforming these images into a vision of a uniquely Brazilian sexuality—a vision built up in the rhythms and movements of *samba,* the trickery and cunning of *malandragem,* and the voluptuous pleasures of the *mulata*—this configuration identifies itself as somehow more "authentic" or "true" to the tropical nature of Brazilian reality, and certainly as more "alive," than the pale conformity of the bourgeois order could ever be. If it reproduces in exaggerated form certain oppressive structures from the world of normal daily life, it simultaneously uses these structures to overthrow others in the kind of constant, playful, sarcastic movement characteristic of a world that has been *carnavalizado* (carnivalized). From the point of view of the elite, it is here that both its fascination and danger lie.[8]

The Greatest Show on Earth

In light of the emphasis it places on the savage, sexual nature of Brazilian life, it is not surprising that for as long as there has been a historical record of the festival, it has been marked by discord and debate. At the same time that the transgressive values of the *carnaval* have been loudly proclaimed in the streets, they have been constantly criticized by the voices of restraint and order. Like the myths of origin that tell of a licentious past, an atmosphere of "sexual intoxication" resulting in the mixture of distinct races, and ultimately, the formation of the Brazilian people, the sometimes violent and always sensual performances of the *carnaval* have been met with a profound ambivalence (see Turner 1983). As much as the *carnaval* has been celebrated, it has also been denegrated as an affront to proper conduct and good taste. Providing unfortunate evidence of what some have seen as the most embarrassing aspects of Brazilian life, and threatening the self-assurance of the established order, it has been the object of extensive criticism as well as outright repression. Over the course of more than a century, there has been an ongoing effort (particularly in Rio de Janeiro, where the festival has been most visible to the wider world) to domesticate the most savage expressions of the carnivalesque tradition, to find a way of organizing its disorder. Ironically, this process has contributed to the attention that has been focused on the festival, to its gradual development as a symbol for an even larger reality.

From the early colonial period on, the celebration of *carnaval* in Brazil was marked by a sharp dichotomy that has continued on up to the present: a distinction between the *carnaval da rua* (*carnaval* in the street) and the *carnaval do salão* (*carnaval* in the large hall or ballroom). This opposition between *rua* and *salão*, in turn, has been translated into any number of other oppositions between the popular classes and the elite, between the influences of African or Amerindian cultures and the predominance of European patterns, and so on. The *carnaval da rua*, perhaps most frequently described as the *entrudo*, was characterized by its unruly and rebellious nature, its violence and dirtiness, as the *foliões* pushed, shoved, and pelted one another with water, mud, urine, and other unidentified substances. It was the *carnaval* of the poor, which meant that its participants were overwhelmingly black—the so-called savage, primitive, African elements in Brazilian society. The *carnaval do salão*, by contrast, was a celebration of the white elite, regulated by invitations or paid admission. Held most often in large theaters, the elaborate *bailes* (balls) were modeled on Portuguese and Italian celebrations and characterized by their elaborate costumes and disguises (see Da Matta 1978, Eneida 1958, Sebe 1986).

By the middle of the nineteenth century, the celebration of the *entrudo* had become the object of considerable concern on the part of the elite, and by 1853, an edict had been issued banning the *entrudo* as a carnivalesque game. While a succession of similar mandates issued over the course of the next fifty years would never completely succeed in doing away with the *entrudo,* the battle lines had clearly been drawn, and an attempt to civilize the *carnaval* had begun. Gradually, this process took shape through the formation of somewhat more organized groups, derived from different classes and communities that came together to celebrate the festival. Beginning in the 1850s, for example, members of the rising middle classes came together to form what were known as *Grandes Sociedades* (Great Societies) which paraded through the streets of the city in elaborate costumes, marching to the music of brass bands and pulling floats that often focused on political issues of the day, as well as organizing balls for the participation of their members. The poorer sectors, in turn, adapted this notion to the more scattered reality of the traditional *entrudo,* joining in somewhat less ordered groups known as *cordões* (cordons), *ranchos* (literally, "strolling persons") and *blocos* (blocks). Composed largely of members of the working class or the petit-bourgeoisie, the *cordões* and the *ranchos,* like the Great Societies, paraded in costume throughout the city, marching to the music of bands and choruses. While less organized than the societies, they still tended to be neighborhood groups that maintained some kind of link outside of the world of *carnaval.* The *blocos,* on the other hand, were made up of the poorest segments of the population, and had little formal structure aside from the spontaneous grouping of the festival, when participants would dress up in old clothes and comic hats in order to parade about as Zé Pereiras or comic clowns (Eneida 1958, Sebe 1986).

 Given the significant presence of poor blacks and mulattos, it was principally in the *blocos* that the influence of *samba* was first felt during the 1920s and 1930s. The earliest samba schools arose out of a number of the larger, better organized *blocos* during the twenties and were closely linked to specific neighborhoods, principally *favelas,* that existed on the margins of Brazilian society:

> The samba schools began in *favelas* and poor neighborhoods. They were seen by the wealthy society as a den of perversion and marginality. The *samba* was a thing of the "rabble" and not of educated and sophisticated people. The police used to beat them up, but received beatings from the drummers and the *sambistas* as well. (Oscar, a forty-nine-year-old heterosexual male from the working class)

As highly visible organizations of poor blacks—and, hence, in the eyes of the elite, of *malandros, vagabundos* (vagrants or vagabonds), and *marginais* (marginals)—the samba schools were subject, especially during this early period, to more than a small amount of harassment on the part of the police, and were themselves extremely concerned with projecting an image that would be respected and accepted by the elite sectors of the society. Their marginal position within society as a whole led to an ongoing struggle over just how they would be incorporated not only within the festival, but within the world of normal daily life.

The position of the samba schools changed radically, however, in the 1930s, with the rise of populist politics and the emergence of Getulio Vargas as president of Brazil. In seeking to recruit support among the lower sectors—and to thus incorporate them into the existing political structure—populist politicians began to turn significant attention to the schools and to offer public funding for their activities. By 1934, the *União Geral de Escolas de Samba* (General Union of Samba Schools) had been formed and had begun, with the blessing of the government of Rio de Janeiro, to sponsor a *carnaval* parade of up to thirty different schools. City authorities, newspapers, and the police had all become involved in planning and organizing the *desfile* (parade or review), and an increasingly elaborate set of rules and regulations had been invented in order to organize a competition between the schools. The most notable requirement was the stipulation that the *enredos* (plots) of the *sambas* presented by the schools were to be based upon "national motifs"—on the events or personalities of Brazilian history. Playing into the rising nationalism of the 1930s and 1940s, such an ordinance is not surprising—but it is instructive. At the same point that elite writers such as Gilberto Freyre were turning to history in order to create myths of origin, the participants in *carnaval* were being pushed to turn to history in order to create ritual, in order to present a reading of the Brazilian past to Brazilians in the present. The elaborate performances of the samba schools would become a way of representing the past, again, not necessarily in terms of any kind of empirical, historical understanding, but along the lines of a particular ideology, a cultural construction.

By the 1950s and 1960s, the samba schools had achieved a remarkable degree of legitimacy within the wider society. The *sambistas* had come down from the hills to perform at the very heart of the *carnaval* in Rio de Janeiro—and like the *carnaval* in Rio more generally, had been held up to Brazil as a whole as a kind of model for the performance of the festival. Indeed, even the membership of the schools had been transformed. While they continued to be based in predominantly poor black neighborhoods, they had been subject to what has been described as an "invasion" on the part of the predominantly white middle and upper classes:

> From the 1960s on, the samba schools became fashionable for every type of social class. They weren't just made up of only blacks and poor people anymore, but of everyone who was attracted by the *batuques* of *agogôs* (a percussion instrument consisting of two different sized bells that are hit with a stick), *tambores chocalhos* (rattling gourd percussion instruments), and every

> type of instrument that awakens in the hearts and minds of the Brazilian the contagious rhythm of the carnivalesque plots. The *carnaval* of the samba schools has come to take on a worldwide position, especially for the Brazilians. The fashionable schools vary a lot from one year to the next—especially when the school is champion of the *carnaval*. The next year, it will be one of the favorites of those who want to parade down the *passarela do samba* (ramp of samba, where the largest schools parade) in Rio. (José)

This invasion of the schools by the middle and upper classes has been interpreted in different ways. It has been seen as a sign of the incorporation of the marginal *sambista* into the structure of the global society, as evidence of the hegemonic appropriation of a popular form of black expression by the white elite, and as a product of the inclusion and *communitas* of the *carnaval* itself. Whatever else it may be, however (and it is all of these things), it is vivid evidence of the extent to which the world of *samba* has come to the center of the carnivalesque world while the festival itself has become a massive spectacle—what by 1965 could be described, without exaggeration, as *o maior espetáculo popular do mundo* (the largest popular spectacle in the world) or *o maior show da terra* (the greatest show on earth) (see Sebe 1986, 72–73).

As befits the greatest show on earth, the parade of the samba schools has moved to the central avenues of downtown Rio—indeed, since the early 1980s, a whole avenue has been set aside for it, and a huge concrete structure known popularly as the *Sambódromo* (Sambadrome) has been constructed as a permanent replacement for the temporary bleachers of the past. The competition between the schools has been divided into three levels: *Grupo I*, the *superdesfile* (superparade) of the largest schools, parading with anywhere from 2,000 to 3,500 members, *Grupo II*, of slightly smaller, intermediate schools, and *Grupo III*, made up of the smallest of the schools. A commission of judges, nominated each year by Riotur, the government agency that administers tourism in Rio de Janeiro, is charged with the responsibility of evaluating the performance of each school in terms of a highly detailed set of criteria ranging from the originality of the theme to the rhythm, melody, and narrative of the music, the design of the costumes, and the quality of the different groups or components that make up the school.

Not surprisingly, given the number of participants, the parade of any given school is in fact a highly organized event that combines *carros alegóricos* (floats), *alas* (literally, "wings," which are subdivisions within the school, and which parade together using matching costumes), and both male and female *destaques* ("eminences," specific individuals who stand out from the crowd because of their elaborate and ornate costumes) and *passistas* (solo dancers, who stand out because of their command of *samba*). To these various elements are added the *comissão de frente* ("front commission," which always marches at the head of the parade and is normally made up of officials of the school), the *mestre-sala* ("majordomo," said to be the finest male dancer in the school) and his partner, the *porta bandeira* ("flag-bearer," said to be the most beautiful woman), and, of course, the *bateria* (percussion band) that creates the music for the *samba*. Placing thousands of performers on the avenue, each school arranges its component parts in slightly different ways, depending upon the demands of its particular theme. Yet even this variation takes place within an overall structure that has itself become an accepted tradition throughout Brazil. The parade of the samba schools has not only become central to the shape of the festival in Rio, but has become largely synonymous with Brazilian *carnaval* more generally—a quintessential expression of everything that the *carnaval* involves and, certainly, among the most widely popular parts of the festival:

> From one year to the next, the parades have come to carry a surprising popularity. Huge lines are formed, and days before they open there are thousands of people waiting to purchase tickets . . . The schools have become so important for the *carnaval* that the government spent millions to construct the new *Sambódromo*, and the parades of the largest schools are realized in two days of spectacle . . . And even with two days of parade, there are millions of people who aren't able to get tickets. (Rose)

Situating itself between the *carnaval da rua* and the *carnaval do salão*, the parade of the samba schools has thus become the best known, most visible, organized, and stylized drama within the festival as a whole. Ordered and controlled by the state, it has also replaced the frightening chaos of carnivalesque play with what is, in its own way, a highly disciplined alternative. However, it has hardly succeeded in silencing the all-encompassing sensuality that is so fundamental to the whole meaning of the festival. It would be more accurate to suggest that the parade, as well as the samba schools more generally, has managed to incorporate the whole carnivalesque system of meanings into its own structure at the same time that it has incorporated itself into the wider structure of the *carnaval*.

Focusing on the world of *samba*, with all of its connotations of savagery, poverty, and marginality, yet recreating this world as a fantastic spectacle of color and movement, the parade creates a kind of utopian illusion. Nowhere is the world created by the festival more completely and absolutely opposed to the world of normal daily life, of work, suffering, and sadness, than in the parade of the samba schools:

> The parade of the samba schools is called the greatest show on earth. The beauty of the colors of the costumes, accompanied by the steps of the *samba* as well as the plot, gives an incredible beauty. The sequins, precious and semi-

precious stones, satins, silks, and purpurins fluttering in plumes . . . It is a parade of great happiness and incredible energy. It is one of the marvels of the world. (Oscar)

Without ever losing sight of the fact that it is only through work that the incredible *luxo* (luxury) of the parade is made possible, this world is as far from the abject poverty of the *favelas* as is imaginable. And without ever losing sight of the often oppressive, exploitative bureaucratization and commercialization of the festival, it is still a world in which the experience of oppression and exploitation is swept away in a sense of freedom—a world in which the masses are healthy and energetic, well fed and well informed. It is a model of the world as it ought to be, yet as it is only during *carnaval*. It is a vision, of course, of *esperança,* of hope, a vision that is presented as the most authentic expression of the Brazilian people.

Linking the passion of the carnivalesque present to the dream of liberty in the future, this utopian vision incorporates, as well, the whole sexual symbolism of the *carnaval*. The sexual imagery of the festival is most vividly displayed in this world of plumes and papier-mâché. As in less organized forms of carnivalesque play—in fact, all the more forcefully because of its highly organized nature—the schools focus on sexuality and sensuality as intimately linked to the deepest meaning of the festival:

> The parade has become a type of stage for sensuality, with its floats and its different sections in their tropical, sensual frenzy . . . The bodies are for the most part semi-nude, showing the energy of hot, happy, virile bodies . . . The couples of *passistas* or *sambistas* intertwine with their legs and with movements of their buttocks in a totally sensual form. The in and out movements of their legs, bellies, sexes, and buttocks give the connotation of an eternal sexual climax. It's a type of theater of sex or *sacanagem,* even in the plots, that touch on all of the meanings of sex beginning with Adam and Eve on to the *bunda* of the Brazilian *mulata*. (José)

Once again, the hidden tradition of a licentious past is recreated in the present, while at the same time offering up an alternative vision of the future.

The symbolism of *carnaval* has responded most clearly (even if in a particularly stylized way) to the changing shape of the Brazilian sexual universe through the parade of the schools. Over the course of the past decade, for example, the increasingly open expression of female sexuality has been pushed, each year, to an extreme in the performances of the schools:

> The image of the *mulher* has changed a lot in the *carnaval*. Going topless and with buttocks exposed has taken an important place in all of the samba schools. Nowadays, there are enormous floats with dozens of beautiful women partially or, many times, totally naked. Wearing only plumes on their heads to cover up from what the most extreme might say, they would otherwise be totally nude. Strong, young, muscular men, with small loincloths, are placed on

these floats also. The demonstration of their sexual attributes, as much of the man as of the woman, has been one of the great attractions of the parade of the samba schools. (Francisco, an eighteen-year-old heterosexual male from the middle class)

As well as women, the most marginalized groups of transvestites and homosexuals have come more to the center of carnivalesque performance in the samba schools, and they can customarily be found not only in the *alas,* but among the most important *destaques* in even the most traditional schools:

> Transvestism and homosexuality have been important parts of the samba schools. There are special floats for male homosexual *destaques* with their luxurious and extremely feminine costumes. They dress up as Gal Costa or Maria Bethânia, or other famous figures from pop music or television. There are even entire *alas* made up of *bichas,* all of them dressed up as Carmen Miranda or old Bahian women . . . The *bichas* have an incredible fascination for the androgynous madness of the *carnaval.* The number of gay groups in the parade has increased every year. They develop all sorts of different types, from the most sophisticated to the most grotesque. They stuff their costumes with large asses, hips, breasts, and bellies. Fruits and vegetables are used often as well . . . Squash, pears, oranges, watermelons, cucumbers, or the traditional manioc root as a phallic symbol . . . the manioc root is used a lot for the joke of the carnivalesque prick. The carrot and the banana also. You're going to see this a lot with the *destaques* on the floats during *carnaval.* (João)

As much as in the symbolism of *samba* itself, then, or for that matter, in the licentious celebrations of the flesh that mark out the unruly play of *carnaval* in the streets, sexual meanings have been fundamental to the highly ordered pageantry of the schools. Indeed, in the drama and spectacle of the parade, as much as in other forms of carnivalesque play, sexual imagery has not only responded to changes taking place in the everyday world, but has pushed the structures and meanings of daily life beyond their limits, incorporating even the most marginal elements of the Brazilian sexual universe into the heart of the carnivalized world.

The impact of this presentation of the sexual universe has been magnified by the attention the schools have received. Broadcast live to every region of the nation, the parade characterizes the festival for the widest possible public. Marketed, both at home and abroad, as the greatest show on earth, the parade has become synonymous with the *carnaval* as a whole. Undercutting the sobriety of daily life in a world of motion, music, and color, this remarkable pageant is the greatest illusion of all. Yet in the reality of fantasy that it creates, it pushes up against the repressive limits that structure the world of convention. It plays with them and stretches them. Like every form of carnivalesque play, it offers an alternative vision of life as it might be rather than as it is. As much as the more haphazard chaos that it was originally designed to replace, the organized chaos of the parade shapes and defines the nature of sexual life in contemporary Brazil. Ironically, in so doing, it has shaped and defined the nature of Brazil itself.

Carnaval as Metaphor

The vision of *carnaval* is quite clearly utopian—a model of the world as it might be rather than as it is. It is also, of course, an illusion, and no matter how fully they throw themselves into its peculiar reality, its participants never completely lose sight of its fleeting quality:

> Everyone knows that *carnaval* is an illusion created to forget about day-to-day life in such difficult times. There are songs that refer to the *carnaval* as "smoke," "wind," "light," or "heat." There is a song that says "for everything comes to an end on Ash Wednesday." Another highlights love: "Love that takes place in the *carnaval* disappears in smoke." They are three days of fun and madness, until Wednesday, when everything begins again. (Maria)

Yet if the ephemeral, imaginary character of the *carnaval* is not lost on the men and women who live it each year, neither is its power to transform experience, and even, perhaps, to change the world around it:

> In spite of being an illusion, the *carnaval* still possesses great psychological power for the Brazilian. They say that liberty went to live in some other place . . . So *carnaval* tries to search for liberty. It is a utopia that in reality is real and not just a dream. Within this surrealism of the *carnaval*, it is possible to imagine a better world, a world that is really made up of true fantasies and freedom. One *carnaval* ends, and you already wait for the next. There are 362 days of waiting and preparations for the realization of the new *carnaval*. (Antônio)

Building, in different ways, on all of the perspectives that we have already examined, the *carnaval* offers yet another. Within the space of the festival, it becomes possible not only to transgress the restrictions of daily life, but to push the limits, to reinvent the possibilities, of that wider social and cultural universe. Built, perhaps, on shifting sand, but rebuilt each year again, this often contradictory capacity for transformation, for the continued search for freedom and happiness, lies at the heart of the whole carnivalesque fantasy. It is central to the meaning of the *carnaval* within Brazilian culture.

Because of its internal contradictions (the illusion that can nonetheless transform the world), one can read this symbolic configuration in any number of different ways. For example, it is impossible to ignore the extent to which the symbolic structures of the festival exaggerate the most oppressive structures of the real world—male fantasies and desires continue to define a particular vision of female sexuality, and for that matter, bourgeois moral-ity continues to organize the expression of what is perceived to be a more "savage" or "primitive" sensuality:

> There are various interpretations—from sexism to the sin of the flesh. Be-cause everything is permitted in these days, there are controversial ideas about what is called "morality" and "proper conduct." There are certain intel-lectuals, or false-intellectuals, that talk about the "opium of the people." Oth-ers deplore the worship of high luxury or of carnality. But, in reality, these people are a pretentious minority. For the majority of Brazilians, playing (*brincar*) the *carnaval* is an authentic expression of the people (*povo*). Playing the *carnaval* is to feel free. It is to feel extremely Brazilian. (Jorge)

Thus it is also impossible to ignore the degree to which carnivalesque im-agery destroys conventional assumptions, offering women as well as men, the *povo* as well as the bourgeoisie, the opportunity to manipulate the webs of meaning and the systems of power in which they find themselves en-meshed, to create a sense of themselves as a whole, an identity as a people. What is most striking about the *carnaval* is its ability to encode and articu-late so many different, often contradictory, meanings, and to thus open it-self up to so many divergent interpretations.[9]

Because of this ability to incorporate contradictory interpretations within a single whole, the *carnaval* has offered a fundamentally popular counterpart to the myths of origin of elite writers such as Paulo Prado and Gilberto Freyre, with their emphasis on the formation of the Brazilian people through the process of racial mixture. With all of its chaos and con-fusion, its contradictions and its juxtapositions, its exaggerated sexuality and its transgressive laughter, the *carnaval* stands as an ironic answer to the search for a sense of identity that has troubled Brazilian thinking for more than a century. As much as the stories that Brazilians have told them-selves about their own formation as a people, it has offered its own reading of Brazilian reality—a reading focused, like the myths of origin, on the sen-sual nature of Brazilian life, on the chaotic mixture of races and cultures that has given rise to a new world in the tropics. While the elite myths of origin have focused on the past as a way of giving meaning to the present, however, the more popular performances of the *carnaval* have themselves cannibalized this past not simply as a way of reinventing the present, but as a means of inventing a future. The symbolic system that they create is ulti-mately less closed than open, and the identity that they suggest, less singu-lar than plural—like the *carnaval* itself, diverse and multiple, based not so much on the fusion of opposites as on the juxtaposition of differences.

In its invention of another (more fundamentally popular) reading of Brazilian reality as still in the process of becoming, the *carnaval* has emerged as far more than a secular ritual marking out the cycle of the year.

It has become a metaphor for Brazil itself—or at the very least, for those qualities that are taken as most essentially Brazilian, as the truest expression of Brazilianness. No less than the myths of origin, it has become a story that Brazilians tell themselves about themselves (about their past, certainly, but also about their future). It is a story that they use as yet another frame of reference that allows them to manipulate, rearrange, and even reinvent the contours of their own sexual universe. Even more than the myths of origin, the *carnaval* has clearly been offered up, as well, as a story that they tell to outsiders—a story about Brazil's peculiarly seductive charms, its exotic sensuality, its tropical pleasures, its erotic diversity and openness. It suggests, to Brazilians and outsiders alike, that here beneath the equator life might best be understood and appreciated as a work in progress, that reality is complex and multiple, and that nothing is ever quite what it appears to be. Even what appears the most absolute can always be transformed, it would seem, in a world where sin ceases to exist and anything is possible.

7

Conclusion

Even in the most small-scale society, it would be impossible to exhaust the full range of sexual meanings within the space of a single analysis. The difficulties are magnified, many times over, when one turns one's attention to a society as large, as diverse, and as profoundly complex as contemporary Brazil.

Because of Brazil's incredible complexity, it is essential to stress that this is an analysis of sexual meanings *in* Brazil rather than *of* Brazil, that it has emerged from research in heavily populated and highly developed urban centers such as Rio de Janeiro and São Paulo, where the greatest diversity could be expected to occur. Without losing sight of this specific context, however, I am still willing to argue that the system of meanings examined here has had a very powerful impact throughout Brazilian society, and that much of the analysis applies in different settings. Because we have focused not on the sexual reality of any particular group or community, but on the broader cultural grammar that individuals, as well as social groups, draw on in building up their sexual realities, it has been possible to isolate certain forms and patterns that remain significant even in the face of varied content. While the specific terms or expressions may vary from region to region and group to group, and while the grammar itself is built up in different ways for the members of different social and economic classes, sexual diversity within Brazil as a whole is made possible by the existence of the wider cultural system that shapes it—a system itself composed of multiple subsystems.

Ultimately, then, even in seeking to examine the widest possible system of sexual meanings, the picture that emerges is less singular than plural. Focusing on the diverse cultural frames of reference that map out the sexual universe, what we find is not a single reading of sexual life, but many varied, competing, and often contradictory readings. On the one hand, as much in what I have described as the myths of origin as in the cultural performances of *carnaval,* we find a kind of self-interpretation of an entire society played out through the idioms of sexuality and sensuality. In a mythic time outside of time, whether in the distant past of colonial chaos or the annual performances of the *carnaval,* sin is said not to exist beneath the equator. Sensuality is celebrated and is linked, at the deepest level, to what it means to be Brazilian. It is elaborately presented, not only by Brazilians to themselves, but by Brazilians to the outside world. Yet it is possible to detect a certain ambivalence lying not far beneath the surface of this celebration of sensuality—an uneasiness, or even a sense of shame, about the perceived immodest excesses of the past, and a certain revulsion, or even indignation, at least on the part of some, about what are seen as the grotesque and decadent celebrations of the present. This underlying ambivalence, or better, ambiguity, I am convinced, is essential to an understanding of the Brazilian sexual universe—as well as to an understanding of Brazilian life more generally. It can be approached, however, only by moving beyond these particular readings of Brazilian existence to the other frames of reference that we have described, and to the complex social and cultural structures that build them up and make them meaningful.

The ambiguity that one finds at the heart of both the myths of origin and the symbolism of *carnaval* must be understood through the fundamental contradictions that emerge as part of the different perspectives, the diverse logics, that structure the sexual universe in Brazil: the ideology of the erotic, with its emphasis on bodies and pleasures; the discourses of sexuality, with their rationalized, reproductive focus; and the hierarchical system of gender, with its calculus of activity and passivity. Situated, both historically and socially, each in relation to the others, these frames of reference offer profoundly different readings of sexual reality. With its transgressive logic, the ideology of the erotic, the world of *sacanagem,* for example, seems to be most closely tied to the world of *carnaval*—indeed, it might well be described as a carnivalization, however brief, of daily life. It reads sexual practices in terms of the possibilities for pleasure that they offer, and through this reading, it invents and reinvents notions of excitement and desire, the sensuality of the body, and even the experience of pleasure. Focusing on satisfaction and totality, it opens up a whole range of otherwise unimaginable possibilities and builds itself up in clear contrast to the rules of normal life that seek to divide, to categorize, to regulate, and to repress the potential for sexual pleasure.

Most sharply opposed to the ideology of the erotic is the highly rationalized interrogation of sexuality. Whether in the debates of the sexologists, the studies of the doctors and hygienists, or the doctrines of the Church, sexual life is examined and questioned. The truth of the self is sought in its deepest, darkest sexual secrets, and the field of possible sexual practices is mapped out in terms of a hierarchy of values that establishes norms while at the same time producing perversions that serve, finally, to reconfirm and reproduce the structure they are said to threaten. Defining procreation as the ultimate goal of sexual interactions, this hierarchy offers a reading of sexual life that has relatively little place for erotic pleasures or the excesses of *carnaval.* Yet while it may be limited in its impact, this too is Brazil, a fundamental part of the wider cultural reality in which Brazilians live. Through the structures of government, the institutions of law and medicine, the technologies of mass communications, and the like, this system impinges upon the lives of individuals in ways that they may be completely unaware of, and that they are often powerless to avoid or resist. As much as the rhythms of *samba,* these discourses of sexuality mark out the sexual field in contemporary Brazil, and it is in the face of the classifications that they encode, as well, that sexual life must be lived.

If the hierarchy of sex defines Brazilian sexual experience, however, it is surely no more central than what we described as the ideology of gender and the gender hierarchy that it constructs. Focused less on the sexual self or the logic of reproduction than on the notions of activity and passivity, this ideology is probably the most deeply rooted in Brazilian life. Nowhere are the meanings of sexual life more immediate, or more widespread, than in this system or subsystem that builds up notions of masculinity and femininity and orders them in relation to one another. Like the discourses of sexuality, this frame of reference articulates a range of categories that simultaneously threaten and reconfirm it and that structure the drama of Brazilian sexual life. Yet just as the ends of the discourses of sexuality are profoundly different from those of erotic ideology, the focus of this ideology of gender is clearly unique. It, too, offers its own reading of sexual reality—a reading which, perhaps more than any other, must be taken into account if we are to make sense of the sexual universe as it is lived in Brazil today.

If each of these perspectives must be situated in relation to the others within the wider structure of a system of sexual meanings in Brazil, it is essential to remember that the various relations between them are at once structural and historical. Indeed, as I have tried to suggest throughout this discussion, each of these systems can be situated historically in relation to certain developments and transformations that have taken place in Brazilian society more generally. Because sexual meanings exist only in relation to a wider historical reality, they continue to change in relation to the broader sets of changes taking place in that society. And even if we wished to minimize the importance of changes such as the processes of modernization or urbanization, the mere mention of an epidemic like AIDS, with all of the immensely complicated transformations that it inevitably entails, should be enough to remind us that the picture of sexual culture that has emerged from this analysis could look very different only a few years from now.

Indeed, the emerging AIDS epidemic in Brazil offers an especially vivid example of how powerfully sexual culture can shape even the most apparently biological dimensions of sexual life, while, at the same time, how fundamentally historical the patterns of culture in fact are. First reported in Brazil, as elsewhere, in the early 1980s, within less than a decade AIDS had cut a path across Brazilian society and had placed Brazil second only to the United States on the list of countries reporting cases of AIDS to the World Health Organization. In keeping with the most basic patterns of Brazilian sexual culture, HIV infection quickly escaped the boundaries of definable "risk groups," and the predominantly homosexual transmission that dominated the epidemiology of AIDS in the early part of the decade gave way to heterosexual contact as the most rapidly expanding mode of HIV transmission by the end of the 1980s (see Parker 1987, 1990).

Yet just as the AIDS epidemic in Brazil has been shaped by the systems of sexual meaning that we have discussed here (with the particular construction of bisexual behavior, the emphasis on anal intercourse, polymorphous erotic pleasures, and the like), it has simultaneously played back into these systems, and has itself profoundly influenced the changes taking place in them in the present. Never have questions related to sexuality been raised as vividly as in the discussion of AIDS, and there are already signs that issues raised by HIV transmission have begun to reshape the sexual landscape in contemporary Brazilian life. While AIDS has reopened old wounds and given rise, once again, to the condemnations that have frequently defined the politics of sexuality in Brazil, it has also provided a focus for social activism, for the expression of demands for greater social justice and more effective medical and social services, and a range of related debates. How, ultimately, Brazilian sexual culture and Brazilian society as a whole will respond to the challenges raised by AIDS is of course a question that remains to be answered, but at least some hope can be found in the fact that the fluidity and flexibility that have contributed to the spread of HIV infection within the Brazilian population may also lead to a more effective response to the AIDS epidemic in the future (see Parker 1987, 1988, 1990).

Ultimately, this entire system of sexual meanings, with all of its complexity, its ambiguity, and its internal contradictions, can be situated within the wider context of Brazilian social history. For some time now, the most insightful interpretations of Brazilian society have consistently focused on the fragmented, multifaceted nature of reality in contemporary Brazilian life. Writers as different as Roger Bastide, Roberto Da Matta, Peter Fry, Gilberto Velho, and Charles Wagley have all emphasized the extent to which, in a society like Brazil, where tradition and modernity seem to coexist, double or multiple ethics take shape and structure the experience of daily life (see, for example, Bastide 1978, Da Matta 1978, Fry 1982, Velho 1981, Wagley 1971). Brazil has been described as a land of contrasts or extremes, and the simultaneous existence of seemingly contradictory systems of thought has been well documented, both from region to region and from class to class (see, for example, Bastide 1978, Wagley 1971). What has been harder to

understand and interpret, yet what is absolutely central to a full appreciation of Brazilian reality, is the degree to which these contrasting systems
are complementary (Da Matta 1978). Because of the multifaceted nature of
social life, multiple ethics can coexist—at times, even in the minds and
experiences of specific individuals—without producing the kinds of internal
conflicts that would be inevitable in a different setting (Da Matta 1978, Fry
1982, Velho 1981).

While the existence of multiple ethics or systems of thought in Brazil is
most obvious in more well-documented and familiar fields such as politics
(patrimonialism as opposed to democracy; hierarchy as opposed to equality)
or religion (Catholicism as opposed to Protestantism; ecstatic trance as opposed to prayer), it is no less real in the world of sexual meanings (see, for
example, Fry 1982; Parker 1985b, 1987). Like the social world more generally, the sexual universe is divided, segmented, and cross-cut by various ethics, by what I have described as diverse perspectives or multiple frames of
reference, that are distinct yet complementary—that are, at one level, opposed, yet at a different level, make sense only through their relations with
one another. Indeed, none of the systems, or subsystems, that we have examined can be considered in and of itself; each takes shape through its relations with the others as part of a more complicated whole. Together they
shape the experience of sexual life in contemporary Brazil, not by creating a
unified whole, but by opening up any number of diverse possibilities. And it
is only within the terms of these possibilities that the sexual experiences and
realities of specific individuals, or even groups, can be constituted in the
ongoing process of social life.

In short, the remarkable diversity of the Brazilian sexual universe re-
flects the complicated structure of social life in contemporary Brazil. Because of the structured nature of such diversity, however, the ways in which
different individuals encounter this complicated system of sexual meanings
are not, of course, simply random. On the contrary, they are themselves
structured, both by the system itself and by the wider constraints imposed
by the organization of Brazilian society more generally. Regardless of class,
region, or any other circumstance, for example, the possibilities that are
open to women throughout Brazil are more limited than those that are open
to men. The ideology of gender, which works almost relentlessly to subju-
gate women, has only been countered in relatively limited ways by the processes of modernization and urbanization, and feminist thought has hardly
had any impact beyond a small, elite segment of society. The social, political, and economic institutions that work together to minimize the opportunities for choice and self-determination on the part of women from all
walks of life in Brazil continue to function with ruthless efficiency, and the
fact that some changes have begun to take place among the most privileged
sectors of Brazilian society must not be allowed to obscure the degree of

oppression that still characterizes the lives of the vast majority of women within a profoundly patriarchal social order.

In addition, for both women and men, the possibilities that exist within this system of sexual meanings are clearly conditioned according to divisions of class and differences in location. As Peter Fry has suggested in examining the meanings associated with homosexuality in Brazil, it is useful to draw on Basil Bernstein's distinction between "restricted" and "elaborated" vocabularies as a way of conceptualizing how this process works along both of these axes (see Fry 1982, Bernstein 1973). While it would be inaccurate to suggest that these vocabularies, and the conceptual frameworks that they open up, are somehow inadequate or inferior for members of the lower sectors, the fact remains that they are indeed more restricted. The same structures that limit access to education, economic security, and social mobility simultaneously limit access to systems of sexual meaning that are available to more privileged sectors. Because of this, the vocabularies, and the range of possibilities, that are open to the members of the elite, the middle or upper classes, for the organization and imagination of sexual life can be more elaborate than those that are open to the popular classes. While members of the middle class continue to draw on the traditional ideology of gender in building up their sexual realities, they are much more likely than members of the lower class to draw, as well, on formal doctrines of the Church or on the highly rationalized discourses of science and medicine. The world of meanings that is open to members of the elite, then, like the material world that they live in, offers them choices that are largely unavailable to the popular sectors—that are perhaps less carefully guarded than the privileges of wealth, but that are nonetheless beyond the reach of the vast majority of the Brazilian people.

Much of what has been said about the structure of sexual meanings for the members of different classes applies to the residents of different regions as well. The inhabitants of rural areas, and even of urban areas in less modernized, less industrialized regions such as the Northeast live in a more restricted universe of sexual meanings than do the inhabitants of urban centers in the highly developed areas of the Southeast and, to a lesser extent, the South. As is true for the popular classes in the larger cities of the Southeast, the traditional ideology of gender continues to play a central role in structuring sexual life for the inhabitants of less urbanized areas, and the discourses of sexuality as well as the ideology of the erotic—linked as they are to the processes of urbanization and modernization—play a considerably less significant part in structuring sexual conceptions. Changes have of course begun to take place, as in every area of Brazilian society, but the restrictions that structure the day-to-day experience of sexual life outside the cities are no less evident than those that define the situation of women or of the popular classes in more urban settings.

Even where the possibilities offered by the cultural system seem most limited, however, it would be a mistake to underestimate the extent to which opposing social forces operate to undermine the rigidity of the structures that we have described. As has been apparent, for example, in our examination of both erotic ideology and the popular-festive structures of the *carnaval,* a whole range of alternatives has been elaborated within popular culture, opening up possibilities that would themselves be "restricted" within the bourgeois moralities of more privileged sectors. And because the system of sexual meanings does in fact offer a range of options, even in the most apparently inflexible situations, there is often room for movement in a variety of unexpected ways. Indeed, in a society that seems to be as rigid and hierarchical as Brazil, it is often hard to fathom the degree of flexibility in the behavior of its inhabitants. Even in the face of immense obstacles, there is, in fact, movement in any number of directions—from rural to urban areas and back again, across the boundaries of class, and even, at times, beyond the oppressive structures of gender. Just as the system of sexual meanings is cross-cut by conflicting ethics, the systems of control that minimize the possibilities of social change are played off against other systems that seem to make change inevitable. And in the larger cities, at least, the understandings and assumptions of different classes are constantly forced to confront one another, whether through face-to-face interactions or through more impersonal means such as the media or the systems of mass communications.

Indeed, because its hierarchical structures seem to contain within themselves the seeds of their own undoing, there are few domains where the occasions for movement are as readily available as in the universe of sexual meanings. Characterized, not only by multiple ethics, but by a sense that these ethics are in fact complementary, this system of sexual meanings is capable of entertaining a degree of fluidity that would seem startling in a setting that was either more absolutely traditional, on the one hand, or more fully rationalized, on the other. Even where one's choices are most restricted, at least some choices do exist; and as one moves into the larger urban arenas where differing ethics, differing styles of life, constantly bump into one another in the flow of daily life, the range of possibilities can be expanded to a remarkable degree.

Shifting from one frame of reference to another, playing one off against the others, building bridges between them, integrating them as fully as possible: these are all among the processes through which meaningful sexual realities are constructed in contemporary Brazilian life, and through which the world of sexual meanings is continually recreated in the flow of collective action. The dilemmas facing flesh-and-blood individuals within this world are naturally as often unconscious as they are conscious, and the ways in which any particular individual responds to the choices that confront him or her is, of course, impossible to predict. But the broader outlines of the cultural systems that structure these choices can be analyzed and interpreted along the lines that I have suggested here, and the kinds of decisions that particular social actors ultimately make can perhaps be understood in relation to these systems.

This focus on the possibilities and choices that are opened up by social and cultural systems to the women and men who make their way within them is significantly different than the emphasis on uniformity or conformity that has tended to characterize anthropological work on the construction of sexual life. Perhaps in part because so much of the most important anthropological work on gender and sexuality has been carried out in relatively small-scale settings, or in sharply delimited subpopulations within larger-scale societies, there has been a tendency to emphasize the essential coherence of sexual meanings within the boundaries of any given society or culture (see, for example, Ortner and Whitehead 1981). Many studies have of course emphasized the very different sexual universes open to women and men, but even here, little attention has been given to variation and diversity in the possibilities open to different women or different men within the wider structure of female or male sexual culture. Indeed, when the question of sexual difference has been raised at all, it has been largely in terms of a dichotomy between conformity and deviance that itself assumes an essential norm which, for whatever reasons, some individuals fail to live up to (see Plummer 1984). At best, an understanding of human sexual diversity has focused on cross-cultural variation, with little or no attention paid to intra-cultural differences; while at worst, even cross-cultural variations have been explained away as little more than the peculiarities of local custom that can ultimately be reduced to some underlying (usually biological or psychological) level of analysis.

Even in much of the best work on the social construction of sexual life, the notion that sexual meanings are "constructed" has itself become little more than a more modern and fashionable substitute for earlier concepts such as socialization or enculturation. Analysis has generally focused on describing what is assumed to be a relatively unified and coherent system of meanings and, in some instances, on analyzing the ways in which this system is transmitted from one generation to the next. Less attention has been given to the kinds of contradictory variations that may exist within the system of sexual meanings as a whole—to the ways in which the cultural system not only delimits the sexual universe, but simultaneously opens it up. As one turns one's attention to a context like contemporary Brazil, however, where assumptions about cultural coherence and continuity dissolve in the face of multiple, often contradictory, and constantly changing social and cultural structures, it becomes necessary to rethink the whole notion of construction along these lines—to focus on systems of sexual meanings in terms of their diversities, their contradictions and discontinuities, their underlying ambiguities. Only by approaching the system of sexual meanings as something built up out of multiple subsystems, diverse frames of reference, conflicting logics, disparate configurations, and the like, is it possible to begin to understand the experience of the men and women whose particular sexual realities are defined within its terms.

These diverse frames of reference and conflicting cultural logics emerge with unusual clarity in a society such as Brazil, where multiple ethics are such an obvious part of all contemporary social life. Yet their presence here, for all its vividness, is not entirely unique. On the contrary, similar systems of difference and diversity, existing and interacting within a wider whole, can be found, if we would look for them, as a part of life in every large, complex society in the contemporary world—even, I think, in the most fully modernized and rationalized settings (see, in particular, Weeks 1985). And while they may seem more difficult to discover in the smaller, more traditional social settings that have often been the focus of anthropological analysis, this may itself be the illusion of an anthropological perspective that has tended to seek out the "unspoiled" and the "authentic" in small-scale societies, while largely ignoring the kinds of social and cultural linkages between these societies and the wider world that are inevitably a part of contemporary life everywhere in the world today (see Mintz 1985). An understanding of sexual life, like an understanding of all modern life, regardless of the specific setting, must ultimately confront these questions of difference in ways that it has thus far failed to explore. Perhaps the first step along these lines will be to examine not only the ways in which social and cultural systems delimit the possibilities of sexual life, but the ways in which they create them, the conscious and unconscious choices that they offer, the changing meanings and the multiple realities that they produce.

Of course, the approach to sexual life that has been developed here is itself but one among a number of possibilities, and it leaves unanswered any number of questions that other approaches might respond to. If there are some questions that it fails to answer, however, it allows us to ask others, and to come to certain insights that perhaps no other method would offer. Focusing, above all else, on language, on cultural forms, on the symbolic vehicles that people use to think with and to feel with, we can begin to examine not so much behavior as practice—we can seek to understand the meanings of sexual life, the construction of meaningful realities in which sexual behavior itself becomes significant. We can begin to understand that the experience of sexual life in different settings is shaped as much by the cultural context of words, images, myths, rituals, and fantasies as by the physiology or biology of the species as a whole. The ways in which human beings think and feel about sex shape the ways in which they live it, and a full understanding of this process is possible only by turning to the intersubjective cultural forms that structure the world of subjective meanings (Weeks 1985; Geertz 1973, 1983; Herdt 1981).

Focusing on this question of meaning, the anthropological interpretation of sexual life across cultures becomes a process of translation that is essentially parallel to the interpretation of any other aspect of human experience. Based, as Clifford Geertz, among others, has pointed out, less on some kind of mystical leap of intuition than on the careful interpretation of intersubjective symbolic forms, it becomes a matter of unraveling the webs of meaning that constitute the sexual universe in any given setting. It involves finding a way to transform "experience-near" concepts such as *tesão, sacanagem,* or *malandragem,* into the "experience-distant" language of anthropological description (Geertz 1983, 57). It is an opening up of the meaningful universe of other human beings that is in fact no different than opening up the belief system of a distinct religion or the values implied in a particular political ideology. Like the interpretation of these more traditional subjects, the anthropological interpretation of sexual meanings is an exercise in close reading that is aimed, ultimately, at elucidating the readings that other men and women have built up in order to make sense out of their own experience.

As Geertz has suggested, this exercise is surely valuable in and of itself, as part of the scientific understanding of human experience—as a contribution to the "consultable record" of the human species in all of its remarkable variety (Geertz 1973, 30). Yet it is just as important, I believe, as part of what might be described as a particular kind of cultural politics—a politics that is implicit in the whole anthropological enterprise and that is based on the conviction that understanding the realities of others allows us to see our own in new and different ways, that it enables us to raise questions about the givenness of our own traditions, our own ways of being (Parker 1985a, 65–66). Even today, there are few certainties in our own society that continue to be more taken for granted, or more deeply invested with fears and prejudices, than the assumptions that map out our sexual realities. In the face of these certainties, the anthropological interpretation of a world of meanings different from our own can help to make possible a process of relativizing in which we might begin to imagine the plausibility of other assumptions, other realities—assumptions and realities that may, at some points, intersect with our own, but that nonetheless remain uniquely different. To the extent that this makes us less self-assured about the superiority of our own way of being, to the extent that it allows us to conceive of other possibilities, and, one would hope, to respect them and those that live them, then it will have served a purpose that is every bit as important as its more strictly scientific mission.

Appendix 1

Notes on Field Research

Like much contemporary work on a range of different issues, this book is a mixture of many different things—a case, no doubt, of what Clifford Geertz has described as "blurred genres" (Geertz 1983, 19–35). Clearly, it cuts across the lines that might, for some, divide social history from cultural anthropology. Yet it took shape as the result of my own training as a social/cultural anthropologist, and through the process of many years of anthropological field research in Brazil, where I currently live and work. In order to situate much of the text, then, it is worth briefly outlining the development of my field research as well as some of the problems I faced in carrying out research on sexual experience in a context as diverse as contemporary Brazil (a briefer discussion of some of these same issues can also be found in Parker 1987).

Originally, I had no intention of focusing my attention on the question of sexual life. Having been trained principally in the field of symbolic or interpretive anthropology, I was primarily interested in the question of ritual, and in particular, in *carnaval*, which I hoped to examine in a historical perspective. This focus gradually began to shift, however, during my initial trip to Brazil in July and August of 1982, when I traveled to Rio de Janeiro to study Portuguese and to make arrangements for more extensive fieldwork the following year. Quite by chance, I lived in a rather run-down section of central Rio where lower-class female and transvestite prostitutes operated. I still remember the vivid impressions, walking back to my hotel in the evenings, of the drama taking place around me—theater in the fullest sense of the word, with elaborate presentations and complicated dialogues that I was only partially able to follow. Even in the necessarily limited relationships that I was able to establish during this first stay, I began to ask a few tentative questions about this particular underworld, and to come away with a sense that it was very different, in a number of ways, from anything comparable in my own society. I felt a bit like Dorothy, I suppose, upon realizing that she and Toto had come a long way from Kansas.

When I returned to Rio for a longer stay in August of 1983, I still intended to focus on a historical and political examination of *carnaval* rather than on a study of sexuality. But as I began to carry out archival research on the festival, I found myself returning, almost unavoidably, to the question of sex. This continued as I began to make contacts with informants, and to talk about the meanings linked to the *carnaval*. The extent to which sexual symbolism seemed to dominate not merely the festival itself, but the Brazilian interpretation of its meaning or significance, was impossible to ignore, and I found myself turning, increasingly, to the wider system of sexual beliefs and customs in Brazilian culture. Within a matter of months, I realized that the festival had become but one aspect of a more extensive project—an analysis of the Brazilian sexual universe.

This change of direction was made possible not only because of the logical ties between the two subjects, but also because of the kinds of informant networks that I had begun to develop. During the first months of my stay, I had lived in Catete, a middle- to lower-middle-class neighborhood located just south of the center of Rio, and afterward I moved to an apartment in the more well-to-do area of Copacabana. I had not focused my attention on the life of any particular community or neighborhood, however, but concentrated instead on making contacts with men and women involved in preparations for *carnaval*. Through the complex social networks built up around the festival, I had come into contact with a fairly wide range of individuals— with *favelados* (shantytown dwellers) and other members of the lower class, with individuals from the lower middle and middle classes, and even with a few quite well-to-do women and men from throughout the city. As the focus of my research began to shift, these people served as my initial informants not only about *carnaval*, but also about the shape of Brazilian sexual culture.

At first, I concentrated my activity on both formal and informal interviewing of the women and men that I had met through these various networks. My informants were nearly equally divided along the lines of gender—though, for a range of different reasons that would be almost impossible to avoid in a society so sharply divided along the lines of gender, the handful of my closest informants included perhaps twice as many men as women. As a whole, though, they included most, if not all, of the sexual subtypes that we, in our own tradition, would be inclined to classify: heterosexually identified men and women, both single and married; couples, with and without children; self-identified lesbians, male homosexuals, and bisexuals; both female and male prostitutes as well as their clients, and so on. These informants were relatively young, as well—almost all between eighteen or nineteen and thirty-five or forty years of age. And my work with them was almost entirely qualitative; I made no attempt to gather detailed statistical information or to conduct quantitative surveys. Indeed, given the sensitive nature of the subject matter, there is no doubt that whatever insights I might have gained were heavily dependent, for better or worse, on the quality of the relationships that I was able to develop with my informants—as in any ethnographic work, I think, on whatever mutual trust and friendship we were able to build up.

By March of 1984, these varied contacts throughout metropolitan Rio had enabled me to form at least some notion of the sexual universe as it seemed to exist there—as well as of the class and status distinctions which seemed to affect it. In an attempt to broaden this view in a number of different directions, I made short trips to São Paulo, Brasília, Salvador, and Maceió, as well as to Recife, where I was able to spend time with the relatives of a number of my informants in Rio. Between March and July of 1984, I split my time and activities between my base in Rio and a predominantly lower-class community situated on the outskirts of a smaller city in the state of Rio de Janeiro, where I lived with the family of one of my closest informants in Rio. Here, within the context of a more clearly defined community, my friends and informants ranged from children of nine or ten to older individuals in their sixties and seventies, and I was able to get a view of family life that was far more intimate and more detailed than anything I had been exposed to in Rio. While Rio would continue to provide the central focus for my work, I sought to situate my findings there in relation to at least some more general understanding of urban life in contemporary Brazil.

On the basis of these various experiences, then, I have sought to examine the sometimes contradictory cultural patterns, the ideological constructs, and the value systems that work to shape and structure the sexual universe in contemporary Brazilian life. I have tried to extrapolate the underlying, and often unconscious, rules that organize sexual life there—a kind of cultural grammar, if you will, in which, I think, most Brazilians (and especially most urban Brazilians) are more or less competent, but which individuals clearly draw on in a variety of ways in generating their own unique performances. Transforming contacts with individual informants into an understanding of this grammar was by no means a simple task, because of the elaborate structure of taboos and prohibitions, repressions and silences, surrounding the subject of sex itself. At the same time, though, the emotional or symbolic danger of the project may have worked to my advantage. Having passed a set of initial barriers, I found that informants often seemed to take a certain pleasure in being part of a project which seemed to break the rules of proper social decorum (a fact which would itself become symptomatic of a wider pattern in Brazilian culture)—that while they often resisted, understandably, speaking too directly about their own sexual lives, they seemed to enjoy (and, at times, to take a positive delight in) the opportunity to speak freely about the question of sex more generally. The content of my discussions with them thus increasingly focused, not simply on their own personal experiences, but on their subjective interpretations of inter-subjective cultural forms—of stories, proverbs and jokes, of socially sanctioned as well as prohibited practices, and perhaps above all else, of the linguistic terms and usages which they drew on in describing such practices.

Treated as texts, these bits and pieces of popular culture which emerged from my contact with particular informants could then be gradually combined with and at times juxtaposed to a wider set of cultural documents which seemed in one way or another to touch on the sphere of sexual meanings and to offer various insights into its complexity and constitution: the images of film and photography, the work of poets and novelists, the writings of journalists, of sociologists, psychologists, and medical doctors, to name but a few of the sources which I found most useful. Not entirely unlike my Brazilian informants before me, I found myself confronted less by a ready-made totality waiting to be adopted and internalized than by an immensely varied set of problems and possibilities offered up by the cultural system as a whole to its social actors. Drawing on these bits and pieces, these multiple texts and textual fragments, whose interrelationships were not always immediately apparent, I tried to lay out the systems of meaning that would become the subject of my own text.

As I have tried to emphasize, this is of course only one of the possible ways of examining the experience of sexual life. Indeed, I have become acutely aware of this over the course of a number of years now, as I have been involved in ongoing research (an outgrowth, really, of the project that led to this book) on the relationship between sexual culture and AIDS in contemporary Brazilian society (Parker 1987, 1988, 1990), and have continued to examine sexual experience in a variety of ways that differ significantly from the methods used in this initial fieldwork. Having lived fulltime in Brazil now since June of 1988, however, and having spent almost all of my time on issues linked to questions of sexual meaning and behavior, I have found little to call into question my original sense of the ways in which Brazilian society and culture open up possibilities for sexual diversity and difference. It is this, I suppose, that made possible, and continues to sustain, my own seduction and my own respect for the Brazilian people as a whole as well as for the particular Brazilians who people the pages of this text, many of whom have become my closest friends.

Appendix 2

Informants Cited in the Text

Informants are briefly identified the first time that they are cited in the text. In subsequent citations, however, only their name is given, and this Appendix has been included with an alphabetical list of all informants for reference. In order to protect informant anonymity, all of the names are pseudonyms and the biographical information has intentionally been limited to key issues such as age, class, sexual identity (when available), and the like.

Alexandre: A twenty-seven-year-old homosexual male from a lower-middle-class background. He grew up in Niterói, across the bay from Rio. Currently unemployed, he studies on and off in Rio.

Angela: A forty-eight-year-old housewife from Rio. From a lower-middle- to middle-class family, she married at the age of seventeen and has raised three children.

Antônio: A twenty-nine-year-old gay male from the middle class. He grew up in a smaller city in the state of Rio de Janeiro. After studying history at the university level, he moved to Rio, where he works as a functionary in a large business.

Carlos: A twenty-seven-year-old bisexual male from a lower-class background. He was born in a small town in the state of Rio, and moved to the city at the age of seventeen, in order to look for work. He has led a somewhat nomadic existence and is currently working in downtown Rio.

Cristina: A twenty-nine-year-old heterosexual female from a middle-class background.

Dora: A twenty-two-year-old female university student from a middle-class family in Rio.

Dulce: A forty-five-year-old heterosexual woman, and the mother of three children. She comes from a relatively poor background and she and her husband would be defined as working class today. She has had virtually no formal education, and was married by the age of fourteen.

Francisco: An eighteen-year-old heterosexual male, currently a student in the state university, from a middle-class family in Rio.

João: A twenty-six-year-old bisexual male from a lower-middle-class background, who was born and raised in the state of Rio de Janeiro. He currently lives and works in the city of Rio.

Jorge: A forty-five-year-old attorney originally from the Northeast. His family was quite well off, and he was able to travel and study abroad before moving to Rio more than twenty years ago.

José: A thirty-two-year-old bisexual male from a working-class background. He works in the record industry in Rio.

José Carlos: A thirty-two-year-old heterosexual male who works as a writer in Rio.

Katia: A twenty-three-year-old heterosexual woman from Porto Alegre in south Brazil. From an upper-middle-class family, she moved to Rio at the age of twenty-one in order to study and is completing a university degree.

Lílian: A twenty-nine-year-old female from a lower-middle-class family from São Paulo.

Luís: A thirty-five-year-old heterosexual male from a relatively poor family. He worked hard to achieve an education and currently works as a teacher in Rio.

Maria: A twenty-seven-year-old woman from a poor family in Rio. She attended school for a number of years as a young girl, but by the time she was a teenager, she needed to begin to work as a cleaning woman.

Miriam: A twenty-six-year-old lesbian, from a lower-middle-class background, who was born and raised in Rio.

Nelson: A thirty-four-year-old heterosexual male.

Néstor: A twenty-eight-year-old heterosexual male from a working-class background. He grew up in Rio, lived for a short time in São Paulo, but returned to Rio, where he currently works as a store clerk.

Oscar: A forty-nine-year-old heterosexual male who works as a carpenter. He is a veteran of the samba schools.

Paulo: A twenty-six-year-old heterosexual male who is currently a student in Rio.

Rose: A twenty-five-year-old heterosexual female from a lower-middle-class family in Rio. She had worked as a salesperson in a number of different stores before taking her current job as a secretary.

Roberto: A twenty-two-year-old gay male, currently attending the university in Rio. Both parents have professional careers, and his upbringing was generally quite liberal.

Rubens: A twenty-four-year-old heterosexual male, from an upper-middle-class family, who is currently studying at a university in Rio.

Sandra: A thirty-six-year-old housewife from an upper-middle-class background.

Sérgio: A twenty-nine-year-old heterosexual male from a lower-middle- to working-class background in Rio. His family went through periods of extreme hardship, but he managed to finish high school and to spend a number of years at the university before going on to work in a variety of different jobs.

Telma: A twenty-year-old heterosexual female from a very poor background. She was born in a rural area; her family subsequently moved to the city of São Paulo. Since the age of seventeen, she has divided her time between Rio and São Paulo and has worked in a variety of service jobs.

Tereza: A twenty-year-old lesbian from São Paulo.

Vera: A twenty-four-year-old woman from a very poor family in rural Minas Gerais. Her family moved to Rio when she was a teenager, and she has worked for nearly a decade, first in domestic service, and later as a cashier.

Vilma: A thirty-two-year-old female from a working-class background. She is married, and has had two children.

Wilson: A fifty-two-year-old heterosexual male, a jack-of-all-trades.

Notes

One: Introduction

1. The literature is of course far too extensive to review here. See, for example, Foucault 1978; Gagnon and Simon 1973; Padgug 1979; Plummer 1981, 1984; Ross and Rapp 1983; Rubin 1984; Vance 1984; Weeks 1977, 1981, 1985.

2. On symbolic analysis and interpretive anthropology, see in particular Geertz 1973, 1983. On the analysis of sexual meanings, see, for example, Caplan 1987, Gregor 1985, Herdt 1981, Newton 1972, Ortner and Whitehead 1981.

Two: Myths of Origin

1. On the notion of *brasilidade* (Brazilianness) generally, see, for example, Burns 1968, Putnam 1948.

2. The reading of cultural forms as stories that people tell themselves about themselves is of course developed most fully in Geertz 1973, 412–53. See also Parker 1985a.

3. Technically, myth is perhaps best defined as a "sacred narrative." For a fuller discussion of this notion, see Dundes 1984. As should be obvious, I am using the term "myth" here not in this technical sense, but as a kind of metaphor connoting stories which may or may not be based in historical fact, but which are important because of the ways in which they structure the perceptions of their believers.

4. On the vision of an earthly paradise during the age of discovery, see Baudet 1965. For a detailed discussion of this theme, and of the "Edenic" motives for the exploration and colonization of Brazil, see Buarque de Holanda 1969.

5. On the vision of the noble savage and its relation to images of native Brazilians, see Mello Franco 1937 and Hemming 1978.

6. See, for example, Cardim 1939, Léry 1941, Staden 1955, Thevet 1944. The reporting of cannibalistic practices has, it is worth noting, long been questioned (see, for example, Arens 1979). My concern here, of course, is clearly *not* the empirical presence or absence of cannibalism but the representation of it, its evocative power, both for early Europeans and later Brazilians.

7. Again, my use of the term "myth" is perhaps somewhat unusual. It is not uncommon in anthropology to speak of the origin myths of a particular people. But the term has generally been reserved for use in the context of relatively small-scale societies which are perceived to live somehow outside of history. Myth—and, in particular, origin myths—have thus generally been opposed to "history" in anthropological discourse. This tendency has begun to change over the course of recent

years, as we have become increasingly aware of the fact that historical processes are themselves often profoundly shaped by cultural meanings, and that history itself is interpreted in specific ways depending upon the cultural frameworks within which it is contextualized (see Sahlins 1981, 1985). In the present context, what particularly interests me is the extent to which historical processes can take on almost mythical qualities because of the ways in which they are culturally elaborated—in what might be described as the mythologization of history itself.

8. Freyre's views on slavery have been extensively debated, and it seems clear that his view of slavery in Brazil as relatively benign is founded less in reality than in his own ideological position. For an especially helpful discussion of slavery in Brazil, and of the scholarly debate concerning its character, see Degler 1971.

9. Milk, and by extension, food more generally, play important roles in the semiotic construction of *Casa-Grande e Senzala*. Freyre pays a great deal of attention to the culinary contributions of both the Amerindian as well as the African in Brazilian culture, and he seems to view these contributions almost as symbols of the dark-skinned woman. This semiotic is rooted in a deeper set of cultural constructs that will be discussed in greater detail below.

Three: Men and Women

1. This examination of Brazilian history is especially appropriate as a point of departure given the fact that the construction of gender in Brazil is deeply rooted in far more widespread cultural patterns found throughout the Mediterranean and Latin worlds. For an overview of these patterns, see Saunders 1981. For a discussion of regional patterns of gender and sexuality, see also Davis and Whitten 1987.

2. Again, this configuration is clearly part of a broader Latin pattern. See, for example, Brandes 1980, Peristiany 1966, Pitt-Rivers 1977.

3. On the distinction between the "penis" and the "phallus," see Lacan 1977, 1981; Mitchell 1974; Rubin 1975.

4. On the cross-cultural association of pollution and femininity, see Douglas 1966, MacCormack and Strathern 1980, Ortner 1974.

5. At least one indication of just how highly charged this area of the sexual domain has traditionally been is the degree of cultural elaboration which it has received. While terms such as *maricas, viado,* and *bicha* are among the most commonly used in contemporary speech, they vie with an extensive number of possible synonyms in offering Brazilians a variety of ways to comment upon and interpret the passivity of *homens* through the discourse of daily life. Indeed, they can be used quite interchangeably with terms such as *boneca* (doll), *coisinha* (little thing), *efeminado* (effeminate), *enxuto* (literally, "dried, without tears or rain, slim"), *florzinha* (little flower), *fresco* (fresh), *fronha* (pillowcase), *frouxo* (limp, cowardly, impotent), *fruta* (fruit), *passivo* (passive), *puto* (defined by informants as a masculine form of *puta,* or "whore," when used as a noun, but meaning "angry" or "enraged" when used as an adjective), or *vinte e quatro* (literally, "twenty-four"—the number assigned to the *veado* in the popular Brazilian numbers game known as the *jogo do bicho,* or "animal game"). In virtually every case, however, this otherwise wide array of terms

seems to draw attention to one quality: the apparent *efeminação* (effeminacy) of the *pederasta passivo* (passive pederast).

6. The cultural emphasis on "active" and "passive" roles in same-sex interactions is, of course, widespread, and can be found not only in Brazil (Fry 1982, 1985; Fry and MacRae 1983; Hutchinson 1957, 140–41; Parker 1985b, 1987, 1989b), but also in other parts of Latin America (see Carrier 1985, Taylor 1985, Lancaster 1988), as well as in any number of other, quite distant, settings (see, for example, Dover 1978, Herdt 1981, Veyne 1985). On the notion of phallic attack, see Brandes 1981, Dundes, Leach and Özkök 1970, Vanggaard 1972.

7. The Brazilian case would certainly seem to parallel that described by Brandes for Andalusia. Taking issue with Pitt-Rivers, Brandes has argued that the cuckold's horns are placed upon his head by the woman who betrays him rather than by the man who sleeps with her. This is, without question, the position that my Brazilian informants took on the matter in their society. See Brandes 1980, 1981; Pitt-Rivers 1966.

8. The cultural salience of the *piranha* or *puta* can be grasped simply in the vocabulary that Brazilians can draw on in speaking of her. Terms as diverse as *aranha* (spider), *ave* (bird), *bicha* (again, a female animal, used particularly in Northeastern Brazil), *borboleta* (butterfly), *dama* (dame or matron), *dama da noite* (matron of the night) or *dama da madrugada* (matron of the early morning), *égua* (mare), *galinha* (chicken or chick), *loba* (she-wolf), *mariposa* (moth or butterfly, associated particularly with the night), *meretriz* (prostitute), *mulher-da-rua* (woman of the street or streetwalker), *mulher-da-vida* (woman in the life), *mulher-da-zona* (woman of the red-light district), *mulher perdida* (lost woman), *mulher profana* (profane woman), *mulher pública* (public woman), *pistoleira* (gunwoman), *prostituta* (prostitute), and *vaca* (cow) can all be used to refer to women either as prostitutes, in the strict sense, as women who sell their sexual favors, or more simply, as loose women, women who give of themselves indiscriminantly and who thus defile the *honra* of their families and betray their husbands. In either case, the epithet is clearly among the most serious condemnations in all of Brazilian culture, as its repercussions are felt not merely by the *puta* herself, but by the men whose lives she touches.

9. The distinction between *sapatão* and *sapatilha* functions much like the differentiation between "butch" and "fem" in the lesbian communities of many North American and European societies. See, for example, Nestle 1981.

10. Without wanting to overstate the value of an overly formal schematization, a number of insights can be obtained from examining the structural relationships between the categories in some detail. The *homem* and the *mulher* can clearly be opposed as "positive" and "negative" figures within a wider system of values. Both male and female sides of this opposition can be further broken down in positive and negative terms as well. The positive *machão* and *pai,* representing virility and potency, can be opposed to the negative *corno* and *bicha,* who seem to represent impotence and passivity: the *machão* controls his women, while the *corno* fails to do so; the *pai* fathers children, while the *bicha* fails to reproduce and pass on his family name. In much the same fashion, the positive *virgem* and *mãe* can be opposed to the negative *puta* and *sapatão:* the *virgem* denies unauthorized sexual access and pro-

tects her family name, while the *puta* invites transgression and brings ruin on her family; the *mãe* produces children, while the *sapatão* does not.

11. On the question of masculinization and the construction of male gender identities, see Chodorow 1974, 1978; Herdt 1981, 1987; Stoller and Herdt 1982.

12. While cultural analysis is especially well suited to laying out the symbolic structures that articulate the gender hierarchy in any given context, it seems clear that both sociological and psychological analyses are also imperative if we hope to understand the complex processes through which such structures are internalized and reproduced. Nancy Chodorow's work offers some sense of the many complicated questions that must be addressed (see Chodorow 1974, 1978).

13. One way of putting this might be to draw on Chomsky's distinction between communicative competence and performance, and to suggest that even those who do not draw on such a language in their concrete performances are nonetheless competent in its particular grammar.

Four: Norms and Perversions

1. As will be apparent, my understanding of this frame of reference has been influenced most directly by Michel Foucault's work on the history of sexuality (Foucault 1978; see also Plummer 1981, Rubin 1984, Weeks 1985). Many of the same issues that have marked Foucault's work have been raised, as well, in a growing literature on the history of sexuality in Brazil that has been extremely important in grounding my own understanding of the ways in which diverse discourses focusing on sexuality have taken shape in Brazilian culture (see, for example, Costa 1979; Engel 1988; Machado et al. 1978; Mott 1988; Trevisan 1986; Vainfas 1986, 1989).

2. It is this kind of debate that most clearly marks the discourses of sexuality. As Foucault has pointed out in analyzing the history of sexuality in Western Europe, it is here that the elaboration of discourse takes shape, that sex most obviously speaks its name, and that sexuality is constituted within this speech.

Five: Bodies and Pleasures

1. On the notion of eroticism see, for example, Bataille 1962. For a helpful psychoanalytic perspective, see Stoller 1979, 1985.

2. The variations on this expression are in fact so numerous that it is impossible to indicate how often it came up in work with informants. My favorite was during a conversation with Lílian, a twenty-nine-year-old woman from a lower-middle-working-class background in São Paulo. She was describing the discussion about sexuality that traditionally precedes marriage in the Catholic church. The priest who conducted the session before her own marriage was very good, she said. None of the expected moralizing. On the contrary, as long as it was with her husband, he had told her, anything that might happen "within four walls" was alright. In short, while the emphasis on marriage and monogamy was maintained, the emphasis on procreation was dissolved into a rather different understanding of erotic practice.

3. The link between sexual excitement and heat is, of course, quite widespread cross-culturally, and it is just as present in contemporary American culture as it is in Brazil. The use of "hot" and "cold" as sexual metaphors is no less common, however, in very different social and cultural contexts, such as the small-scale groups of New Guinea (see, for example, Lewis 1980, 125–27).

4. For a particularly helpful discussion developing a psychoanalytic theory of fantasy, see Laplanche and Pontalis 1968.

5. This transformation of the parts of the body into mental images or symbols has been addressed most directly in psychoanalysis. While it only gradually seems to enter into Freud's *Three Essays on the Theory of Sexuality* (Freud 1962b) in the later revisions, it is more clearly at issue in *The Complete Introductory Lectures on Psychoanalysis* (Freud 1966) as well as in the essays collected in *Sexuality and the Psychology of Love* (Freud 1962a). The discussion of this process has generally focused on the specific symbolisms of particular individuals, and the collective representations of the body have received relatively less attention.

6. The notion of sexual (and, by extension, erotic) scripts has been most usefully developed in the work of Gagnon and Simon. See, in particular, Gagnon 1977, Gagnon and Simon 1973, Simon 1973, Simon and Gagnon 1984. For a discussion linking their emphasis on conscious scripting to the dynamics of the unconscious, see Stoller 1979.

7. Since the argument that I am making here might easily lead to some confusion, it is worth underlining the fact that I am exploring an ideological system rather than empirical behaviors. This system serves as a kind of backdrop for behavior, making behavior meaningful—in short, transforming it into practice or conduct. While it enables particular individuals to imagine the range of possible sexual practices open to them, it does not in any direct sense determine which of these practices they will in fact integrate into their own individual performances. On the contrary, such individual performances emerge from a complicated calculus of both conscious and unconscious choices—choices that are themselves both possible and necessary because individuals live in a sexual universe with conflicting prescriptions. In short, the fact that the ideology of the erotic places high value, for example, on anal intercourse does not mean that all individuals will practice anal intercourse; it simply means that the culture offers at least one very important erotic script in which anal intercourse plays a key role. Other scripts exist, in the same cultural context, which no less clearly have absolutely no place for such a practice. Because of this, the transition from the imaginary to the real, from the cultural system of meanings to the actual practices that individuals are engaged in, must be negotiated within highly specific circumstances and contexts, and an analysis of the cultural system cannot be taken as an analysis of behavioral frequencies.

Six: The Carnivalization of the World

1. Chico Buarque de Hollanda, "Não Existe Pecado Ao Sul do Equador," FM Rádio Nacional, February 12, 1984. The untranslated terms, *sarapatel, caruru, tucupi,* and *tacacá,* all refer to specific foods or dishes in Afro-Brazilian cooking—a cuisine that is noted for its hot, spicy, sensual foods.

2. For a discussion of the "tropicalist" movement of the late 1960s and the early 1970s, and of its relation to the modernist movement of the 1920s, see Tavaretto 1979.

3. "100 Anos de Carnaval," Polydor Records, 1974. As one example of the carnivalesque play with language, it is worth noting the joking reinvention of this song. In the *carnaval* of 1989, for example, groups of young heterosexual males could be found parading through the streets, singing *"Mamãe Eu Quero,"* but substituting the term *boceta* (cunt) for *chupeta* (pacifier): "Mommy I want, Mommy I want, Mommy I want to suck, give me a cunt, give me a cunt, give me a cunt so that your baby won't cry." At the same time, groups of young gay men substituted *caceta* (prick) for *chupeta:* "Mommy I want, Mommy I want, Mommy I want to suck, give me a prick, give me a prick, give me a prick so that your baby won't cry."

4. The allusion here, of course, is to Geertz's analysis of the ways in which the Balinese cockfight plays with hierarchical notions of rank and status. Clearly, this emphasis on gender classifications is only one possible reading of the meaning of transvestism. Another obvious possibility might be the symbolic expression of male hostility toward women—or even, perhaps at a deeper level, male envy of women. Because of the multivocal nature of all carnivalesque symbolism, I do not think that the reading offered here in any way precludes these other interpretations. For an interpretation developed along rather different lines, see Counihan 1985. For a useful interpretation linking the symbolism of transvestism to a more general emphasis on *ambiguidade* (ambiguity) in the symbolism of Brazilian *carnaval,* see Da Matta 1981.

5. Like *tristeza,* the notion of *esperança* is an especially powerful metaphor in Brazilian culture more generally, and could itself be the focus for an extended study. However, while the symbolism of *tristeza* generally focuses, as we saw in chapter 2, on the past or the present, the symbolism of *esperança* of course focuses on the future. These different orientations, and the interrelations between them, will be examined in somewhat greater detail below.

6. In the same way, more recent developments in Brazilian dance and popular culture, such as the *lambada,* can be understood as extensions of this same tradition and situated within the same system of meanings.

7. On the importance of the *malandro* and of *malandragem* in contemporary Brazilian culture, see in particular Da Matta 1978. For a somewhat different, but equally insightful, analysis, see Oliven 1983, 29–60.

8. On the notion of "carnivalization," see Bakhtin 1968. On the importance of *carnavalização* in Brazil, see Da Matta 1978.

9. The number of studies that have been published in Brazil interpreting the *carnaval* is an obvious sign of its incredible wealth of meanings. I hope that by now it will be evident that my own reading is but one among many, and does not seek to claim some kind of privileged or definitive status. At the same time, it should also be noted that even if developed in a somewhat different direction, my own analysis of the *carnaval* as a complex symbol for Brazil as a whole links up, in a number of ways, with other discussions of the appropriation of popular cultural forms as national symbols. See in particular Fry 1982, 47–53; Oliven 1983, 61–73.

Bibliography

Alencar, José de. 1984. *Iracema*. 15th edition. São Paulo: Ática.

Almeida, Horacio de. 1981. *Dicionário de Termos Eróticos e Afins*. 2d edition. Rio de Janeiro: Civilização Brasileira.

Almeida, Maria Suely Kofes de, et al. 1982. *Colcha de Retalhos: Estudos sobre a Família no Brasil*. São Paulo: Editora Brasiliense.

Alves, Branca Maria Moreira, and Jacqueline Pitanguy. 1983. *O Que É Feminismo*. São Paulo: Editora Brasiliense.

Alves, Branca Maria Moreira, et al. 1980. "Sexualidade e Desconhecimento: A Negação do Saber." In *Vivência: História, Sexualidade, e Imagens Femininas*, ed. Maria Cristina A. Bruschini and Fúlvia Rosemberg, 257–88. São Paulo: Editora Brasiliense.

Anchieta, José de. 1933. *Cartas, Informações, Fragmentos Históricos, e Sermões*. Rio de Janeiro: Civilização Brasileira.

Andrade, Mário de. 1983. *Macunaíma: O Herói sem Nenhum Caráter*. 19th edition. Belo Horizonte: Editora Itatiaia.

Andrade, Oswald de. 1967. *Trechos Escolhidos*. Rio de Janeiro: AGIR.

Arens, W. 1979. *The Man-Eating Myth: Anthropology and Anthropophagy*. New York: Oxford University Press.

Aufderheide, Patricia. 1973. "True Confessions: The Inquisition and Social Attitudes in Brazil at the Turn of the 17th Century." *Luso-Brazilian Review* 10(2):208–40.

Azevedo, Aluizio. 1941. *O Mulato*. 11th edition. Rio de Janeiro: F. Briquiet and Cia.

———. 1943. *O Cortiço*. 9th edition. Rio de Janeiro: F. Briquiet and Cia.

Azevedo, Thales de. 1953. "Catholicism in Brazil: A Personal Evaluation." *Thought* 28:253–74.

Bakhtin, Mikhail. 1968. *Rabelais and His World*. Cambridge, Mass.: MIT Press.

Barlaeus, Gaspar. 1980. *História dos Feitos Recentemente Praticados durante Oito Anos no Brasil*. Recife: Fundação de Cultura Cidade do Recife.

Baroja, Julio Caro. 1979. *El Carnaval: Analisis Historico-Cultural*. Madrid: Taurus Ediciones.

Bastide, Roger. 1951. "Religion and the Church in Brazil." In *Brazil: Portrait of a Half Continent*, ed. T. Lynn Smith and Alexander Marchant, 334–55. New York: Dryden Press.

———. 1978. *Brasil, Terra de Contrastes*. 8th edition. Rio de Janeiro and São Paulo: Difel/Difusão.

Bataille, Georges. 1962. *Eroticism*. London: John Calder.

Baudet, Henri. 1965. *Paradise on Earth: Some Thoughts on European Images of Non-European Man*. New Haven: Yale University Press.

Bernstein, Basil. 1973. *Class, Codes, and Control*. London: Paladin.

Bourdieu, Pierre. 1977. *Outline of a Theory of Practice*. Cambridge: Cambridge University Press.

Bourdieu, Pierre, and Jean-Claude Passeron. 1977. *Reproduction: In Education, Society, and Culture*. London and Beverly Hills: Sage Publications.

Boxer, C. R. 1957. *The Dutch in Brazil, 1624–1654*. Oxford: Clarendon Press.

Brandes, Stanley. 1980. *Metaphors of Masculinity: Sex and Status in Andalusian Folklore*. Philadelphia: University of Pennsylvania Press.

———. 1981. "'Like Wounded Stags': Male Sexual Ideology in an Andalusian Town." In *Sexual Meanings: The Cultural Construction of Gender and Sexuality*, ed. Sherry B. Ortner and Harriet Whitehead, 216–39. New York: Cambridge University Press.

Brito, Mário de Silva. 1971. *História do Modernismo Brasileiro*. 3d edition. Rio de Janeiro: Civilização Brasileira.

Buarque de Holanda, Sérgio. 1969. *Visão do Paraíso: Os Motivos Edênicos no Descobrimento e Colonização do Brasil*. 2d edition. São Paulo: Companha Editora Nacional, Editôra da Universidade de São Paulo.

Burke, Peter. 1978. *Popular Culture in Early Modern Europe*. New York: Harper and Row.

Burns, E. Bradford. 1968. *Nationalism in Brazil: A Historical Survey*. New York: Fredrick A. Praeger.

Caminha, Adolfo. 1983. *Bom-Crioulo*. São Paulo: Ática.

Caminha, Pero Vaz de. 1943. "A Carta de Pero Vaz de Caminha." In *A Carta de Pero Vaz de Caminha*, ed. Jaime Cortesão. Rio de Janeiro: Livros de Portugal.

Cândido, Antônio. 1951. "The Brazilian Family." In *Brazil: Portrait of a Half Continent*, ed. T. Lynn Smith 291–312. New York: Dryden Press.

———. 1968. "Literature and the Rise of Brazilian National Self-Identity." *Luso-Brazilian Review* 5(1):27–43.

Caplan, Pat. 1987. *The Cultural Construction of Sexuality*. London: Tavistock Publications.

Cardim, Fernão. 1939. *Tratados da Terra e Gente do Brasil*. 2d edition. São Paulo: Companha Editora Nacional.

Carneiro, Edison. 1982. *Folguedos Tradicionais*. 2d edition. Rio de Janeiro: Edições FUNARTE/INF.

Carrier, Joseph M. 1985. "Mexican Male Bisexuality." *Journal of Homosexuality* 11(1/2):75–85.

Chodorow, Nancy. 1974. "Family Structure and Feminine Personality." In *Woman, Culture, and Society*, ed. Michelle Zimbalist Rosaldo and Louise Lamphere, 43–66. Stanford: Stanford University Press.

———. 1978. *The Reproduction of Mothering*. Berkeley and Los Angeles: University of California Press.

Conniff, Michael L. 1981. *Urban Politics in Brazil: The Rise of Populism, 1925–1945*. Pittsburgh: University of Pittsburgh Press.

Conrad, Robert. 1972. *The Destruction of Brazilian Slavery, 1850–1888*. Berkeley and Los Angeles: University of California Press.

Cortesão, Jaime. 1943. *A Cara de Pero Vaz de Caminha*. Rio de Janeiro: Livros de Portugal.

Costa, João Cruz. 1964. *A History of Ideas in Brazil: The Development of Philosophy in Brazil and the Evolution of National History*. Berkeley and Los Angeles: University of California Press.

Costa, Jurandir Freire. 1979. *Ordem Médica e Norma Familiar*. Rio de Janeiro: Edições Graal.

Counihan, Carole M. 1985. "Transvestism and Gender in a Sardinian Carnival." *Anthropology* 8(1/2):11–24.

Cunha, Euclydes da. 1940. *Os Sertões*. 15th edition. Rio de Janeiro: Livraria Francisco Alves.

Da Matta, Roberto. 1973. "Carnaval como um Rito de Passagem." In *Ensaios de Antropologia Estrutural*, 121–68. Petrópolis: Editora Vozes.

———. 1978. *Carnavais, Malandros, e Heróis: Para uma Sociologia do Dilema Brasileiro*. Rio de Janeiro: Zahar Editores.

———. 1981. *Universo do Carnaval: Imagens e Reflexões*. Rio de Janeiro: Edições Pinakotheke.

———. 1983. "Para uma Teoria da Sacanagem: Uma Reflexão sobre a Obra de Carlos Zéfiro." In *A Arte Sacana de Carlos Zéfiro*, ed. Joaquim Marinho, 22–39. Rio de Janeiro: Editora Marco Zero.

———. 1985. *A Casa e a Rua: Espaço, Cidadania, Mulher, e Morte no Brasil*. São Paulo: Editora Brasiliense.

d'Assunção, Otacílio. 1984. *O Quadro Erótico de Carlos Zéfiro*. Rio de Janeiro: Record.

Davis, D. L., and R. G. Whitten. 1987. "The Cross-Cultural Study of Human Sexuality." *Annual Review of Anthropology* 16:69–98.

Davis, Natalie Zemon. 1975. *Society and Culture in Early Modern France*. Stanford: Stanford University Press.

Degler, Carl N. 1971. *Neither Black nor White*. New York: Macmillan.

Douglas, Mary. 1966. *Purity and Danger: An Analysis of Concepts of Pollution and Taboo*. London: Routledge and Kegan Paul.

Dover, Kenneth J. 1978. *Greek Homosexuality*. New York: Vintage Books.

Dundes, Alan, ed. 1984. *Sacred Narrative: Readings in the Theory of Myth*. Berkeley and Los Angeles: University of California Press.

Dundes, Alan, Jerry W. Leach, and Bora Özkök. 1970. "The Strategy of Turkish Boys' Verbal Dueling Rhymes." *Journal of American Folklore* 83:325–49.

Eneida. 1958. *História do Carnaval Carioca.* Rio de Janeiro: Editora Civilização Brasileira.

Engel, Magali. 1988. *Meretrizes e Doutores: Saber Médico e Prostituição no Rio de Janeiro (1840–1890).* São Paulo: Editora Brasiliense.

Faoro, Raymundo. 1979. *Os Donos do Poder: Formação do Patronato Político Brasileiro.* 5th edition. Porto Alegre: Editora Globo.

Filho, Hermilo Borba. 1972. *Sobrados e Mocambos.* Rio de Janeiro: Civilização Brasileira.

Forman, Shepard. 1975. *The Brazilian Peasantry.* New York: Columbia University Press.

Foucault, Michel. 1978. *The History of Sexuality.* Volume 1: *An Introduction.* New York: Random House.

Freud, Sigmund. 1962a. *Sexuality and the Psychology of Love.* New York: Collier Books.

————. 1962b. *Three Essays on the Theory of Sexuality.* New York: Basic Books.

————. 1966. *The Complete Introductory Lectures on Psychoanalysis.* New York: W. W. Norton.

Freyre, Gilberto. 1956. *The Masters and the Slaves: A Study in the Development of Brazilian Civilization.* New York: Alfred A. Knopf.

————. 1963. *The Mansions and the Shanties.* New York: Alfred A. Knopf.

————. 1970. *Order and Progress.* New York: Alfred A. Knopf.

————. 1983. *Casa-Grande e Senzala: Formação da Família Brasileira sob o regime da Economia Patriarcal.* 22d edition. Rio de Janeiro: Livraria José Olympio Editora.

Fry, Peter. 1982. *Para Inglês Ver: Identidade e Política na Cultura Brasileira.* Rio de Janeiro: Zahar Editores.

————. 1985. "Male Homosexuality and Spirit Possession in Brazil." *Journal of Homosexuality* 11(3/4):137–53.

Fry, Peter, and Edward MacRae. 1983. *O Que É Homossexualidade.* São Paulo: Editora Brasiliense.

Furtado, Celso. 1963. *The Economic Growth of Brazil: A Survey from Colonial to Modern Times.* Berkeley and Los Angeles: University of California Press.

Gagnon, John H. 1977. *Human Sexualities.* Glenview, Ill.: Scott, Foresman.

Gagnon, John H., and William Simon. 1973. *Sexual Conduct: The Social Sources of Human Sexuality.* Chicago: Aldine.

Gaignebet, Claude, and Marie-Claude Florentin. 1974. *Le Carnaval: Essais de Mythologie Populaire.* Paris: Payot.

Geertz, Clifford. 1973. *The Interpretation of Cultures.* New York: Basic Books.

————. 1983. *Local Knowledge: Further Essays in Interpretive Anthropology.* New York: Basic Books.

Graça Aranha, José Pereira da. 1913. *Chanaan.* Rio de Janeiro: Livraria Granier.

Greenlee, William Brooks. 1937. *The Voyages of Pedro Álvares Cabral to Brazil and India.* London: The Hakluyt Society.

Gregor, Thomas. 1985. *Anxious Pleasures: The Sexual Lives of An Amazonian People.* Chicago: University of Chicago Press.

Haberly, David T. 1983. *Three Sad Races: Racial Identity and National Consciousness in Brazilian Literature.* New York: Cambridge University Press.

Haring, C. H. 1958. *Empire in Brazil: A New World Experiment with Monarchy.* New York: W. W. Norton and Company.

Hemming, John. 1978. *Red Gold: The Conquest of the Brazilian Indians, 1500–1760.* Cambridge, Mass.: Harvard University Press.

Herdt, Gilbert H. 1981. *Guardians of the Flutes: Idioms of Masculinity.* New York: McGraw-Hill.

———. 1987. *The Sambia: Ritual and Gender in New Guinea.* New York: Holt, Rinehart and Winston.

Herédia de Sá, Miguel. 1845. "Algumas Reflexões sobre a Cópula, o Onanismo, e a Prostituição, em Especial na cidade do Rio de Janeiro." Thesis. Faculdade de Medicina, Rio de Janeiro.

Hutchinson, Harry. 1957. *Village and Plantation Life in Northeastern Brazil.* Seattle: Washington University Press.

Inez, Antônio Leal de Santa, ed. 1983. *Hábitos e Atitudes Sexuais dos Brasileiros.* São Paulo: Editora Cultrix.

Ivo, Lêdo. 1981. *Snakes' Nest.* New York: New Directions Books.

Lacan, Jacques. 1977. *Écrits: A Selection.* New York: W. W. Norton.

———. 1981. *Speech and Language in Psychoanalysis.* Baltimore, Md.: Johns Hopkins University Press.

Ladurie, Emmanuel Le Roy. 1979. *Carnival in Romans.* New York: Braziller.

Lancaster, Roger N. 1988. "Subject Honor and Object Shame: The Cochon and the Milieu-Specific Construction of Stigma and Sexuality in Nicaragua." *Ethnology* 27:111–25.

Laplanche, Jean, and J. B. Pontalis. 1968. "Fantasy and the Origins of Sexuality." *International Journal of Psycho-Analysis* 49:1–18.

Leach, Edmund. 1961. *Rethinking Anthropology.* London: Athlone Press.

Leach, Maria, ed. 1972. *Funk and Wagnall's Standard Dictionary of Folklore, Mythology, and Legend.* New York: Funk and Wagnall's.

Léry, Jean de. 1941. *Viagem à Terra do Brasil.* São Paulo: Livraria Martins.

Lewis, Gilbert. 1980. *Day of Shining Red: An Essay on Understanding Ritual.* Cambridge: Cambridge University Press.

Lima, Delcio Monteiro de. 1978. *Comportamento Sexual do Brasileiro.* 3d edition. Rio de Janeiro: Livraria Francisco Alves Editora.

MacCormack, Carol, and Marilyn Strathern, eds. 1980. *Nature, Culture, and Gender.* New York: Cambridge University Press.

Machado, Roberto, et al. 1978. *Danação da Norma: Medicina Social e Constituição da Psiquiatria no Brasil.* Rio de Janeiro: Edições Graal.

Maior, Mário Souto. 1980. *Dicionário do Palavrão e Termos Afins.* 3d edition. Recife: Editora Guararapes.

Marinho, Joaquim, ed. 1983. *A Arte Sacana de Carlos Zéfiro.* Rio de Janeiro: Editora Marco Zero.

Martins, Wilson. 1970. *The Modernist Idea: A Critical Survey of Brazilian Writing in the Twentieth Century.* New York: New York University Press.

Mazín, Rafael. 1983a. "Anatomia e Fisiologia Sexual Humana." In *Sexo e Juventude,* ed. Carmen Barroso and Cristina Bruschini, 22–27. São Paulo: Editora Brasiliense.

———. 1983b. "Controle Voluntário da Reprodução." In *Sexo e Juventude,* ed. Carmen Barroso and Cristina Bruschini, 54–60. São Paulo: Editora Brasiliense.

———. 1983c. "Homossexualidade." In *Sexo e Juventude,* ed. Carmen Barroso and Cristina Bruschini, 73–79. São Paulo: Editora Brasiliense.

Mello Franco, Affonso Arinos de. 1937. *O Índio Brasileiro e a Revolução Francesa: As Origens Brasileiras da Teoria da Bondade Natural.* Rio de Janeiro: Livraria José Olympio Editora.

Míccolis, Leila, and Herbert Daniel. 1983. *Jacarés e Lobisomens: Dois Ensaios sobre a Homossexualidade.* Rio de Janeiro: Edições Achiamé.

Mintz, Sidney W. 1985. *Sweetness and Power: The Place of Sugar in Modern History.* New York: Viking Penguin.

Misse, Michel. 1981. *O Estigma do Passivo Sexual.* Rio de Janeiro: Achiamé.

Mitchell, Juliet. 1974. *Psychoanalysis and Feminism.* New York: Random House.

Morse, Richard M. 1958. *From Community to Metropolis: A Biography of São Paulo, Brazil.* Gainesville: University of Florida Press.

———. 1978. "Cities and Society in Nineteenth-Century Latin America: The Illustrative Case of Brazil." In *Urbanization in the Americas from Its Beginnings to the Present,* ed. Richard P. Schaedel, Jorge E. Hardoy, and Nora Scott Kinzer, 283–302. The Hague: Mouton.

Mott, Luiz. 1988. *Escravidão, Homossexualidade, e Demonologia.* São Paulo: Ícone.

Nestle, Joan. 1981. "Butch-Fem Relationships." *Heresies* 12:21–24.

Newton, Esther. 1972. *Mother Camp: Female Impersonators in America.* Englewood Cliffs, N.J.: Prentice-Hall.

Nobrega, Manoel da. 1931. *Cartas do Brasil, 1549–1560.* Rio de Janeiro: Officina Industrial Graphica.

Novinsky, Ilana W. 1980. "Heresia, Mulher, e Sexualidade (Algumas notas sobre o Nordeste Brasileiro nos séculos XVI e XVII)." In *Vivência: História, Sexualidade, e Imagens Femininas,* ed. Maria Cristina A. Bruschini and Fúlvia Rosemberg, 227–56. São Paulo: Editora Brasiliense.

Oliven, Ruben George. 1983. *Violência e Cultura no Brasil.* Petrópolis: Editora Vozes.

Ortiz, Renato. 1976. "Reflexões sobre o Carnaval." *Ciência e Cultura* 28(12):1407–12.

———. 1978. "Carnaval, Reflexões II." *Cadernos* 11:66–76.

———. 1985. *Cultura Brasileira e Identidade Nacional.* São Paulo: Editora Brasiliense.

Ortner, Sherry B. 1974. "Is Female to Male as Nature is to Culture?" In *Woman, Culture, and Society,* ed. Michelle Zimbalist Rosaldo and Louise Lamphere, 67–87. Sanford: Stanford University Press.

Ortner, Sherry B., and Harriet Whitehead, eds. 1981. *Sexual Meanings: The Cultural Construction of Gender and Sexuality.* New York: Cambridge University Press.

Padgug, Robert A. 1979. "Sexual Matters: On Conceptualizing Sexuality in History." *Radical History Review* 20:3–23.

Parker, Richard G. 1985a. "From Symbolism to Interpretation: Reflections on the Work of Clifford Geertz." *Anthropology and Humanism Quarterly* 10(3): 62–67.

———. 1985b. "Masculinity, Femininity, and Homosexuality: On the Anthropological Interpretation of Sexual Meanings in Brazil." *Journal of Homosexuality* 11(3/4):155–63.

———. 1987. "Acquired Immunodeficiency Syndrome in Urban Brazil." *Medical Anthropology Quarterly,* n.s. 1(2):155–75.

———. 1988. "Sexual Culture and AIDS Education." In *AIDS 1988: AAAS Symposia Papers,* ed. Ruth Kulstad, 169–73. Washington, D.C.: American Association for the Advancement of Science.

———. 1989a. "Bodies and Pleasures: On the Construction of Erotic Meanings in Contemporary Brazil." *Anthropology and Humanism Quarterly* 14(2):58–64.

———. 1989b. "Youth, Identity, and Homosexuality: The Changing Shape of Sexual Life in Contemporary Brazil." *Journal of Homosexuality* 17(3/4):269–89.

———. 1990. "Responding to AIDS in Brazil." In *Action on AIDS: National Policies in Comparative Perspective,* ed. Barbara A. Misztal and David Moss, Westport, Conn.: Greenwood Press.

Peristiany, J. G., ed. 1966. *Honor and Shame: The Values of Mediterranean Society.* Chicago: University of Chicago Press.

Pitt-Rivers, Julian R. 1961. *The People of the Sierra.* Chicago: University of Chicago Press.

———. 1977. *The Fate of Shechem, or the Politics of Sex: Essays in the Anthropology of Sex.* Cambridge: Cambridge University Press.

Plummer, Kenneth. 1984. "Sexual Diversity: A Sociological Perspective." In *Sexual Diversity,* ed. K. Howells, 219–53. Oxford: Basil Blackwell.

———., ed. 1981. *The Making of the Modern Homosexual.* Totowa, N.J.: Barnes and Noble Books.

Prado, Paulo. 1931. *Retrato do Brasil: Ensaio sobre a Tristeza Brasileira.* 3d edition. Rio de Janeiro: F. Briguiet and Cia.

Putnam, Samuel. 1948. *Marvelous Journey: A Survey of Four Centuries of Brazilian Writing.* New York: Alfred A. Knopf.

Queiroz, Maria Isaura Pereira de. 1981. "Evolução do Carnaval Latino-Americano." *Diógenes* 1:1–17.

Rasmussen, Kenneth Welden. 1971. "Brazilian Portuguese Words and Phrases for Certain Aspects of Love and Parts of the Body." Doctoral dissertation, University of Wisconsin, Madison.

Read, Kenneth E. 1980. *Other Voices: The Style of a Male Homosexual Tavern.* Novato, Cal.: Chandler and Sharp Publishers.

Reiter, Rayna, ed. 1975. *Toward an Anthropology of Women.* New York: Monthly Review Press.

Ribeiro, Leonídio. 1949. *Medicina Legal e Criminologia.* Rio de Janeiro: Livraria Avenida.

Risério, Antonio. 1981. *Carnaval Ijexá.* Salvador: Corrupio.

Rosaldo, Michelle Zimbalist, and Louise Lamphere, eds. 1974. *Woman, Culture, and Society.* Stanford: Stanford University Press.

Ross, Ellen, and Rayna Rapp. 1983. "Sex and Society: A Research Note from Social History and Anthropology." In *Powers of Desire: The Politics of Sexuality,* ed. Ann Snitow, Christine Stansell, and Sharon Thompson, 51–73. New York: Monthly Review Press.

Rubin, Gayle. 1975. "The Traffic in Women: Notes on the 'Political Economy' of Sex." In *Toward an Anthropology of Women,* ed. Rayna Reiter, 157–210. New York: Monthly Review Press.

———. 1984. "Thinking Sex: Notes for a Radical Theory of the Politics of Sexuality." In *Pleasure and Danger: Exploring Female Sexuality,* ed. Carole S. Vance, 267–319. Boston: Routledge and Kegan Paul.

Sahlins, Marshall. 1981. *Historical Metaphors and Mythical Realities: Structure in the Early History of the Sandwich Islands Kingdom.* Ann Arbor: University of Michigan Press.

———. 1985. *Islands of History.* Chicago: University of Chicago Press.

Sant'Anna, Affonso Romano. 1984. *O Canibalismo Amoroso.* São Paulo: Editora Brasiliense.

Saunders, George R. 1981. "Men and Women in Southern Europe: A Review of Some Aspects of Cultural Complexity." *Journal of Psychoanalytic Anthropology* 4(4):435–66.

Scheper-Hughes, Nancy. 1988. "The Madness of Hunger: Sickness, Delirium, and Human Needs." *Culture, Medicine, and Psychiatry* 12(4):1–30.

Sebe, José Carlos. 1986. *Carnaval, Carnavais.* São Paulo: Editora Ática.

Simon, William. 1973. "The Social, the Erotic, and the Sensual: The Complexities of Erotic Scripts." In *Nebraska Symposium on Motivation,* ed. J. K. Cole and Richard Deinstbier, 61–82. Lincoln, Neb.: University of Nebraska Press.

Simon, William, and John H. Gagnon. 1984. "Sexual Scripts." *Society* 23(1):53–60.

Siqueira, Sonia A. 1978. *A Inquisição Portuguesa e a Sociedade Colonial*. São Paulo: Editora Ática.

Skidmore, Thomas E. 1974. *Black into White: Race and Nationality in Brazilian Thought*. New York: Oxford University Press.

Soares de Sousa, Gabriel. 1971. *Tratado Descritivo do Brasil em 1587*. São Paulo: Companhia Editora Nacional, Editôra da Universidade de São Paulo.

Staden, Hans. 1955. *Viagem ao Brasil*. Salvador: Livraria Progresso Editora.

Stein, Stanley J. 1957. *Vassouras: A Brazilian Coffee County, 1850–1900*. Cambridge, Mass.: Harvard University Press.

Stepan, Nancy. 1976. *Beginnings of Brazilian Science: Oswaldo Cruz, Medical Research, and Policy, 1890–1920*. New York: Science History Publications.

Stoller, Robert J. 1979. *Sexual Excitement: Dynamics of Erotic Life*. New York: Pantheon Books.

———. 1985. *Observing the Erotic Imagination*. New Haven: Yale University Press.

Stoller, Robert J., and Gilbert H. Herdt. 1982. "The Development of Masculinity: A Cross-Cultural Contribution." *Journal of the American Psychoanalytic Association* 30:29–59.

Suplicy, Marta. 1983. *Conversando sobre Sexo*. São Paulo: Edição da Autora.

Tavaretto, Celso. 1979. *Tropicália: Alegria/Alegria*. São Paulo: Kairós.

Taylor, Clark L. 1985. "Mexican Male Homosexual Interaction in Public Contexts." *Journal of Homosexuality* 11(3/4):117–36.

Thevet, André. 1944. *Singularidades da França Antarctica*. São Paulo: Companhia Editora Nacional.

Toplin, Robert Brent. 1975. *The Abolition of Slavery in Brazil*. New York: Atheneum.

Toschi, Paolo. 1955. *Le Origini del Teatro Italiano*. Torino: Einaudi.

Trevisan, João Silvério. 1986. *Perverts in Paradise*. London: GMP Publishers.

Turner, Victor. 1969. *The Ritual Process: Structure and Anti-Structure*. Chicago: University of Chicago Press.

———. 1983. "*Carnaval* in Rio: Dionysian Drama in an Industrializing Society." In *The Celebration of Society: Perspectives on Contemporary Cultural Performance*, ed. Frank E. Manning, 103–24. Bowling Green, Ohio: Bowling Green University Popular Press.

Vainfas, Ronaldo, ed. 1986. *História e Sexualidade no Brasil*. Rio de Janeiro: Edições Graal.

———. 1989. *Trópico dos Pecados: Moral, Sexualidade, e Inquisição no Brasil*. Rio de Janeiro: Editora Campus.

Vance, Carole S. 1984. "Pleasure and Danger: Toward a Politics of Sexuality." In *Pleasure and Danger: Exploring Female Sexuality*, ed. Carole S. Vance, 1–27. Boston: Routledge and Kegan Paul.

Vanggaard, Thorkil. 1972. *Phallós: A Symbol and Its History in the Male World*. New York: International Universities Press.

Vasconcellos, Carlos Rodrigues de. 1888. "Higiene Escolar, Suas Aplicações à Cidade do Rio de Janeiro." Thesis. Rio de Janeiro.

Vasconcelos, Naumi A. de. 1972. *Resposta Sexual Brasileira*. Rio de Janeiro: Editora Paz e Terra.

Velho, Gilberto. 1981. *Individualismo e Cultura: Notas para uma Antropologia da Sociedade Contemporânea*. Rio de Janeiro: Zahar Editores.

Vespucci, Amerigo. 1954. "Mundus Novus." In *Amerigo Vespucci e Suas Viagens*, ed. T. O. Marcondes de Souza, 159–67. São Paulo: Instituto Cultural Italo-Brasileiro.

Veyne, Paul. 1985. "Homosexuality in Ancient Rome." In *Western Sexuality: Practice and Precept in Past and Present Times*, ed. Philippe Ariès and André Béjin, 26–35. Oxford: Basil Blackwell.

Vianna, Oliveira. 1955. *Instituições Políticas Brasileiras*. Rio de Janeiro: Livraria José Olympio Editora.

Voloshinov, V. N. 1973. *Marxism and the Philosophy of Language*. New York: Seminar Press.

Wagley, Charles. 1971. *An Introduction to Brazil*. Revised edition. New York: Columbia University Press.

Weeks, Jeffrey. 1977. *Coming Out: Homosexual Politics in Britain from the Nineteenth Century to the Present*. New York: Horizon Press.

———. 1981. *Sex, Politics, and Society: The Regulation of Sexuality Since 1800*. New York: Longman.

———. 1985. *Sexuality and Its Discontents: Meanings, Myths, and Modern Sexualities*. London: Routledge and Kegan Paul.

Willems, Emílio. 1953. "The Structure of the Brazilian Family." *Social Forces* 31(4):339–45.

Index

Abortion, 3, 97
Activity and passivity, 166; as criteria for sexual classification, 43, 45, 46, 47, 48–49, 53, 82; and gender hierarchy, 41–43, 65, 66, 96, 167; and sexual socialization, 55, 56, 60
African influences, 19; and carnival, 144, 149–50, 155. *See also* Racial mixture
Afro-Brazilian religious cults, 144, 150
AIDS epidemic, 3, 94, 167–68
Alencar, José de, 15
Amerindian influences, 155; and carnival, 144–45, 149. *See also* Racial mixture
Anal intercourse, 72, 82; and AIDS epidemic, 168; as alternative to vaginal intercourse, 128–29; and early sexual play, 127–28; and erotic ideology, 116–19, 122, 127–29, 132; language used to describe, 41–42; and modernization of sexual life, 92–95; and sexual classification system, 45, 46, 47
Anchieta, Joseph de, 15
Andrade, Mário de, 16, 27
Andrade, Oswald de, 16, 20, 27, 139
Androgynes, 145
Anthropological perspective, 1–2, 172–74
Anthropophagy. *See* Cannibalism
Azevedo, Aluízio, 15

Barlaeus, Gaspar von, 136, 137, 138, 139
Bastide, Roger, 168
Bernstein, Basil, 170
Bicha, 44, 45–47, 51, 53, 124
Birth control pill, 91
Bisexuality, 83; and AIDS epidemic, 168; and modernization of sexual life, 92–95; and structuring of erotic practice, 122, 124
Blocos de sujos, 145–46
Boas, Frank, 21
Bourdieu, Pierre, 37
Brazilian *carnaval. See* Carnival
Brazilian sadness, concept of, 14–20, 21, 23, 27
Breasts, symbolism of, 55, 113–14, 115, 116
Brincar, 141–43
Brothel, 62, 82. *See also* Prostitution

Buarque de Hollanda, Chico, 138–39
Bunda, 116–19. *See also* Anal intercourse

Cabral, Pedro Álvares, 9, 11
Caminha, Adolfo, 15
Caminha, Pero Vaz de, 9–11, 13, 17, 29, 136
Cândido, Antônio, 31, 33, 35
Cannibalism, 12, 13–14; symbolism of, 149, 150
Carnival, 28, 135, 166, 167, 171; and celebrations of the flesh, 139–48; costumes of, 144–46, 149, 152, 155, 156; and hidden traditions of Brazil, 136–39, 140; as metaphor, 162–64; nature of sexual life reflected in, 155–62; profound ambivalence toward, 155–56, 166; and the wheel of samba, 148–54
Catholicism, Brazilian, 166, 169; declining influence of, 98–99, 133; and erotic ideology, 98–99; and medical/scientific view, 77, 78–79, 83; and modernization of sexual life, 88, 91, 92; and organization of sexual life, 67–75, 96, 98–99; and sexual classification system, 46; and social class, 170
Coffee plantations, 76
Coitus interruptus, 91
Colonial era, 78; decentralization characteristic of, 75; and gold rush, 76; and heightened sensuality of Brazilian life, 25; and influence of Catholicism, 68, 69; and patriarchal system, 31–35, 75; and racial mixture in Brazil, 19–20; and writings of early explorers, 9–14, 16, 17–18, 20, 22, 28
Concubines, 31, 32–33, 35
Contraception, 91, 92, 97
Costumes, carnival, 144–46, 149, 152, 155, 156
Courting, 58, 59
Cuckold, 44, 45, 47–49, 96
Cunnilingus, 92

Da Matta, Roberto, 100–101, 168
Dance: music and, 149–54; samba, 148–54, 156–62, 167

199